Birnbaum
Montreal &
Quebec City

A BIRNBAUM TRAVEL GUIDE

Alexandra Mayes Birnbaum
EDITORIAL CONSULTANT

Lois Spritzer
Editorial Director

Laura L. Brengelman
Managing Editor

Mary Callahan
Senior Editor

David Appell
Patricia Canole
Gene Gold
Jill Kadetsky
Susan McClung
Associate Editors

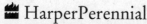 HarperPerennial
A Division Of HarperCollins*Publishers*

To Stephen, who merely made all this possible.

FIRST EDITION

ISSN 0749-2561 (Birnbaum Travel Guides)
ISSN 1061-5415 (Montreal & Quebec City)
ISBN 0-06-278179-0 (pbk.)

94 95 96 97 ❖/RRD 5 4 3 2 1

Cover design © Drenttel Doyle Partners
Cover photograph © Nicholas Devore III/Bruce Coleman
Chateau Frontenac, Quebec City

BIRNBAUM TRAVEL GUIDES

Bahamas, and Turks & Caicos
Berlin
Bermuda
Boston
Canada
Cancun, Cozumel & Isla Mujeres
Caribbean
Chicago
Country Inns and Back Roads
Disneyland
Eastern Europe
Europe
Europe for Business Travelers
France
Germany
Great Britain
Hawaii
Ireland
Italy
London
Los Angeles
Mexico
Miami & Ft. Lauderdale
Montreal & Quebec City
New Orleans
New York
Paris
Portugal
Rome
San Francisco
Santa Fe & Taos
South America
Spain
United States
USA for Business Travelers
Walt Disney World
Walt Disney World for Kids, By Kids
Washington, DC

Contributing Editors

Hazel Lowe
Peter Simon

Maps

Mark Stein Studios

Contents

Diversions

*A selective guide to a variety of unexpected
pleasures, pinpointing the best places to pursue them.*

Exceptional Pleasures and Treasures

Directions

*Nine of the best walks in and around
Montreal and Quebec City.*

Montreal

Quebec City

Glossary

Foreword

My husband, Steve Birnbaum, would fly hundreds of miles out of his way to order a plate of dry garlic spareribs at the late (and very lamented) *Ruby Foo's* restaurant in Montreal. And at the drop of a calorie, he would suggest a side trip to *Schwartz's* for a heaping helping of their French fries sprinkled with vinegar—the Canadian way. My introduction to this city was when Steve took me there as a surprise birthday present.

I well remember my initial Montreal meeting: the first of what became many a romantic calèche ride around this charming city and, most particularly, a lighter-than-air chocolate soufflé that would have been the envy of any chef in Paris. It was Gallic heaven this side of the Atlantic. And not just because I come from a family of Anglophiles did I enjoy the city's enclaves that continue to cling to their very British heritage.

Several months later I first saw Quebec City and paid a visit to the then current hot spot, which blared the then unknown-to-me Patti LaBelle singing the refrain, "Voulez-Vous Coucher avec Moi?" A blizzard started at some point during the third chorus, and no, neither Steve nor I wanted to spend the night with Patti. We did, however, spend the next few days all but snowed in, occasionally making snowbound forays around Quebec's Old City, marveling at this beautiful French-speaking metropolis.

For visitors from the US, the foreign quality of Canada has a unique cast. As a vacation alternative to Paris, Montreal and Quebec City have substantial appeal both in their ambience and in the fact that the US dollar continues to fare far better in Canada than in Europe. And the ever-present separatist spirit shows its face in myriad ways, including the frequent reluctance of Montreal cabdrivers to speak English to US visitors. For the visitor, however, this slight inconvenience may prove welcome; it means that setting foot in a Montreal taxi now more closely approximates a foreign visitor's introduction to France.

We have tried to create a guide to Montreal and Quebec City that's specifically organized, written, and edited for today's demanding traveler, one for whom qualitative information is infinitely more desirable than mere quantities of unappraised data. We realize that it's impossible for any single travel writer to visit thousands of restaurants (and nearly as many hotels) in any given year and provide accurate appraisals of each. And even if it were physically possible for one human being to survive such an itinerary, it would of necessity have to be done at a dead sprint, and the perceptions derived therefrom would probably be less valid than those of any other intelligent individual visiting the same establishments. It is, therefore, both impractical and undesirable (especially in a large, annually revised and updated guidebook *series* such as we offer) to have only one person provide all the data on the entire world. Instead, we have chosen what we like to describe as the "thee and me" approach to restaurant and hotel evaluation and, to a somewhat more limited degree, to the sites and sights we have included in the other sections of our text. What this really reflects is a personal sampling tempered by intelligent counsel from informed local sources.

This guidebook is directed to the "visitor," and such elements as restaurants have been picked specifically to provide the visitor with a representative, enlightening, and, above all, pleasant experience. Since so many extraneous considerations can affect the reception and service accorded a regular restaurant patron, our choices can in no way be construed as an exhaustive guide to resident dining. We think we've listed all the best places, in various price ranges, but they were chosen with a visitor's enjoyment in mind.

Other evidence of how we've tried to tailor our text to reflect modern travel habits is most apparent in the section we call DIVERSIONS. Where once it was common for travelers to spend an urban visit seeing only the obvious sights, today's traveler is more likely to want to pursue a special interest or to venture off the beaten path. In response to this trend, we have collected a series of special experiences so that it is no longer necessary to wade through a pound or two of superfluous prose just to find exceptional pleasures and treasures.

Finally, I also should point out that every good travel guide is a living enterprise; that is, no part of this text is carved in stone. In our annual revisions, we refine, expand, and further hone all our material to serve your travel needs better. To this end, no contribution is of greater value to us than your personal reaction to what we have written, as well as information reflecting your own experiences while using the book. Please write to us at 10 E. 53rd St., New York, NY 10022.

We sincerely hope to hear from you.

Alexandra Mayes Birnbaum

ALEXANDRA MAYES BIRNBAUM, editorial consultant to the *Birnbaum Travel Guides,* worked with her late husband, Stephen Birnbaum, as co-editor of the series. She has been a world traveler since childhood and is known for her travel reports on radio on what's hot and what's not.

Montreal & Quebec City

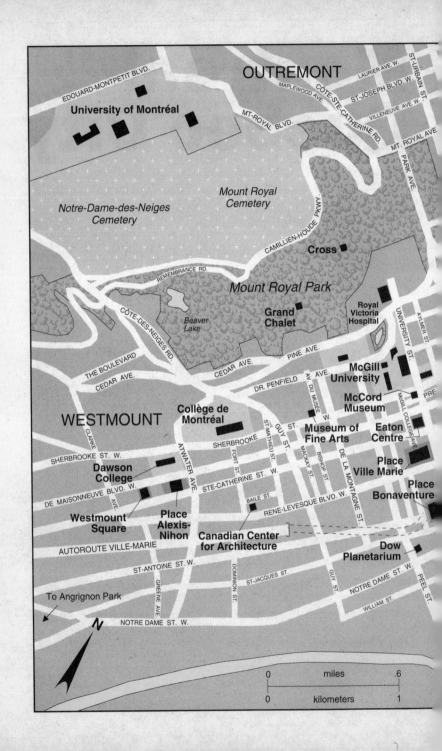

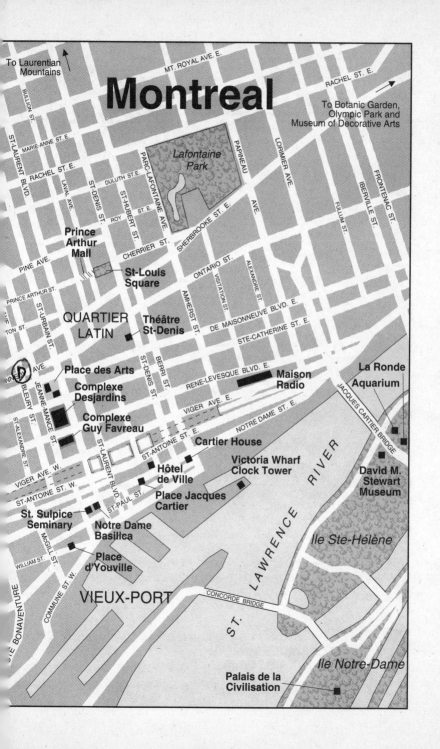

Montreal

To Laurentian Mountains

MT. ROYAL AVE. E.

RACHEL ST. E.

To Botanic Garden, Olympic Park and Museum of Decorative Arts

BULLION ST.

ST-LAURENT BLVD.

MARIE-ANNE ST. E.

RACHEL ST. E.

LAVAL AVE.

ST-DENIS ST.

DULUTH STE.

ST-HUBERT ST.

ROY ST. E.

PARC-LAFONTAINE AVE.

Lafontaine Park

PAPINEAU

LORIMIER AVE.

AVE.

FULLUM ST.

IBERVILLE ST.

FRONTENAC ST.

PINE AVE.

CHERRIER ST.

SHERBROOKE ST. E.

Prince Arthur Mall

St-Louis Square

PRINCE ARTHUR ST.

ST-URBAIN ST.

TON ST.

ONTARIO ST.

AMHERST ST.

VISITATION ST.

ALEXANDRE ST.

QUARTIER LATIN

Théâtre St-Denis

DE MAISONNEUVE BLVD. E.

STE-CATHERINE ST. E.

Place des Arts

BLEURY ST.

JEANNE-MANCE ST.

ST-ALEXANDRE ST.

Complexe Desjardins

ST-DENIS ST.

BERRI ST.

RENE-LEVESQUE BLVD. E.

Maison Radio

La Ronde Aquarium

JACQUES CARTIER BRIDGE

Complexe Guy Favreau

VIGER AVE. E.

NOTRE DAME ST. E.

ST-LAURENT BLVD.

ST-ANTOINE ST. E.

Cartier House

VIGER AVE. W.

ST-ANTOINE ST. W.

Hôtel de Ville

Victoria Wharf Clock Tower

ST.

LAWRENCE

RIVER

David M. Stewart Museum

ST-PAUL ST.

Place Jacques Cartier

St. Sulpice Seminary

Notre Dame Basilica

Ile Ste-Hélène

McGILL ST.

WILLIAM ST.

Place d'Youville

COMMUNE ST. W.

E BONAVENTURE

VIEUX-PORT

CONCORDE BRIDGE

ST.

LAWRENCE

Ile Notre-Dame

Palais de la Civilisation

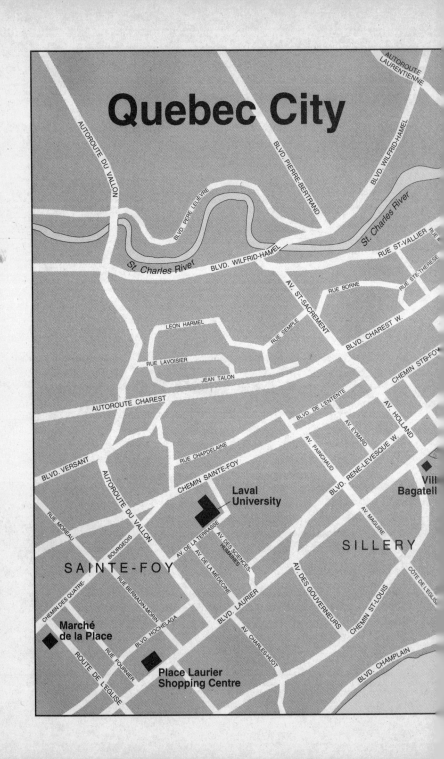

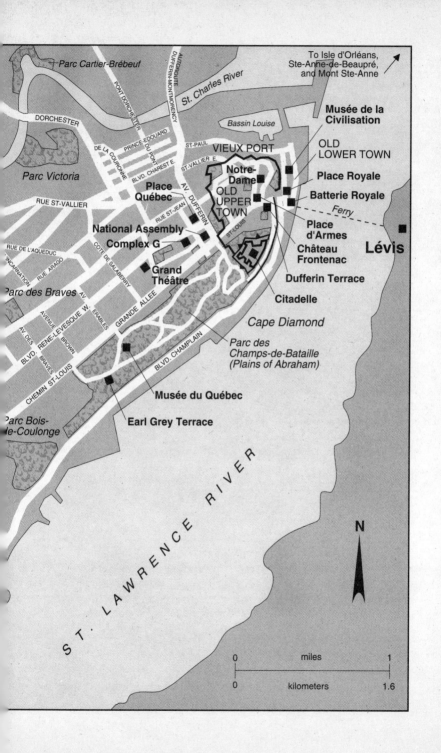

Parc Cartier-Brébeuf

To Isle d'Orléans,
Ste-Anne-de-Beaupré,
and Mont Ste-Anne

St. Charles River

DORCHESTER

PONT DORCHESTER

AUTOROUTE DUFFERIN-MONTMORENCY

PRINCE-EDOUARD

DE LA COURONNE

BLVD. CHAREST E.

ST-PAUL

ST-VALLIER E.

Bassin Louise

VIEUX PORT

Musée de la Civilisation

OLD LOWER TOWN

Parc Victoria

RUE ST-VALLIER

Place Québec

AV. DUFFERIN

RUE ST-JEAN

Notre-Dame

OLD UPPER TOWN

Place Royale

Batterie Royale

Ferry

National Assembly

Complex G

CÔTE DE SALABERRY

ST-LOUIS

Place d'Armes

Lévis

RUE DE L'AQUEDUC

L'INCARNATION

RUE ARAGO

Grand Théâtre

Château Frontenac

Parc des Braves

AV. ÉRABLES

BROWN

GRANDE ALLÉE

Dufferin Terrace

AVENUE RENÉ-LÉVESQUE W.

Citadelle

AV. DES BRAVES

BLVD. BRAVES

Cape Diamond

CHEMIN ST-LOUIS

BLVD. CHAMPLAIN

Parc des Champs-de-Bataille
(Plains of Abraham)

Parc Bois-de-Coulonge

Musée du Québec

Earl Grey Terrace

S T · L A W R E N C E   R I V E R

N

| 0 | miles | 1 |
| 0 | kilometers | 1.6 |

How to Use This Guide

A great deal of care has gone into the special organization of this guidebook, and we believe it represents a real breakthrough in the presentation of travel material.

Our text is divided into five basic sections in order to present information in the best way on every possible aspect of a vacation to Montreal and/or Quebec City. Our aim is to highlight what's where and to provide basic information—how, when, where, how much, and what's best—to assist you in making the most intelligent choices possible.

Here is a brief summary of what you can expect to find in each section. We believe that you will find both your travel planning and en route enjoyment enhanced by having this book at your side.

GETTING READY TO GO

A mini-encyclopedia of practical travel facts with all the precise data necessary to create a successful trip to Montreal and Quebec City. Here you will find how to get where you're going, plus selected resources—including useful publications and companies and organizations specializing in discount and special-interest travel—providing a wealth of information and assistance useful both before and during your trip.

THE CITIES

Our individual reports on Montreal and Quebec City offer a short-stay guide, including an essay introducing each city as a historic entity and a contemporary place to visit; an *At-a-Glance* section that's a site-by-site survey of the most important, interesting, and unique sights to see and things to do; *Sources and Resources,* a concise listing of pertinent tourism information, such as the address of the local tourist office, which sightseeing tours to take, where to find the best nightspot, which are the shops that have the finest merchandise and/or the most irresistible bargains, and where the best museums and theaters are to be found; and *Best in Town,* which lists our collection of cost-and-quality choices of the best places to eat and sleep on a variety of budgets.

DIVERSIONS

This section is designed to help travelers find the best places in which to engage in a variety of exceptional experiences, without having to wade through endless pages of unrelated text. In every case, our particular suggestions are intended to guide you to that special place where the quality of experience is likely to be highest.

DIRECTIONS

Here are nine walks that cover Montreal and Quebec City, their main thoroughfares and side streets, and their most spectacular landmarks and lovely parks.

GLOSSARY

This compendium of helpful travel information includes a weights and measures table and *Useful Words and Phrases,* a brief introduction to the French language that will help you make a hotel or dinner reservation, order a meal, mail a letter, and even buy toothpaste. Though most hotels and restaurants in Montreal and Quebec City have English-speaking staff, at smaller establishments a little knowledge of French will go a long way.

To use this book to full advantage, take a few minutes to read the table of contents and random entries in each section to get a firsthand feel for how it all fits together. You will find that the sections of the book are building blocks designed to help you put together the best possible trip. Use them selectively as a tool, a source of ideas, a reference work for accurate facts, and a guidebook to the best buys, the most exciting sights, the most pleasant accommodations, and the tastiest foods—*the best travel experience* that you can possibly have.

Getting
Ready to Go

Getting Ready to Go

When to Go

With the exception of long, cold, and snowy winters, Montreal and Quebec City both have fairly temperate climates. Summer weather can be pleasant, with temperatures averaging from 55 to 80F—although hotter weather is not unknown. Spring also is mild, with temperatures between 50 and 70F; fall temperatures average between 40 and 55F. Early spring and fall are the rainiest times of year.

June through September traditionally is the peak period for travel to Montreal and Quebec City, but excellent skiing nearby makes these cities attractive winter destinations as well. In addition, there is a consistent flow of business travelers to these cities throughout the year. And Montreal and Quebec City are attractive long-weekend destinations in any season.

If you have a touch-tone phone, you can call *The Weather Channel Connection* (phone: 900-WEATHER) for current worldwide weather forecasts. This service, available from *The Weather Channel* (2600 Cumberland Pkwy., Atlanta, GA 30339; phone: 404-434-6800), costs 95¢ per minute; the charge will appear on your phone bill.

Traveling by Plane

SCHEDULED FLIGHTS

Montreal has two airports, *Dorval International Airport* and *Mirabel International Airport;* Quebec City is served by *Jean-Lesage International Airport*. Airlines offering flights to Montreal and/or Quebec City include *Air Canada, American, Canadian Airlines International, Delta, Northwest, NW Airlink,* and *USAir*.

FARES The great variety of airfares can be reduced to the following basic categories: first class, business class, coach (also called economy or tourist class), excursion or discount, and standby, as well as various promotional fares. For information on applicable fares and restrictions, contact the airlines listed above or ask your travel agent. Most airfares are offered for a limited time. Once you've found the lowest fare for which you can qualify, purchase your ticket as soon as possible.

RESERVATIONS Reconfirmation is strongly recommended for all international flights. It is essential that you confirm your round-trip reservations—*especially the return leg*—as well as any flights within Canada.

SEATING Airline seats usually are assigned on a first-come, first-served basis at check-in, although you may be able to reserve a seat when purchasing your ticket. Seating charts sometimes are available from airlines and also are included in the *Airline Seating Guide* (Carlson Publishing Co., 11132 Los Alamitos Blvd., Los Alamitos, CA 90720; phone: 310-493-4877).

SMOKING US law prohibits smoking on flights scheduled for six hours or less within the US and its territories on both domestic and international carriers. Although these restrictions do not apply to nonstop flights between the US and international destinations, none of the major US carriers permit smoking on flights to Canada, and *Air Canada* and *Canadian Airlines International* both prohibit smoking on *all* domestic and international flights. A free wallet-size guide that describes the rights of nonsmokers under current regulations is available from *ASH* (*Action on Smoking and Health;* DOT Card, 2013 H St. NW, Washington, DC 20006; phone: 202-659-4310).

SPECIAL MEALS When making your reservation, you can request one of the airline's alternate menu choices for no additional charge. Though not always required, it's a good idea to reconfirm your request the day before departure.

BAGGAGE On major international airlines, passengers usually are allowed to carry on board one bag that will fit under a seat or in an overhead bin and to check two bags in the cargo hold. Specific regulations regarding dimensions and weight restrictions vary among airlines, but a checked bag usually cannot exceed 62 inches in combined dimensions (length, width, and depth), or weigh more than 70 pounds. There may be charges for additional, oversize, or overweight luggage, and for special equipment or sporting gear. Note that baggage allowances may be more limited for children (depending on the percentage of full adult fare paid) and on some domestic routes in Canada. Check that the tags the airline attaches are correctly coded for your destination.

CHARTER FLIGHTS

By booking a block of seats on a specially arranged flight, charter operators frequently can offer travelers bargain airfares. If you do fly on a charter, however, read the contract's fine print carefully. Federal regulations permit charter operators to cancel a flight or assess surcharges of as much as 10% of the airfare up to 10 days before departure. You usually must book in advance, and once booked, no changes are permitted, so buy trip cancellation insurance. Also, make your check out to the company's escrow account, which provides some protection for your investment in the event that the charter operator fails. For further information, consult the publication *Jax Fax* (397 Post Rd., Darien, CT 06820; phone: 203-655-8746; fax: 203-655-6257).

DISCOUNTS ON SCHEDULED FLIGHTS

COURIER TRAVEL In return for arranging to accompany some kind of freight, a traveler pays only a portion of the total airfare (and sometimes a small registration fee). One agency that matches up would-be couriers with courier companies is *Now Voyager* (74 Varick St., Suite 307, New York, NY 10013; phone: 212-431-1616; fax: 212-334-5243).

Courier Companies

Discount Travel International (169 W. 81st St., New York, NY 10024; phone: 212-362-3636; fax: 212-362-3236; and 801 Alton Rd., Suite 1, Miami Beach, FL 33139; phone: 305-538-1616; fax: 305-673-9376).

F.B. On Board Courier Club (10225 Ryan Ave., Suite 103, Dorval, Quebec H9P 1A2, Canada; phone: 514-633-0740; fax: 514-633-0735).

Halbart Express (147-05 176th St., Jamaica, NY 11434; phone: 718-656-8279; fax: 718-244-0559).

Midnite Express (925 W. Hyde Park Blvd., Inglewood, CA 90302; phone: 310-672-1100; fax: 310-671-0107).

Way to Go Travel (6679 Sunset Blvd., Hollywood, CA 90028; phone: 213-466-1126; fax: 213-466-8994).

Publications

Insiders Guide to Air Courier Bargains, by Kelly Monaghan (The Intrepid Traveler, PO Box 438, New York, NY 10034; phone: 212-569-1081 for information; 800-356-9315 for orders; fax: 212-942-6687).

Travel Unlimited (PO Box 1058, Allston, MA 02134-1058; no phone).

CONSOLIDATORS AND BUCKET SHOPS These companies buy blocks of tickets from airlines and sell them at a discount to travel agents or directly to consumers. Since many bucket shops operate on a thin margin, be sure to check a company's record with the *Better Business Bureau*—before parting with any money.

Council Charter (205 E. 42nd St., New York, NY 10017; phone: 800-800-8222 or 212-661-0311; fax: 212-972-0194).

International Adventures (60 E. 42nd St., Room 763, New York, NY 10165; phone: 212-599-0577; fax: 212-599-3288).

Travac Tours and Charters (989 Ave. of the Americas, New York, NY 10018; phone: 800-872-8800 or 212-563-3303; fax: 212-563-3631).

Unitravel (1177 N. Warson Rd., St. Louis, MO 63132; phone: 800-325-2222 or 314-569-0900; fax: 314-569-2503).

LAST-MINUTE TRAVEL CLUBS Members of such clubs receive information on imminent trips and other bargain travel opportunities. There usually is an annual fee, although a few clubs offer free membership. Despite the names of some of the clubs listed below, you don't have to wait until literally the last minute to make travel plans.

Discount Travel International (114 Forrest Ave., Suite 203, Narberth, PA 19072; phone: 215-668-7184; fax: 215-668-9182).

FLY ASAP (PO Box 9808, Scottsdale, AZ 85252-3808; phone: 800-FLY-ASAP or 602-956-1987; fax: 602-956-6414).

Last Minute Travel (1249 Boylston St., Boston, MA 02215; phone: 800-LAST-MIN or 617-267-9800; fax: 617-424-1943).

> ***Moment's Notice*** (425 Madison Ave., New York, NY 10017; phone: 212-486-0500/1/2/3; fax: 212-486-0783).
>
> ***Spur of the Moment Cruises*** (411 N. Harbor Blvd., Suite 302, San Pedro, CA 90731; phone: 800-4-CRUISES or 310-521-1070 in California; 800-343-1991 elsewhere in the US; 24-hour hotline: 310-521-1060; fax: 310-521-1061).
>
> ***Traveler's Advantage*** (3033 S. Parker Rd., Suite 900, Aurora, CO 80014; phone: 800-548-1116 or 800-835-8747; fax: 303-368-3985).
>
> ***Vacations to Go*** (1502 Augusta Dr., Suite 415, Houston, TX 77057; phone: 713-974-2121 in Texas; 800-338-4962 elsewhere in the US; fax: 713-974-0445).
>
> ***Worldwide Discount Travel Club*** (1674 Meridian Ave., Miami Beach, FL 33139; phone: 305-534-2082; fax: 305-534-2070).

GENERIC AIR TRAVEL These organizations operate much like an ordinary airline standby service, except that they offer seats on not one but several scheduled and charter airlines. One pioneer of generic flights is *Airhitch* (2790 Broadway, Suite 100, New York, NY 10025; phone: 212-864-2000).

BARTERED TRAVEL SOURCES Barter—the exchange of commodities or services in lieu of cash payment—is a common practice among travel suppliers. Companies that have obtained travel services through barter may sell these services at substantial discounts to travel clubs, who pass along the savings to members. One organization offering bartered travel opportunities is *Travel World Leisure Club* (225 W. 34th St., Suite 909, New York, NY 10122; phone: 800-444-TWLC or 212-239-4855; fax: 212-564-5158).

CONSUMER PROTECTION

Passengers whose complaints have not been satisfactorily addressed by the airline can contact the *US Department of Transportation* (*DOT;* Consumer Affairs Division, 400 Seventh St. SW, Room 10405, Washington, DC 20590; phone: 202-366-2220). Also see *Fly Rights* (Publication #050-000-00513-5; *US Government Printing Office,* PO Box 371954, Pittsburgh, PA 15250-7954; phone: 202-783-3238; fax: 202-512-2250). If you have safety-related questions or concerns, write to the *Federal Aviation Administration* (*FAA;* 800 Independence Ave. SW, Washington, DC 20591) or call the *FAA Consumer Hotline* (phone: 800-322-7873). If you have a complaint against a local travel service in Montreal or Quebec City, contact the provincial tourist authorities.

On Arrival

FROM THE AIRPORT TO THE CITY

Montreal's *Dorval International Airport* is located about 12 miles (20 km) from the city and *Mirabel International Airport* is about 34 miles (55 km) from the city. Quebec City's *Jean-Lesage International Airport* is located about 11 miles (18 km) outside the city.

It takes 25 minutes to get from *Dorval* to Montreal; cab fare is about CN$24 ($18 US at press time). A cab ride from *Mirabel* to Montreal takes 45 minutes; the fare is about CN$58 ($44 US). The 35-minute ride from *Jean-Lesage* to Quebec City costs about CN$20 ($15 US).

A more economical way to get from the airports to downtown Montreal is to take the *Autocar Connoisseur* shuttle bus (phone: 514-934-1222), which costs CN$9 (about $6.75 US) one way and CN$16.50 ($12.40 US) round trip from *Dorval,* and CN$14.50 ($11 US) one way and CN$20.50 ($15.40 US) round trip from *Mirabel.* From *Jean-Lesage, Maple Leaf Sightseeing Tours and Dupont* (phone: 418-649-9226) operates a shuttle bus (from mid-May to early October only) to all major downtown hotels in Quebec City; the fare is CN$8.50 ($6.40 US) one way and $16 ($12 US) round trip.

RENTING A CAR

You can rent a car through a travel agent or international rental firm before leaving home, or from a regional or local company once in Canada. Reserve in advance.

Most car rental companies require a credit card, although some will accept a substantial cash deposit. The minimum age to rent a car is set by the company; some also may impose special conditions on drivers above a certain age. Electing to pay for collision damage waiver (CDW) protection will add to the cost of renting a car, but releases you from financial liability for the vehicle. Additional costs include drop-off charges or one-way service fees.

Unless otherwise indicated, all of the companies listed below serve both Montreal and Quebec City.

Car Rental Companies

Auto Europe (phone: 800-223-5555).
Avis (phone: 800-331-1084).
Budget (phone: 800-472-3325).
Dollar Rent A Car (phone: 800-800-4000).
   Serves Montreal only.
Economic (phone: 514-871-1166).
   Serves Montreal only.
Hertz (phone: 800-654-3001).
Kemwel Group (phone: 800-678-0678).
National (phone: 800-CAR-RENT;
   affiliated with *Tilden Rent-A-Car* in Canada).
Sears (phone: 800-527-0770).
Thrifty (phone: 800-367-2277).
Via Route (phone: 514-871-1166).

Package Tours

A package is a collection of travel services that can be purchased in a single transaction. Its principal advantages are convenience and economy—the cost usually is lower than that of the same services purchased separately. Tour programs generally can be divided into two categories: escorted or locally hosted (with a set itinerary) and independent (usually more flexible).

When considering a package tour, read the brochure *carefully* to determine exactly what is included and any conditions that may apply, and check the company's record with the *Better Business Bureau*. The *United States Tour Operators Association* (*USTOA;* 211 E. 51st St., Suite 12B, New York, NY 10022; phone: 212-750-7371; fax: 212-421-1285) also can be helpful in determining a package tour operator's reliability. As with charter flights, to safeguard your funds, always make your check out to the company's escrow account.

Many tour operators offer packages focused on special interests such as the arts, local history, sports, and other recreations. *All Adventure Travel* (5589 Arapahoe St., Suite 208, Boulder, CO 80303; phone: 800-537-4025 or 303-440-7924; fax: 303-440-4160) represents such specialized packagers. Many also are listed in the *Specialty Travel Index* (305 San Anselmo Ave., Suite 313, San Anselmo, CA 94960; phone: 415-459-4900 in California; 800-442-4922 elsewhere in the US; fax: 415-459-4974). In addition, a number of local companies offer half- or full-day sightseeing tours in and around Montreal and Quebec City.

Package Tour Operators

Adventure Tours (10612 Beaver Dam Rd., Hunt Valley, MD 21030-2205; phone: 410-785-3500 in Baltimore; 800-638-9040 elsewhere in the US; fax: 410-584-2771).

American Express Vacations (offices throughout the US; phone: 800-YES-AMEX).

Brendan Tours (15137 Califa St., Van Nuys, CA 91411; phone: 800-421-8446 or 818-785-9696; fax: 818-902-9876).

Cartan Tours (2809 Butterfield Rd., Suite 350, Oak Brook, IL 60521; phone: 800-422-7826 or 708-571-1400; fax: 708-574-8074).

Certified Vacations (110 E. Broward Blvd., Ft. Lauderdale, FL 33302; phone: 800-233-7260 or 305-522-1440; fax: 305-468-4781).

Classic Adventures (PO Box 153, Hamlin, NY 14464-0153; phone: 800-777-8090 or 716-964-8488).

Collette Tours (162 Middle St., Pawtucket, RI 02860; phone: 800-752-2655 in New England; 800-832-4656 elsewhere in the US; fax: 401-727-4745).

Delta's Dream Vacations (PO Box 1525, Ft. Lauderdale, FL 33302; phone: 800-872-7786).

Educational Adventures (815 North Rd., Westfield, MA 01085; phone: 800-628-9655 or 413-568-2855; fax: 413-562-3621).

EuroConnection (2004 196th St. SW, Suite 4, Lynnwood, WA 98036; phone: 800-645-3876 or 206-670-1140; fax: 206-775-7561).

Gadabout Tours (700 E. Tahquitz Canyon Way, Palm Springs, CA 92262-6767; phone: 800-952-5068 or 619-325-5556; fax: 619-325-5127).

Jefferson Tours (1206 Currie Ave., Minneapolis, MN 55403; phone: 800-767-7433 or 612-338-4174; fax: 612-332-5532).

Kerrville Tours (PO Box 79, Shreveport, LA 71161-0079; phone: 800-442- 8705 or 318-227-2882; fax: 318-227-2486).

Le Ob's Tours (4635 Touro St., New Orleans, LA 70122-3933; phone: 504-288-3478; fax: 504-288-8517).

Liberty Travel (for the nearest location, contact the central office: 69 Spring St., Ramsey, NJ 07446; phone: 201-934-3500; fax: 201-934-3888).

Marsans International (19 W. 34th St., Suite 302, New York, NY 10001; phone: 800-777-9110 or 212-239-3880; fax: 212-239-4129).

Maupintour (PO Box 807, Lawrence, KS 66044; phone: 800-255-4266 or 913-843-1211; fax: 913-843-8351).

Mayflower (1225 Warren Ave., Downers Grove, IL 60515; phone: 800-323-7604 or 708-960-3430; fax: 708-960-3575).

New England Vacation Tours (PO Box 560, West Dover, VT 05356; phone: 800-742-7669 or 802-464-2076; fax: 802-464-2629).

Panorama Tours (600 N. Sprigg St., Cape Girardeau, MO 63701; phone: 800-962-8687 in Missouri and adjacent states; 314-335-9098 elsewhere in the US; fax: 314-335-7824).

Tauck Tours (PO Box 5027, Westport, CT 06881; phone: 800-468-2825 or 203-226-6911; fax: 203-221-6828).

Thomas Cook (headquarters: 45 Berkeley St., Piccadilly, London W1A 1EB, England; phone: 44-171-499-4000; fax: 44-171-408-4299; main US office: 100 Cambridge Park Dr., Cambridge, MA 02140; phone: 800-846-6272; fax: 617-349-1094).

Tours and Travel Odyssey (230 E. McClellan Ave., Livingston, NJ 07039; phone: 800-527-2989 or 201-992-5459; fax: 201-994-1618).

Yankee Holidays (435 Newbury St., Suite 210, Danvers, MA 01923-1065; phone: 800-225-2550 or 508-750-9688; fax: 508-750-9692).

Insurance

The first person with whom you should discuss travel insurance is your own insurance broker. You may discover that the insurance you already carry protects you adequately while traveling and that you need little additional coverage. If you charge travel services, the credit card company also may provide some insurance coverage (and other safeguards).

Types of Travel Insurance

Automobile insurance: Provides collision, theft, property damage, and personal liability protection while driving.

Baggage and personal effects insurance: Protects your bags and their contents in case of damage or theft at any point during your travels.

Default and/or bankruptcy insurance: Provides coverage in the event of default and/or bankruptcy on the part of the tour operator, airline, or other travel supplier.

Flight insurance: Covers accidental injury or death while flying.

Personal accident and sickness insurance: Covers cases of illness, injury, or death in an accident while traveling.

Trip cancellation and interruption insurance: Guarantees a refund if you must cancel a trip; may reimburse you for additional travel costs incurred in catching up with a tour or traveling home early.

Combination policies: Include any or all of the above.

Disabled Travelers

Make travel arrangements well in advance. Specify to all services involved the nature of your disability to determine if there are accommodations and facilities that meet your needs. Publications issued by *Tourisme Québec,* the provincial tourist office (see *For Further Information,* below, for address), use the standard symbol (person in a wheelchair) to indicate facilities accessible to the disabled. For additional information on accessibility in Montreal and Quebec City, contact *Keroul* (PO Box 1000, Station M, Montreal, Quebec H1V 3R2, Canada; phone: 514-252-3104; fax: 514-254-0766), which publishes *Accessible Montreal,* a guide to accessible hotels, restaurants, and tourist attractions, and *Accessible Tourism Guide,* which lists accessible hotels throughout the province of Quebec.

Organizations

ACCENT on Living (PO Box 700, Bloomington, IL 61702; phone: 800-787-8444 or 309-378-2961; fax: 309-378-4420).

Access: The Foundation for Accessibility by the Disabled (PO Box 356, Malverne, NY 11565; phone/fax: 516-887-5798).

American Foundation for the Blind (15 W. 16th St., New York, NY 10011; phone: 800-232-5463 or 212-620-2147; fax: 212-727-7418).

Canadian Paraplegic Association (520 Sutherland Dr., Toronto, Ontario M4G 3V9, Canada; phone: 416-422-5644; fax: 416-422-5943).

Canadian Rehabilitation Council for the Disabled (45 Sheppard Ave. E., Suite 801, Toronto, Ontario M2N 5W9, Canada; phone: 416-250-7490; fax: 416-229-1371).

Holiday Care Service (2 Old Bank Chambers, Station Rd., Horley, Surrey RH6 9HW, England; phone: 44-1293-774535; fax: 44-1293-784647).

Information Center for Individuals with Disabilities (Ft. Point Pl., 27-43 Wormwood St., Boston, MA 02210; phone: 800-462-5015 in Massachusetts; 617-727-5540 elsewhere in the US; TDD: 617-345-9743; fax: 617-345-5318).

Mobility International (main office: 228 Borough High St., London SE1 1JX, England; phone: 44-171-403-5688; fax: 44-171-378-1292; US office: *MIUSA,* PO Box 10767, Eugene, OR 97440; phone/TDD: 503-343-1284; fax: 503-343-6812).

Moss Rehabilitation Hospital Travel Information Service (telephone referrals only; phone: 215-456-9600; TDD: 215-456-9602).

National Rehabilitation Information Center (8455 Colesville Rd., Suite 935, Silver Spring, MD 20910; phone: 301-588-9284; fax: 301-587-1967).

Paralyzed Veterans of America (*PVA;* PVA/ATTS Program, 801 18th St. NW, Washington, DC 20006; phone: 202-872-1300 in Washington, DC; 800-424-8200 elsewhere in the US; fax: 202-785-4452).

Royal Association for Disability and Rehabilitation (*RADAR;* 12 City Forum, 250 City Rd., London EC1V 8AF, England; phone: 44-171-250-3222; fax: 44-171-250-0212).

Society for the Advancement of Travel for the Handicapped (*SATH;* 347 Fifth Ave., Suite 610, New York, NY 10016; phone: 212-447-7284; fax: 212-725-8253).

Travel Industry and Disabled Exchange (*TIDE;* 5435 Donna Ave., Tarzana, CA 91356; phone: 818-368-5648).

Tripscope (The Courtyard, Evelyn Rd., London W4 5JL, England; phone: 44-181-994-9294; fax: 44-181-994-3618).

Publications

Access Travel: A Guide to the Accessibility of Airport Terminals (Consumer Information Center, Dept. 578Z, Pueblo, CO 81009; phone: 719-948-3334).

Air Transportation of Handicapped Persons (Publication #AC-120-32; *US Department of Transportation,* Distribution Unit, Publications Section, M-443-2, 400 Seventh St. SW, Washington, DC 20590; phone: 202-366-0039).

The Diabetic Traveler (PO Box 8223 RW, Stamford, CT 06905; phone: 203-327-5832; fax: 203-975-1748).

Directory of Travel Agencies for the Disabled and Travel for the Disabled, both by Helen Hecker (Twin Peaks Press, PO Box 129, Vancouver, WA 98666; phone: 800-637-CALM or 206-694-2462; fax: 206-696-3210).

Guide to Traveling with Arthritis (Upjohn Company, PO Box 989, Dearborn, MI 48121; phone: 800-253-9860).

The Handicapped Driver's Mobility Guide (*American Automobile Association,* 1000 AAA Dr., Heathrow, FL 32746-5080; phone: 407-444-7000; fax: 407-444-7380).

Handicapped Travel Newsletter (PO Box 269, Athens, TX 75751; phone/fax: 903-677-1260).

Handi-Travel: A Resource Book for Disabled and Elderly Travellers, by Cinnie Noble (*Canadian Rehabilitation Council for the Disabled,* 45 Sheppard Ave. E., Suite 801, Toronto, Ontario M2N 5W9, Canada; phone/TDD: 416-250-7490; fax: 416-229-1371).

Holidays and Travel Abroad, edited by John Stanford (*Royal Association for Disability and Rehabilitation,* address above).

Incapacitated Passengers Air Travel Guide (*International Air Transport Association,* Publications Sales Department, 2000 Peel St., Montreal, Quebec H3A 2R4, Canada; phone: 514-844-6311; fax: 514-844-5286).

Ticket to Safe Travel (*American Diabetes Association,* 1660 Duke St., Alexandria, VA 22314; phone: 800-232-3472 or 703-549-1500; fax: 703-836-7439).

Travel for the Patient with Chronic Obstructive Pulmonary Disease (Dr. Harold Silver, 1601 18th St. NW, Washington, DC 20009; phone: 202-667-0134; fax: 202-667-0148).

Travel Tips for Hearing-Impaired People (*American Academy of Otolaryngology,* 1 Prince St., Alexandria, VA 22314; phone: 703-836-4444; fax: 703-683-5100).

Travel Tips for People with Arthritis (*Arthritis Foundation,* 1314 Spring St. NW, Atlanta, GA 30309; phone: 800-283-7800 or 404-872-7100; fax: 404-872-0457).

Traveling Like Everybody Else: A Practical Guide for Disabled Travelers, by Jacqueline Freedman and Susan Gersten (Modan Publishing, PO Box 1202, Bellmore, NY 11710; phone: 516-679-1380; fax: 516-679-1448).

The Wheelchair Traveler, by Douglass R. Annand (123 Ball Hill Rd., Milford, NH 03055; phone: 603-673-4539).

Package Tour Operators

Accessible Journeys (35 W. Sellers Ave., Ridley Park, PA 19078; phone: 800-846-4537 or 215-521-0339; fax: 215-521-6959).

Accessible Tours/Directions Unlimited (Attn.: Lois Bonnani, 720 N. Bedford Rd., Bedford Hills, NY 10507; phone: 800-533-5343 or 914-241-1700; fax: 914-241-0243).

Beehive Business and Leisure Travel (1130 W. Center St., N. Salt Lake, UT 84054; phone: 800-777-5727 or 801-292-4445; fax: 801-298-9460).

Classic Travel Service (8 W. 40th St., New York, NY 10018; phone: 212-869-2560 in New York State; 800-247-0909 elsewhere in the US; fax: 212-944-4493).

Evergreen Travel Service (4114 198th St. SW, Suite 13, Lynnwood, WA 98036-6742; phone: 800-435-2288 or 206-776-1184; fax: 206-775-0728).

Flying Wheels Travel (143 W. Bridge St., PO Box 382, Owatonna, MN 55060; phone: 800-535-6790 or 507-451-5005; fax: 507-451-1685).

Good Neighbor Travel Service (124 S. Main St., Viroqua, WI 54665; phone: 800-338-3245 or 608-637-2128; fax: 608-637-3030).

The Guided Tour (7900 Old York Rd., Suite 114B, Elkins Park, PA 19117-2339; phone: 800-783-5841 or 215-782-1370; fax: 215-635-2637).

Hinsdale Travel (201 E. Ogden Ave., Hinsdale, IL 60521; phone: 708-325-1335 or 708-469-7349; fax: 708-325-1342).

MedEscort International (*ABE International Airport,* PO Box 8766, Allentown, PA 18105-8766; phone: 800-255-7182 or 215-791-3111; fax: 215-791-9189).

Prestige World Travel (5710-X High Point Rd., Greensboro, NC 27407; phone: 800-476-7737 or 910-292-6690; fax: 910-632-9404).

Sprout (893 Amsterdam Ave., New York, NY 10025; phone: 212-222-9575; fax: 212-222-9768).

Weston Travel Agency (134 N. Cass Ave., Westmont, IL 60559; phone: 708-968-2513 in Illinois; 800-633-3725 elsewhere in the US; fax: 708-968-2539).

Single Travelers

The travel industry is not very fair to people who vacation by themselves—they often end up paying more than those traveling in pairs. There are services catering to single travelers, however, that match travel companions, offer travel arrangements with shared accommodations, and provide information and discounts. Useful publications include *Going Solo* (Doerfer Communications, PO Box 123, Apalachicola, FL 32329; phone/fax: 904-653-8848) and *Traveling on Your Own,* by Eleanor Berman (Random House, Order Dept., 400 Hahn Rd., Westminster, MD 21157; phone: 800-733-3000; fax: 800-659-2436).

Organizations and Companies

Contiki Holidays (300 Plaza Alicante, Suite 900, Garden Grove, CA 92640; phone: 800-466-0610 or 714-740-0808; fax: 714-740-0818).

Gallivanting (515 E. 79th St., Suite 20F, New York, NY 10021; phone: 800-933-9699 or 212-988-0617; fax: 212-988-0144).

Globus/Cosmos (5301 S. Federal Circle, Littleton, CO 80123; phone: 800-221-0090, 800-556-5454, or 303-797-2800; fax: 303-347-2080).

Jane's International and Sophisticated Women Travelers (2603 Bath Ave., Brooklyn, NY 11214; phone: 718-266-2045; fax: 718-266-4062).

Marion Smith Singles (611 Prescott Pl., N. Woodmere, NY 11581; phone: 516-791-4852, 516-791-4865, or 212-944-2112; fax: 516-791-4879)

Partners-in-Travel (11660 Chenault St., Suite 119, Los Angeles, CA 90049; phone: 310-476-4869).

Singles in Motion (545 W. 236th St., Riverdale, NY 10463; phone/fax: 718-884-4464).

Singleworld (401 Theodore Fremd Ave., Rye, NY 10580; phone: 800-223-6490 or 914-967-3334; fax: 914-967-7395).

Solo Flights (63 High Noon Rd., Weston, CT 06883; phone: 800-266-1566 or 203-226-9993).

Suddenly Singles Tours (161 Dreiser Loop, Bronx, NY 10475; phone: 718-379-8800 in New York City; 800-859-8396 elsewhere in the US; fax: 718-379-8858).

Travel Companion Exchange (PO Box 833, Amityville, NY 11701; phone: 516-454-0880; fax: 516-454-0170).

Travel Companions (Atrium Financial Center, 1515 N. Federal Hwy., Suite 300, Boca Raton, FL 33432; phone: 800-383-7211 or 407-393-6448; fax: 407-451-8560).

Travel in Two's (239 N. Broadway, Suite 3, N. Tarrytown, NY 10591; phone: 914-631-8301 in New York State; 800-692-5252 elsewhere in the US).

Umbrella Singles (PO Box 157, Woodbourne, NY 12788; phone: 800-537-2797 or 914-434-6871; fax: 914-434-3532).

Older Travelers

Special discounts and more free time are just two factors that have given older travelers a chance to see the world at affordable prices. Many travel suppliers offer senior discounts—sometimes only to members of certain senior citizens organizations (which provide benefits of their own). When considering a particular package, make sure the facilities—and the pace of the tour—match your needs and physical condition.

Publications

Going Abroad: 101 Tips for Mature Travelers (*Grand Circle Travel,* 347 Congress St., Boston, MA 02210; phone: 800-221-2610 or 617-350-7500; fax: 617-423-0445).

The Mature Traveler (PO Box 50820, Reno, NV 89513-0820; phone: 702-786-7419).

The Senior Citizen's Guide to Budget Travel in the US and Canada, by Paige Palmer (Pilot Books, 103 Cooper St., Babylon, NY 11702; phone: 516-422-2225; fax: 516-422-2227).

Take a Camel to Lunch and Other Adventures for Mature Travelers, by Nancy O'Connell (Bristol Publishing Enterprises, PO Box 1737, San Leandro, CA 94577; phone: 510-895-4461 in California; 800-346-4889 elsewhere in the US; fax: 510-895-4459).

Unbelievably Good Deals & Great Adventures That You Absolutely Can't Get Unless You're Over 50, by Joan Rattner Heilman (Contemporary Books, 1200 Stetson Ave., Chicago, IL 60601; phone: 312-782-9181; fax: 312-540-4687).

Organizations

GETTING READY TO GO

American Association of Retired Persons (*AARP;* 601 E St. NW, Washington, DC 20049; phone: 202-434-2277).

Golden Companions (PO Box 754, Pullman, WA 99163-0754; phone: 208-858-2183).

Mature Outlook (Customer Service Center, 6001 N. Clark St., Chicago, IL 60660; phone: 800-336-6330).

National Council of Senior Citizens (1331 F St. NW, Washington, DC 20004; phone: 202-347-8800; fax: 202-624-9595).

Package Tour Operators

Elderhostel (75 Federal St., Boston, MA 02110-1941; phone: 617-426-7788; fax: 617-426-8351).

Evergreen Travel Service (4114 198th St. SW, Suite 13, Lynnwood, WA 98036-6742; phone: 800-435-2288 or 206-776-1184; fax: 206-775-0728).

Gadabout Tours (700 E. Tahquitz Canyon Way, Palm Springs, CA 92262; phone: 800-952-5068 or 619-325-5556; fax: 619-325-5127).

Grand Circle Travel (347 Congress St., Boston, MA 02210; phone: 800-221-2610 or 617-350-7500; fax: 617-423-0445).

Grandtravel (6900 Wisconsin Ave., Suite 706, Chevy Chase, MD 20815; phone: 800-247-7651 or 301-986-0790; fax: 301-913-0166).

Interhostel (*University of New Hampshire,* Division of Continuing Education, 6 Garrison Ave., Durham, NH 03824; phone: 800-733-9753 or 603-862-1147; fax: 603-862-1113).

Mature Tours (c/o *Solo Flights,* 63 High Noon Rd., Weston, CT 06883; phone: 800-266-1566 or 203-226-9993).

OmniTours (104 Wilmot Rd., Deerfield, IL 60015; phone: 800-962-0060 or 708-374-0088; fax: 708-374-9515).

Saga International Holidays (222 Berkeley St., Boston, MA 02116; phone: 800-343-0273 or 617-262-2262; fax: 617-375-5950).

Money Matters

Travelers from the US should have little difficulty with matters of exchange in Canada. Both countries have monetary systems based on dollars and cents, although US and Canadian currency are not equal in value. Canadian currency is distributed in coin denominations of $1, 25¢, 10¢, 5¢, and 1¢, and in bills of $1,000, $500, $100, $50, $20, $10, $5, and $2. Although 50¢ coins and $1 bills are no longer issued, these still are in circulation and are legal tender. At the time of this writing, the exchange rate for the Canadian dollar was CN$1.33 to $1 US.

Exchange rates are posted in international newspapers such as the *International Herald Tribune.* Foreign currency information and related services are provided by banks and companies such as *Thomas Cook Foreign Exchange* (for the nearest location, call 800-621-0666 or 312-236-0042; fax: 312-807-4895); *Harold Reuter and Company* (200 Park Ave., Suite 332E, New York, NY 10166; phone: 800-258-0456 or 212-661-0826; fax: 212-557-6622); and *Ruesch International* (for the nearest location, call 800-424-2923 or 202-408-1200; fax: 202-408-1211). In Montreal and Quebec City, you will find the official rate of exchange posted in banks, airports, money exchange houses, hotels, and some shops. Since you will get more Canadian currency for your US dollar at banks and money exchanges, don't change more than $10 at other commercial establishments. Ask how much commission you're being charged and the exchange rate, and don't buy money on the black market (it may be counterfeit). Estimate your needs carefully; if you overbuy, you lose twice—buying and selling back.

CREDIT CARDS AND TRAVELER'S CHECKS

Most major credit cards enjoy wide domestic and international acceptance; however, not every hotel, restaurant, or shop in Montreal or Quebec City accepts all (or in some cases any) credit cards. When making purchases with a credit card, note that the rate of exchange depends on when the charge is processed; most credit card companies charge a 1% fee for converting foreign currency charges.

It's also wise to carry traveler's checks while on the road, since they are widely accepted and replaceable if stolen or lost. You can buy traveler's checks at banks and some are available by mail or phone. Keep a separate list of all traveler's checks (noting those that you have cashed) and the names and numbers of your credit cards. Both traveler's check and credit card companies have international numbers to call for information or in the event of loss or theft.

CASH MACHINES

Automated teller machines (ATMs) are increasingly common worldwide, and most banks participate in international ATM networks such as *CIRRUS* (phone: 800-4-CIRRUS) and *PLUS* (phone: 800-THE-PLUS). Cardholders can withdraw cash from any machine in the same network using either a "bank" card or, in some cases, a credit card. Additional information on ATMs and networks can be obtained from your bank or credit card company.

SENDING MONEY ABROAD

Should the need arise, you can have money sent to you in Montreal or Quebec City via the services provided by *American Express MoneyGram* (phone: 800-926-9400 for information; 800-866-8800 for money transfers) or *Western Union Financial Services* (phone: 800-325-6000 or 800-325-4176). If you are down to your last cent and have no other way to obtain cash, the nearest *US Consulate* will let you call home to set these matters in motion.

Accommodations

For specific information on hotels and other selected accommodations see *Checking In* in THE CITIES. Quebec's provincial tourist office also publishes accommodations booklets that provide information (including ratings) about licensed establishments in the Montreal and Quebec City areas.

BED AND BREAKFAST ESTABLISHMENTS

Commonly known as B&Bs, bed and breakfast establishments provide exactly what the name implies. A private bath isn't always offered, so check before you reserve. Although some hosts may be contacted directly, most prefer that arrangements be made through reservations services, some of which are listed below. The Quebec provincial tourist office also can provide information on bed and breakfast establishments and reservations services in Montreal and Quebec City.

Reservations Services

Bed & Breakfast à Montreal (PO Box 575, Snowdon Station, Montreal, Quebec H3X 3T8, Canada; phone: 514-738-9410; fax: 514-735-7493).

Hospitalité Canada (1001 Dorchester Square, Montreal, Quebec H3B 4V4, Canada; phone: 514-393-9049; fax: 514-393-8942).

Relais Montréal Hospitalité (3977 Laval St., Montreal, Quebec H2W 2H9, Canada; phone: 800-363-9635).

RENTAL OPTIONS

An attractive accommodations alternative for the visitor content to stay in one spot is a vacation rental. For a family or group, the per-person cost can be reasonable. To have your pick of the properties available, make inquiries at least six months in advance. The *Worldwide Home Rental Guide* (3501 Indian School Rd. NE, Albuquerque, NM 87106; phone/fax: 505-255-4271) lists rental properties and managing agencies.

Rental Property Agents

Coast to Coast Resorts (64 Inverness Dr. E., Englewood, CO 80112; phone: 800-368-5721 or 303-790-2267; fax: 303-792-7360).

Keith Prowse & Co. (USA) Ltd. (234 W. 44th St., Suite 1000, New York, NY 10036; phone: 800-669-8687 or 212-398-1430; fax: 212-302-4251).

Property Rentals International (1 Park W. Circle, Suite 108, Midlothian, VA 23113; phone: 800-220-3332 or 804-378-6054; fax: 804-379-2073).

HOME EXCHANGES

For comfortable, reasonable living quarters with amenities that no hotel could possibly offer, consider trading homes with someone abroad. The following companies provide information on exchanges:

Home Base Holidays (7 Park Ave., London N13 5PG, England; phone/fax: 44-181-886-8752).

Intervac US/International Home Exchange (PO Box 590504, San Francisco, CA 94159; phone: 800-756-HOME or 415-435-3497; fax: 415-386-6853).

Loan-A-Home (2 Park La., Apt. 6E, Mt. Vernon, NY 10552-3443; phone: 914-664-7640; no fax).

Vacation Exchange Club (PO Box 650, Key West, FL 33041; phone: 800-638-3841 or 305-294-3720; fax: 305-294-1448).

Worldwide Home Exchange Club (main office: 50 Hans Crescent, London SW1X 0NA, England; phone: 44-171-589-6055; no fax; US office: 806 Brantford Ave., Silver Spring, MD 20904; phone: 301-680-8950; no fax).

HOME STAYS

United States Servas (11 John St., Room 407, New York, NY 10038; phone: 212-267-0252; fax: 212-267-0292) maintains a list of hosts worldwide willing to accommodate visitors free of charge. The aim of this nonprofit cultural program is to promote international understanding and peace, and *Servas* emphasizes that member travelers should be interested mainly in their hosts, not in sightseeing, during their stays.

ACCOMMODATIONS DISCOUNTS

Unless specified otherwise, the following organizations offer discounts of up to 50% on accommodations in both Montreal and Quebec City.

Entertainment Publishing (2125 Butterfield Rd., Troy, MI 48084; phone: 800-477-3234 or 313-637-8400; fax: 313-637-9779). Provides discounts in Montreal only.

Hotel Express (4405 Beltwood Pkwy. N., Dallas, TX 75244; phone: 800-580-2083 for reservations; 800-866-2015 or 214-991-5482 for information; fax: 214-770-3575).

International Travel Card (6001 N. Clark St., Chicago, IL 60660; phone: 800-342-0558 or 312-465-8891; fax: 312-764-8066).

Privilege Card (3391 Peachtree Rd., Suite 110, Atlanta, GA 30326; phone: 800-236-9732 or 404-262-0255; fax: 404-262-0235).

Quest International (402 E. Yakima Ave., Suite 1200, Yakima, WA 98901; phone: 800-325-2400 or 509-248-7512; fax: 509-457-8399).

Time Zone

Montreal and Quebec City are in the eastern standard time zone, which means that the time is the same as in East Coast US cities. As in the US, daylight saving time is observed from the first Sunday in April until the last Sunday in October. Canadian timetables use a 24-hour clock to denote arrival and departure times, which means that hours are expressed sequentially from 1 AM—for example, in Montreal and Quebec City, 1:30 PM would be "1330 hours" (in English) or "13h30" (in French-speaking areas).

Business and Shopping Hours

Business hours throughout Canada are fairly standard and similar to those in the US: 9 AM to 5 PM, Mondays through Fridays. Retail stores usually are open weekdays from 9 or 9:30 AM to around 6 PM, and Saturdays from 8:30 AM to 5 PM; some stores also are open on Sundays (usually from around 10 AM to 5 PM). Department stores and malls may be open from 10 AM to 9 PM during the week, 10 AM to 6 PM on Saturdays, and noon to 5 PM on Sundays.

Banks usually are open from 10 AM to 3 PM, Mondays through Thursdays, and until 6 PM on Fridays, but the trend is toward longer hours. Although most banks are closed on weekends, some may have Saturday morning hours.

Holidays

Quebec celebrates its own provincial holiday, *St-Jean-Baptiste Day* (also known as *Quebec Day*), on June 24. The province also observes all Canadian national holidays, which are listed below with the dates they will occur this year. (Note that the dates of some holidays vary from year to year; others occur on the same day every year.)

> *New Year's Day* (January 1)
> *Good Friday* (April 14)
> *Easter Monday* (April 17)
> *Victoria Day* (May 22)
> *Canada Day* (July 1)
> *Labour Day* (September 4)
> *Thanksgiving* (October 9)
> *Remembrance Day* (November 11)
> *Christmas Day* (December 25)
> *Boxing Day* (December 26)

Mail

The main post office in Montreal (Station A, 1025 St-Jacques St. W., Montreal, Quebec H3C 1G0, Canada; phone: 514-846-5390) is open weekdays from 8 AM to 5:45 PM. Quebec City's main post office, or *Bureau Post Principal* (300 Rue St-Paul, Quebec City, Quebec G1K 3W0, Canada; phone: 418-694-6175), is open weekdays from 8 AM to 5:45 PM. For the locations of other branches, contact the main post office. Post offices in Montreal and Quebec City are not open on weekends. Stamps also are available at most hotel desks, tobacconists, drug stores, and convenience stores (called *Depanneurs* in Quebec), as well as from public vending machines.

Note that the inclusion of postal codes in Canadian addresses is essential; delivery of your letter or parcel may depend on it. Allow at least seven days for delivery of letters between the US and Canada. If your correspondence is especially important, you may want to send it via an international courier service, such as *Federal Express* or *DHL Worldwide Express*.

You can have mail sent to you care of your hotel (marked "Guest Mail, Hold for Arrival") or the main post office in Montreal or Quebec City (sent "c/o General Delivery" or "c/o *Poste Restante*"—either term is acceptable— to the applicable address above). *American Express* offices in Montreal and Quebec City also will hold mail for customers ("c/o Client Letter Service"); information is provided in their pamphlet *Travelers' Companion*. Note that *US Embassies* and *Consulates* abroad will hold mail for US citizens *only* in emergency situations.

Telephone

The procedure for making calls between the US and Canada, as well as within Canada, is the same as in the US. You simply dial the area code + the local number. (The area code for Montreal is 514; the area code for Quebec City is 418.) To call a number within the same area code, dial the local number.

Although most public telephones in Canada still take coins, pay phones that accept special phone cards are increasingly common. *Bell Quebec,* the provincial phone company, sells the "Hello! Phone Pass"—a phone debit card designed for use by foreign travelers. Available in denominations of CN$5, CN$10, and CN$20, these cards can be purchased at "Phone Centers" (called *"Teleboutiques"* in Quebec) throughout the province and may be used for both domestic and international calls.

You can use a telephone calling card number on any phone, and some pay phones take major credit cards (*American Express, MasterCard, Visa,* and so on). Also available are combined telephone calling/bank credit cards, such as the *AT&T Universal Card* (PO Box 44167, Jacksonville, FL 32231-4167; phone: 800-423-4343). Similarly, *Sprint* (8140 Ward Pkwy., Kansas City, MO 64114; phone: 800-THE-MOST or 800-800-USAA) offers the *VisaPhone* program, through which you can add phone card privileges to your existing *Visa* card. Companies offering long-distance phone cards without additional credit card privileges include *AT&T* (phone: 800-CALL-ATT), *Executive Telecard International* (4260 E. Evans Ave., Suite 6, Denver, CO 80222; phone: 800-950-3800), *MCI* (323 Third St. SE, Cedar Rapids, IA 52401; phone: 800-444-4444; and 12790 Merit Dr., Dallas, TX 75251; phone: 800-444-3333), *Metromedia Communications* (1 International Center, 100 NE Loop 410, San Antonio, TX 78216; phone: 800-275-0200), and *Sprint* (address above).

Hotels routinely add surcharges to the cost of phone calls made from their rooms. Long-distance telephone services that may help you avoid this added expense are provided by a number of companies, including *AT&T* (International Information Service, 635 Grant St., Pittsburgh, PA 15219; phone: 800-874-4000), *MCI* (address above), *Metromedia Communications* (address above), and *Sprint* (address above). Note that even when you use such long-distance services, some hotels still may charge a fee for line usage.

Useful resources for travelers include the *AT&T 800 Travel Directory* (phone: 800-426-8686 for orders), the *Toll-Free Travel & Vacation Information Directory* (Pilot Books, 103 Cooper St., Babylon, NY 11702; phone: 516-422-2225; fax: 516-422-2227), and *The Phone Booklet* (Scott American Corporation, PO Box 88, W. Redding, CT 06896; no phone).

Important Phone Numbers

Emergency assistance: 911 or 0 (for an operator, who will connect you)
Local and long-distance operator: 0
Local information: 555-1212 or 411
Countrywide information: Area code + 555-1212

Electricity

Like the US, Canada uses 110-volt, 60-cycle, alternating current (AC). Travelers from the US can use appliances they have brought from home without converters or plug adapters.

Staying Healthy

For up-to-date information on current health conditions, call the Centers for Disease Control's *International Travelers' Hotline:* 404-332-4559.

Travelers to Canada face few serious health risks. Tap water generally is clean and potable, although in rural areas the water supply may not be thoroughly purified. Milk is pasteurized throughout Canada, and dairy products are safe to eat, as are fresh fruit, vegetables, meat, poultry, and fish.

Although Canada has a government-supported medical system, and health care is free (or inexpensive) for Canadian citizens, this does not apply to travelers from the US. Unlike many foreign countries, however, US health insurance policies *may* cover care in Canada; check with your insurance company before your trip.

All Canadian hospitals are prepared for emergency cases, and some also have walk-in clinics. Should you need non-emergency medical attention, ask at your hotel for the house physician or for help in reaching a doctor. Referrals also are available from the *US Embassy* or a *US Consulate.* In an emergency: Go to the emergency room of the nearest hospital, dial the nationwide emergency assistance number provided in *Telephone,* above, or call an operator for assistance.

Hospitals

In Montreal

Montreal Children's Hospital (2300 Tupper St.; phone: 514-934-4499).
Montreal General Hospital (1650 Cedar Ave.; phone: 514-937-6011).
Royal Victoria Hospital (687 Pine Ave. W.; phone: 514-842-1231).

In Quebec City

Jeffrey Hale Hospital (1250 St-Foy Rd.; phone: 418-683-4471).
Hôpital l'Hôtel-Dieu de Québec (11 Côte du Palais; phone: 418-691-5042).

Dentists

In Montreal

Dental Center (1414 Drummond St., Suite 412, Montreal; phone: 514-281-1023).

In Quebec City

Clinique Dentale (1175 La Vigerie, Quebec City; phone: 418-653-5412 weekdays; 418-656-6060 weekends).

24-Hour Pharmacies

In Montreal

Dubois Pharmacy (5122 Côte-des-Neiges, Montreal; phone: 514-738-8464).
Pharmatrix (901 Ste-Catherine E., Montreal; phone: 514-842-4915).

In Quebec City

Pharmacy Brunet (*Les Galeries Charlesbourg* mall, 4266 First Ave., Charlesbourg, near Quebec City; phone: 418-623-1571).

Other Services

Quebec Poison Control Center (phone: 418-656-8090 for Quebec province's emergency information hotline).

Additional Resources

International Association for Medical Assistance to Travelers (*IAMAT;* 417 Center St., Lewiston, NY 14092; phone: 716-754-4883; and 40 Regal Rd., Guelph, Ontario N1K 1B5, Canada; phone: 519-836-0102; fax: 519-836-3412).

International Health Care Service (440 E. 69th St., New York, NY 10021; phone: 212-746-1601).

International SOS Assistance (PO Box 11568, Philadelphia, PA 19116; phone: 800-523-8930 or 215-244-1500; fax: 215-244-2227).

Medic Alert Foundation (2323 Colorado Ave., Turlock, CA 95382; phone: 800-ID-ALERT or 209-668-3333; fax: 209-669-2495).

Travel Care International (*Eagle River Airport,* PO Box 846, Eagle River, WI 54521; phone: 800-5-AIR-MED or 715-479-8881; fax: 715-479-8178).

TravMed (PO Box 10623, Baltimore, MD 21285-0623; phone: 800-732-5309 or 410-296-5225; fax: 410-825-7523).

Consular Services

The American Services section of the *US Consulate* is a vital source of assistance and advice for US citizens abroad. If you are injured or become seriously ill, the consulate can direct you to sources of medical attention and notify your relatives. If you become involved in a dispute that could lead to legal action, the consulate can provide a list of local attorneys. In cases of natural disasters or civil unrest, consulates handle the evacuation of US citizens if necessary.

The US Embassy and Consulates

Embassy

Ottawa: 100 Wellington St., Ottawa, Ontario K1P 5T1, Canada (phone: 613-238-5335; fax: 613-238-5720).

Consulates

Montreal: *Consulate General,* 1155 St-Alexandre St. (phone: 514-398-9695; fax: 514-398-0973); mailing address: PO Box 65, Station Desjardins, Montreal, Quebec H5B 1G1, Canada.

Quebec City: *Consulate General,* 1 Ste-Genevieve Ave., Quebec City, Quebec G1R 4C9, Canada (phone: 418-692-2095; fax: 418-692-4640).

The *US State Department* operates an automated 24-hour *Citizens' Emergency Center* travel advisory hotline (phone: 202-647-5225). You also can reach a duty officer at this number from 8:15 AM to 10 PM, eastern standard time on weekdays, and from 9 AM to 3 PM on Saturdays. At all other times, call 202-647-4000. For faxed travel warnings and other consular information, call 202-647-3000 using the handset on your fax machine; instructions will be provided. With a PC and a modem, you can access the consular affairs electronic bulletin board (phone: 202-647-9225).

Entry Requirements
and Customs Regulations

ENTERING CANADA

To cross the Canadian border, US citizens need either a valid passport or *two* other official forms of identification (such as a driver's license, original or certified birth certificate, baptismal certificate, or voter registration card). Proof of current residency also may be requested. Naturalized US citizens should carry their naturalization certificate or some other evidence of citizenship. Permanent residents of the US who are not American citizens should have Alien Registration Receipt cards (US Form I-151 or Form I-551). Visitors under 18 years of age not accompanied by an adult must carry a letter from a parent or guardian giving them permission to travel to Canada.

Travelers from the US can stay in Canada for up to six months as tourists. Vehicles and trailers are allowed into the country for this period duty-free. Sporting equipment also can be brought into Canada duty-free, although, in some cases, a (refundable) deposit may be required to ensure that such items are not being imported to be sold. Although a permit is not required to bring tackle for sport fishing into the country, provincial governments require travelers to obtain a license to fish in Canada.

You are allowed to enter Canada with the following items duty-free: 50 cigars, 200 cigarettes, and 400 grams (approximately one pound) of processed tobacco, and a "reasonable" amount of food for your stay. If you are over the legal drinking age (which varies between provinces and territories), you also can bring up to 40 ounces (1.1 liters) of liquor or wine, or 288 ounces of beer or ale (equal to 24 12-ounce cans or bottles). All plants and plant material must be declared at the border; house plants from the continental US generally are permitted, but bonsai and all outdoor plants, including bulbs, require permits.

DUTY-FREE SHOPS

Located in international airports, duty-free shops provide bargains on the purchase of goods imported to Canada from other countries. But beware: Not all foreign goods are automatically less expensive. You *can* get a good deal on some items, but know what they cost elsewhere. Also note that although these goods are free of the duty that *Canadian Customs* normally would assess, they will be subject to US import duty upon your return to the US (see below).

GOODS AND SERVICES TAX (GST)

Similar to the Value Added Tax imposed in many European countries, this Canadian sales tax is applicable to most goods and services. Although everyone must pay the tax, foreign visitors with total purchases of at least CN$100 during their stay are eligible for a refund. The procedure is as follows: Request a rebate application at the store at the time of purchase. Then, send this application, along with the original receipts, to *Revenue Canada* (Customs and Excise Visitors' Rebate Program, Ottawa, Ontario K1A 1J5, Canada; phone: 800-66-VISIT in Canada; 613-991-3346 in the US). A refund check (in US dollars) will be mailed to you in the US.

Quebec's provincial sales tax also is refundable to foreign visitors. The procedure for obtaining a refund is the same as for the Canadian Goods and Services Tax, and provincial and national tax refund forms can be sent together to *Revenue Canada,* at the address above.

RETURNING TO THE US

You must declare to the *US Customs* official at the point of entry everything you have acquired in Canada. The standard duty-free allowance for US citizens is $400. If your trip is shorter than 48 continuous hours, or if you have been outside the US within 30 days of your current trip, the duty-free allowance is reduced to $25. Families traveling together may make a joint customs declaration. To avoid paying duty unnecessarily on expensive items (such as computer equipment) that you plan to take with you on your trip, register these items with *US Customs* before you depart.

A flat 10% duty is assessed on the next $1,000 worth of merchandise; additional items are taxed at a variety of rates (see *Tariff Schedules of the United States* in a library or any *US Customs Service* office). Some articles are duty-free only up to certain limits. The $400 allowance includes one carton of (200) cigarettes, 100 cigars (not Cuban), and one liter of liquor or wine (for those over 21); the $25 allowance includes 10 cigars, 50 cigarettes, and four ounces of perfume. With the exception of gifts valued at $50 or less sent directly to the recipient, *all* items shipped home are dutiable.

Antiques (at least 100 years old) and paintings or drawings done entirely by hand are duty-free. However, you must obtain a permit (from any office of *Canadian Customs*) to take original works of art out of the country.

FORBIDDEN IMPORTS

Note that US regulations prohibit the import of some goods sold abroad, such as fresh fruits and vegetables, most meat products (except certain canned goods), and dairy products (except for fully cured cheeses). Also prohibited are articles made from plants or animals on the endangered species list.

FOR ADDITIONAL INFORMATION Consult one of the following publications, available from the *US Customs Service* (PO Box 7407, Washington, DC 20044): *Currency Reporting; GSP and the Traveler; Importing a Car; International Mail Imports; Know Before You Go; Pets, Wildlife, US Customs;* and *Pocket Hints. Travelers' Tips on Bringing Food, Plant, and Animal Products into the United States* is available from the *United States Department of Agriculture, Animal, and Plant Health Inspection Service (USDA-APHIS;* 6505 Belcrest

Rd., Room 613-FB, Hyattsville, MD 20782; phone: 301-436-7799; fax: 301-436-5221). For tape-recorded information on customs-related topics, call 202-927-2095 from any touch-tone phone.

For Further Information

The best source of information about Montreal and Quebec City is the Quebec provincial tourist office. *Tourisme Québec* (PO Box 979, Montreal, Quebec H3C 2W3, Canada; phone: 800-363-7777 or 514-873-2015) is open seven days a week, from 9 AM to 5 PM. Tourist information for Montreal also is available from the *Greater Montreal Convention and Tourist Bureau* (1555 Peel St., Office 600, Montreal, Quebec H3A 1X6, Canada; phone: 514-844-5400; fax: 514-844-5757), and information for Quebec City can be obtained from the *Quebec City Tourist Information Center* (60 Auteuil Rd., Quebec City, Quebec G1R 4C4, Canada; phone: 418-692-2471; fax: 418-692-1481). For information on entry requirements and customs regulations, contact the *Canadian Embassy* or a *Canadian Consulate.*

The Canadian Embassy and Consulates in the US

Embassy
Washington, DC: 501 Pennsylvania Ave. NW, Washington, DC 20001 (phone: 202-682-1740; fax: 202-682-7726).

Consulates
California: *Consulate General,* 300 S. Grand Ave., 10th Floor, Los Angeles, CA 90071 (phone: 213-346-2700; fax: 213-620-8827).

Georgia: *Consulate General,* 1 CNN Center, Suite 400, Atlanta, GA 30303-2705 (phone: 404-577-6810; fax: 404-524-5046).

Illinois: *Consulate General,* 2 Prudential Plaza, 180 N. Stetson Ave., Suite 2400, Chicago, IL 60601 (phone: 312-616-1860; fax: 312-616-1877).

Massachusetts: *Consulate General,* 3 Copley Place, Suite 400, Boston, MA 02116 (phone: 617-262-3760; fax: 617-262-3415).

Michigan: *Consulate General,* 600 Renaissance Center, Suite 1100, Detroit, MI 42843-1704 (phone: 313-567-2340; fax: 313-567-2164).

Minnesota: *Consulate General,* 701 Fourth Ave. S., Minneapolis, MN 55415 (phone: 612-333-4641; fax: 612-332-4061).

New York: *Consulate General,* 1 Marine Midland Center, Suite 3000, Buffalo, NY 14203-2884 (phone: 716-858-9500; fax: 716-852-4340); *Consulate General,* 1251 Ave. of the Americas, New York, NY 10020-1175 (phone: 212-596-1600; fax: 212-596-1790).

Texas: *Consulate General,* 750 N. St. Paul St., Suite 1700, Dallas, TX (phone: 214-922-9806; fax: 214-922-9815).

Washington State: *Consulate General,* 412 Plaza 600, Sixth and Stewart Sts., Seattle, WA 98101-1286 (phone: 206-443-1777; fax: 206-443-1782).

The Cities

Montreal

Since 1535—when Jacques Cartier first laid eyes on the St. Lawrence River village of Hochelaga, climbed with its native residents to the top of its 764-foot mountain, took a look at the 50-mile view, and exclaimed, "What a royal mount!"—the place has emerged as Canada's second-largest city. Yet some of the most dramatic changes on the face of Montreal have been etched in the past 30 years, with the construction of luxury hotels; the addition of a vast underground network of shops and services linked by a clean, efficient *Métro* (subway) system; an accretion of fashionable boutiques and excellent restaurants; and careful restorations in the historic quarter. Montreal's current look was sparked by a midtown face-lift during the 1960s, and the renovation gained momentum during *EXPO '67,* a world's fair that brought the city international attention. A concomitant increase in tourism reached its peak in 1976, when Montreal hosted the *Summer Olympic Games.*

A second building boom in the 1980s transformed the downtown area, with the completion of a dozen major projects that included the conversion of two former hotels on Rue Peel into chic commercial complexes, along with the construction of several showy office towers. Indeed, the transformation was so complete that some residents claim they can't remember what Montreal used to look like. However, a key priority when construction began was the preservation of Vieux Montréal (Old Montreal). The protection of special buildings extended to modern Montreal as well: The city's *Stade Olympique* (Olympic Stadium) has become a spectacular public sports facility, and the *EXPO '67* grounds on Ile Notre-Dame are now the site of the *Casino de Montréal,* Quebec's province-operated gambling casino, which opened in 1993.

Compelling and cosmopolitan, Montreal sits on a flat (except for Mont-Royal), anvil-shape island 32 miles long and 10 miles wide in the middle of the St. Lawrence River, some 170 miles (272 km) northeast of Lake Ontario. The river, which borders the city on the south and east, provides a crucial navigable link between the inland Great Lakes and the Atlantic Ocean. A narrow branch of the St. Lawrence, known as Rivière des Prairies, borders Montreal on the west and the north.

The most appealing thing about Montreal, especially for Americans, is its Frenchness. Without jet lag and with a minimum of cost and bother, Americans have easy access to what is essentially a North American city, yet one that provides the very best of the traditional French experience. Two-thirds of greater Montreal's more than three million inhabitants are of French origin, and the French Canadian patois is heard all around town. Though nearly everyone in the urban center is bilingual, there is no question of the primary tongue.

Montreal's cosmopolitan ambience is due in part to the city's diverse population, which includes more than a hundred ethnic groups. Sixteen percent of the non-French population is Anglo-Saxon; the remainder have roots in Germany, Greece, Italy, Hungary, the West Indies, or China. Montreal has the country's largest Jewish population and a Chinese community of more than 50,000.

Perhaps because Montreal was never the headquarters of the Catholic church (as was Quebec City, its cousin 153 miles/245 km to the north), or because it passed part of this century as a "sin city," it seems more ebullient and easygoing than Quebec City. The reasons for this subtle flavor of life lie in part in its history.

When explorer-entrepreneur Samuel de Champlain reached Montreal's shores in 1603, he foresaw the great value of this natural transportation crossroad as an inland port, and he returned in 1611 to erect a trading post near the foot of the Rapides de Lachine. (The ravages of warring tribes had left no trace of the native village of Hochelaga, first seen by Cartier.) The spot, later christened Place Royale, still is a nucleus of commercial activity.

In 1642 the permanent community of Ville Marie was founded at Place Royale (in what is now Vieux Montréal) by a small group led by the French career soldier Paul de Chomedey, Sieur de Maisonneuve. Shortly after their arrival, the colonists narrowly escaped being swept away in a disastrous flood. As a token of gratitude to God for their survival, they climbed Mont-Royal's eastern slope and planted a wooden cross at the top. Today, the illuminated hundred-foot steel cross that stands in its stead—and on a different site—can be seen for miles on clear nights.

While the flood did not obliterate Ville Marie, the natives very nearly did. During the next 60 years, the rapidly growing colony of traders, explorers, and missionaries was besieged by numerous attacks; an open state of war existed with the Iroquois until 1701, when a treaty was signed.

In the 18th century, Montreal (the name Ville Marie was dropped during this period) prospered through its burgeoning fur trade, though not without difficulties. The natives were quieted, but trouble with the English and Americans took its toll on the French settlement. In 1759, when Quebec City fell to the British after the battle on the Plaines d'Abraham (Plains of Abraham), the capital of New France moved briefly to Montreal. A year later Montreal, too, fell to the British.

During the American Revolution, the Americans eyed Montreal and Quebec City as potential extensions of the original 13 colonies. In November 1775, General Richard Montgomery marched on Montreal and occupied it without firing a shot. American domination lasted only seven months; Montgomery failed to capture Quebec City, and Montreal returned to British rule.

Montreal's expansion under the British gained momentum during the early 19th century, when fur trading, shipbuilding, and railroading reached a crescendo. In 1832 Montreal was incorporated as a city, and by 1843 it was the capital of the province of Canada. The city's expansion during the early 1900s led to Montreal's reputation as a "wicked city"; prostitution, illegal gambling, and other vices flourished, mostly under the well-paid protection of the authorities. By the end of the 1940s, Montreal's central section was a dreary core of slums and run-down buildings. But this has completely vanished since; a war on corruption, mounted during the 1950s by city official Jean Drapeau, wiped out the blot on the face of Montreal.

The first renovation was the construction of *Place Ville-Marie,* an underground complex of shops, restaurants, and services in the heart of downtown, built to hide the ugly pit yards of the *Canadian National Railways. Place Ville-Marie* was the first of six underground complexes to be built in the heart of Montreal, each of which provides weatherproof access to hotels, office buildings, banks, stores, and two railway stations in different parts of the city.

In the 1960s and 1970s, Montreal put up a stunning cultural and performing arts center, *Place des Arts;* it also became one of the two Canadian cities with a major league baseball team, the Montreal *Expos* (Toronto has the *Blue Jays*), and hosted the *1976 Summer Olympics.* As the city was acquiring its new look, municipal and provincial ordinances wisely assured the preservation of Vieux Montréal, designating the 95-acre waterfront sector a historical site.

The city spreads out in all directions from Mont-Royal, and probably the best way to appreciate the mountain and its surrounding *Parc du Mont-Royal* is to hire a calèche (horse-drawn carriage). Meandering through the park, it's possible to assimilate a little local sociology along with an appreciation of the scenic beauty. A certain tension has always existed between the descendants of the original French founders and those of the British conquerors. They enjoy a fairly cordial coexistence today, although former antipathies are still evident in Montreal's neighborhood patterns. To the west is Westmount, the "bedroom" for Montreal's prosperous English community. On the other side of the mountain is Outremont, the turf of the wealthy French inhabitants. Each community is equally affluent but entirely separate, and it is easy to distinguish the lines of demarcation. As you ride along, just note the names of the passing apartment buildings. When the names cease being such Anglophilic gems as *The Trafalgar* and begin to take on the markedly Gallic cast of *Le Trianon,* you'll know that you have "crossed the Channel."

Whichever course the province of Quebec chooses to follow in the near future—continued confederation or possible separation from the rest of Canada—it's safe to say that the city of Montreal always will offer a wide spectrum of sights and sounds for visitors from both near and far.

Montreal At-a-Glance

SEEING THE CITY

There are several vantage points from which to capture the sweep of Montreal. Two lookout points on 764-foot Mont-Royal offer spectacular views. To reach the *Belvédère Mont-Royal* at the *Grand Chalet,* follow the path up from the *Parc du Mont-Royal* parking lot or walk up Rue Peel from downtown. Those traveling by car have access to an impressive view of the north and east at the *Observatoire de l'Est* lookout on the eastern slope of Voie Camillien-Houde, the only road over the mountain on which automobiles are permitted. And from the *Stade Olympique*'s 620-foot-high tower, the view extends more than 50 miles on a clear day. A cable car with bay windows takes visitors to the top in two minutes. It's closed mid-January to mid-February; admission charge (phone: 252-TOUR).

The *Belvédère Westmount* (on Chemin Belvédère in Westmount), also accessible by car, affords an excellent view of the southwestern section of the city and surroundings. Arrows on the lookout's ledge indicate 22 points of interest, extending to the Green Mountains of Vermont and New York's Adirondacks. Iles Ste-Hélène and Notre-Dame offer magnificent views of downtown with a mountain backdrop.

The old *Tour de l'Horloge* (Clock Tower) on *Quai de l'Horloge* (phone: 496-7678), now an interpretive center tracing the Vieux (Old) Port's past, commands a vista of the harbor from its top story. It's closed *Labour Day* through May; no admission charge. The *Oratoire St-Joseph* (see *Special Places*) offers an excellent view of the northern part of the city. Other panoramas of Montreal can be seen from the *Château Champlain*'s *L'Escapade* restaurant and the *Radisson-Gouverneurs*'s *Le Tour de Ville* dining room (see *Checking In* for both).

SPECIAL PLACES

To get a feel for Montreal, walk through its streets and parks; the city's layout makes it easy to navigate on foot. Though not exactly true in direction, Montreal's street plan is laid out on a north-south, east-west axis. Each block covers approximately a hundred numbers. East-west numbering starts at Boulevard St-Laurent, so the street number 900 Ouest, for example, is nine blocks west of St-Laurent. (The directionals E and O—designating *est,* or east, and *ouest,* or west—follow the addresses.) North-south numbers start at the river and run north, following the same formula. Most interesting to the visitor is the area wedged between the river on the south and east and Mont-Royal on the north and west.

Anyone who wearies quickly or would like to visit places farther afield should head for the nearest *Métro* station and hop aboard a train on one of the city's four subway lines; most put visitors near the important attractions.

MUSÉE DES BEAUX-ARTS DE MONTRÉAL (MUSEUM OF FINE ARTS OF MONTREAL)

The main neoclassical structure of Canada's oldest fine-arts museum (1860) boasts an airy, glass-walled atrium and space for more than 3,000 works. The permanent collection of this first-rate institution includes Western European art from the medieval period to the present, as well as relics of ancient civilizations in Europe, Egypt, China, Japan, and pre-Columbian America. Works by Canadian, Inuit, and Amerindian artists are noteworthy, as is the collection of period furnishings. The building also hosts important touring shows, including recent exhibitions from the *Vatican Collection* and works by Leonardo, Picasso, and Miró. Closed Mondays. Admission charge. 1379 and 1380 Rue Sherbrooke O. (phone: 285-1600).

RUES MACKAY TO DE LA MONTAGNE

A concentration of restaurants, pubs, discos, trendy fashion boutiques, and art galleries ensconced in brownstone and gray-stone Victorian houses is centered in this nine-square-block downtown area. Whether for browsing, shopping, or barhopping, this is where the action is, and in good weather much of it takes place out on the street. Rues Mackay, Bishop, Crescent, and de la Montagne, between Rue Sherbrooke and Blvd. René-Lévesque.

UNIVERSITÉ MCGILL (MCGILL UNIVERSITY)

Chartered in 1821, this prestigious school was built with funds from the estate of Scottish immigrant James McGill, who amassed a fortune as a fur trader and served in Lower Canada's Parliament. The campus is on the site of the 16th-century native village of Hochelaga, "discovered" by Cartier in 1535. A stroll around the campus and down fashionable Rue Sherbrooke reveals a number of interesting façades, including some fine old mansions that now belong to the university. Guided tours of the grounds can be arranged by calling 398-6555. During the summer, *McGill* provides inexpensive accommodations in its dormitories, with cafeteria service and sports facilities available to guests. Call 398-6367 for information.

VOIE PIÉTONNIÈRE PRINCE-ARTHUR (PRINCE-ARTHUR PEDESTRIAN MALL)

Once a quiet residential street and then part of *McGill*'s low-cost student ghetto from the 1950s to the early 1970s, today the stretch of Rue Prince-Arthur from Boulevard St-Laurent to Square St-Louis is an attractive mall. Enhanced by a fountain, overflowing tubs of flowers, and street lamps, it is home to an array of moderately priced restaurants running the gamut of ethnicities from Greek and Italian to Vietnamese, Polish, and Québécois. In summer, people watchers take advantage of the many outdoor cafés lining this lovely street. Most of the restaurants are BYOW (bring your own wine). Summer is also the season for outdoor performances by local musicians, magicians, and acrobats.

RUE ST-DENIS Known as Montreal's Latin Quarter, this area is the site of the *Université du Québec à Montréal (UQAM)* campus. The façade of historic *Eglise St-Jacques* has been integrated into the institution's main building. Rue St-Denis and its *Théâtre St-Denis* were the original hosts to the city's annual *Festival International de Jazz de Montréal,* and they still provide the sites for many events in this now much-expanded 10-day music fest (see *Special Events*). Also popular for its restaurants, the street attracts an academic crowd to its bookshops, art galleries, and coffeehouses. St-Denis, above Rue Sherbrooke, has gained a reputation as a fashion hub due to the many Quebec designers who have showrooms and boutiques here.

1000 DE LA GAUCHETIÈRE Montreal's tallest building, this 51-story office tower soars above the *Bonaventure Métro* station and is linked to the underground pedestrian network. It's the home of *l'Amphithéâtre Bell,* a huge indoor public skating rink, with café and restaurant facilities, plus skate-rental and -sharpening services. 1000 de la Gauchetière (phone: 395-0555).

VILLE SOUTERRAINE
(UNDERGROUND MONTREAL)

This below-street-level network of downtown commercial-business-residential complexes is for many as vital a part of Montreal as the city above ground. *Place Ville-Marie,* Montreal's first subterranean complex, opened in 1962; its successful reception prompted a gradual expansion into other sections of the city, and today the network extends some 18 pedestrian miles. All the centers, known as *"places,"* are linked by the *Métro* system. Plans exist for further subterranean development in the first decade of the 21st century.

It's possible to spend days in Montreal without ever going outside. Many Montrealers do just that—especially when winter dumps a hundred inches of snow on the city. The complex networks offer access to the city's main sports facilities, exhibits, and performing arts centers, about 1,700 shops, 200 restaurants, eight major hotels, the two main rail stations and a bus terminal, numerous banks and apartment buildings, more than 30 cinemas and theaters, some 13,000 indoor parking spaces, and even a municipal library branch at the *McGill Métro* station. Reasonably priced tours of the Ville Souterraine are conducted by *Gray Line* (phone: 934-1222); *Guidatour* (phone: 844-4021); *Hertz Tourist Guide* (phone: 937-6690); *Les Tours Diamant* (phone: 744-3009); and *Visites de Montréal* (phone: 933-6674).

PLACE VILLE-MARIE Conceived by architect I. M. Pei and developer William Zeckendorf during the 1950s, the city's first underground complex now houses over 85 boutiques and stores as well as *Les Cours de la Place,* an elegant marble-and-brass fast-food market with everything from Baskin-Robbins ice cream to Asian snacks. Promenades link *Place Ville-Marie* with *Place Bonaventure* and *Place du Canada,* forming an underground core of some 200 shops, 20 restaurants and bars, and entrances to three major hotels—the *Queen Elizabeth, Bonaventure Hilton International,* and *Château Champlain.* A tunnel links *Place Ville-Marie* to the *Centre Eaton* and the Rue Ste-Catherine shopping strip. Enter *Place Ville-Marie* through the *Queen Elizabeth* (900 René-Lévesque Blvd.) or on Rue Cathcart at the foot of Av. McGill College.

PLACE BONAVENTURE Linked to *Place Ville-Marie* by walkways leading through the *Gare Centrale* (Central Station), this six-acre arcade houses about a hundred shops and restaurants. Above the shopping concourse are a merchandise market, the *Bonaventure Hilton International* hotel, and an exhibition hall, which hosts numerous shows, ranging from Canada's largest antiques show to boat and camping exhibits. Enter *Place Bonaventure* through the *Bonaventure Hilton International* (Rues de la Gauchetière and Mansfield) or through the *Château Champlain* (1050 Rue de la Gauchetière O.).

PLACE MONTREAL TRUST This five-level underground atrium houses 120 specialty stores, boutiques, and restaurants in a sunny, California-style setting of cool pastels, waterfalls, reflecting pools, and greenery. Sunlight filters through a rooftop skylight into the second basement level. The *place* has underground links with its neighbors above and below Rue Ste-Catherine. Following the *Métro* corridors, shoppers can walk from here to the *Centre Eaton, Les Promenades de la Cathédrale,* and *La Baie* (The Bay). Enter via the *McGill Métro* station or 1600 Av. McGill College.

CENTRE EATON Downtown's largest shopping center has five tiers of boutique-lined galleries under its glass roof. Linked to *Eaton's* department store, the center maintains more than 200 stores and also houses restaurants and fast-food outlets. A complex of five cinemas is on the top floor. Part of the Ville Souterraine, it opens into the *McGill Métro* station. Street-level entrance at 705 Rue Ste-Catherine O.

LES PROMENADES DE LA CATHÉDRALE Two levels of underground shopping are hidden away beneath *Cathédrale Christ Church,* with more than a hundred shops linked to *La Baie, Centre Eaton,* and the *Métro.* Enter via the *McGill Métro* station or 652 Rue Ste-Catherine O.

LES COURS MONT-ROYAL Within the *Sheraton Mount Royal* hotel are four levels of elegant commercial space housing 60 boutiques, three restaurants, a fast-food court, and a movie theater. Enter via the *Peel Métro* station; street-level entrances at 1455 Rue Peel and 1550 Rue Metcalfe.

TOURS BELL AND BANQUE NATIONALE (BELL AND NATIONAL BANK TOWERS) Joined to the pedestrian passageway between *Place Victoria* and the *Edifice Beaver Hall Hill,* these two office towers have increased the Ville Souterraine's shopping and dining potential with a two-tiered mall of boutiques plus a large restaurant complex on the lower level. They also are connected to the *Place Victoria Métro* station.

PLACE VICTORIA Facing Square Victoria, this massive office tower is home to the *Bourse de Montréal* (Montreal Stock Exchange) and a small underground shopping mall. The complex is connected to the *Radisson-Gouverneurs* hotel and the *Place Victoria Métro* station. *Bourse* tours are given by reservation only; admission charge (phone: 871-2424).

PLACE ALEXIS-NIHON A short subway ride from the central core, this plaza offers more weatherproof shopping. Some 80,000 people pass through the complex daily en route to the office building, apartment tower, three-floor shopping mall, and covered parking levels. 1500 Av. Atwater; take the *Métro* to *Atwater*.

COMPLEXE WESTMOUNT SQUARE High fashion shops share this posh underground plaza with *Le Marché Westmount Square,* an extensive food mart featuring everything from imported fancy food to fast-food snacks. Linked by underground passage to *Place Alexis-Nihon,* the upscale marketplace is situated directly beneath three gleaming office towers designed by Mies van der Rohe. Take the *Métro* to *Atwater*.

PLACE DES ARTS The heart of Montreal's cultural life is its lavish performing arts center, which contains a stunning and acoustically superb concert hall and theater accommodating over 5,000 people. Home of the *Orchestre Symphonique de Montréal, Les Grands Ballets Canadiens,* and the *Opéra de Montréal,* it is also the setting for chamber music concerts, ballet recitals, and plays. On Sunday mornings, the lobby of the center hosts "Sons et Brioches," informal concerts served up with a continental breakfast. (Very reasonably priced tickets are available at *Place des Arts* half an hour prior to performance.) 260 Blvd. de Maisonneuve O.; take the *Métro* to the *Place des Arts* stop (phone: 842-2112).

COMPLEXE DESJARDINS This impressive complex contains meeting halls, offices, and an enclosed shopping center with some one hundred boutiques and specialty stores, four movie theaters, a miniature golf course, a hotel, and 20 restaurants. Sculptures, fountains, plants, and a regular series of entertainment events and special exhibits make it a popular gathering place. It's linked by underground walkways to *Place des Arts, Complexe Guy-Favreau,* the *Palais des Congrès* (Convention Center), and the *Musée d'Art Contemporain* (Museum of Contemporary Art).

COMPLEXE GUY-FAVREAU Yet another complex, this one houses offices, apartments, and boutiques, as well as the *National Film Board*'s movie theater. It connects to the *Complexe Desjardins* and the city's convention center. The convention center mall also melds with the Chinatown pedestrian plaza, lined with Asian shops and restaurants.

VIEUX MONTRÉAL (OLD MONTREAL)

Private enterprise and government funds are contributing to the restoration of important buildings in Vieux Montréal, the city's historic waterfront section. The area can be toured by car or horse-drawn calèche, but the best way to get a feel for it is by strolling through the narrow streets. Get a free copy of *A Walking Tour of Vieux Montréal* from *INFOTOURISTE* (Sq. Dorchester at Rue Peel; phone: 873-2015) or its satellite center (corner of Pl. Jacques-Cartier and Rue Notre-Dame in Vieux Montréal). Also see *Walk 2: Vieux Montréal* in DIRECTIONS—MONTREAL. Highlights include the following:

BASILIQUE NOTRE-DAME Opened in 1829, this building was designed in Gothic Revival style by New York architect James O'Donnell, whose grave lies in the crypt. Closed weekdays. Admission charge. Adjacent to the main church is the restored *Chapelle du Sacré-Coeur* (Sacred Heart Chapel). For more information, see *Historic Churches* in DIVERSIONS. Pl. d'Armes (phone: 849-1070).

VIEUX SÉMINAIRE ST-SULPICE (OLD ST-SULPICE SEMINARY) Sightseers aren't welcome inside the oldest building in Montreal (1685) because it's still a private home for Sulpician priests, but they can admire its weathered graystone façade through the wrought-iron gateway to the front courtyard. Photographers and students of historic architecture admire the symmetrical windows and dormers and the campanile over the main entrance, which, according to local historians, is the oldest outdoor clock in North America (1710). 130 Rue Notre-Dame O.

PLACE JACQUES-CARTIER This cobblestone square, the largest in Vieux Montréal, was once the main marketplace. Now the hub of the area's activity, it's lined with attractive restaurants and restored houses. Dominating the square is a statue of Horatio Nelson atop a 35-foot column (erected in 1809). In warm weather, the base of the column is the venue for a flower market that offers blossoms of every conceivable size and hue; in autumn, apples and pumpkins are sold. Alfresco cafés line both sides of the square, perfect for relaxing and drinking in the early-19th-century flavor. Between Rues St-Paul and Notre-Dame.

VIEUX PORT (OLD PORT) Developed as a government project more than a decade ago, the Vieux Port is now a summertime entertainment center. Strollers may rest on a bench and take in the waterfront; bikers can rent wheels at the port to explore its river-view trails; and pleasure craft dock at the marina at *Bassin Bon Secours.* The restored piers are departure points for harbor cruises and Rapides de Lachine jet-boat excursions (see *Getting Around*). The *Fête du Vieux Port* (Vieux Port Festival) begins on the *Fête Nationale* (St-Jean-Baptiste Day; June 24), running through *Labour Day* (for details, see *Special Events*). There also are summer exhibitions in the Vieux Port at the *Expotec* (phone: 496-4629) and *Image du Futur* (phone: 849-1612). The *Cinéma IMAX* has a giant seven-story-high screen (phone: 496-IMAX). An immense flea market with piles of secondhand bargains takes place here. The Vieux Port also provides a summer stage for the touring *Cirque* *du Soleil,* an internationally acclaimed circus of tumblers, contortionists, and clowns. A favorite summer stop is the garden restaurant at *Gibby's* (see *Eating Out*). In winter, the Vieux Port is one of the sites for the city's annual *Fête des Neiges* (see *Special Events*).

CHÂTEAU RAMEZAY The manor, built in 1705, was the official residence of Claude de Ramezay, 11th Governor of Montreal, who occupied this modest version of a Norman château during his 20 years in office. It later housed the offices of the West India Company and, still later, was the residence of English governors. During the American occupation (1775–76), the Continental Army, under Generals Richard Montgomery and Benedict Arnold, established its headquarters here. Today the château is a museum, with a collection of Amerindian and other artifacts. The big cellar kitchen, with its cavernous fireplace and the latest innovations in 18th-century appliances, is particularly noteworthy. Some of the rooms, such as the richly paneled *Grand Salon,* represent a later period. Open daily June through August; closed Mondays September through May. Admission charge. 280 Rue Notre-Dame E. (phone: 861-3708).

CHAPELLE NOTRE-DAME-DE-BON-SECOURS One of the city's oldest churches, it is also called the *Eglise des Matelots* (Sailors' Chapel) because of the large number of sailors who worship here. Built originally in 1657, it was destroyed by fire and twice rebuilt and modified. The on-site museum pays homage to Marguerite Bourgeoys, the first Catholic saint to live and die in Canada. For more information, see *Historic Churches* in DIVERSIONS. Museum closed Mondays. Admission charge to the museum. 400 Rue St-Paul E. (phone: 845-9991).

CENTRE D'HISTOIRE (HISTORY CENTER) Place d'Youville—one of Montreal's first civic centers—is now surrounded by monuments and historic sites. One interesting landmark is the restored *Caserne de Pompiers* (Fire Station 1), which houses the *Centre d'Histoire.* It offers exhibits on the cultural mosaic of the city; an audiovisual presentation that leads visitors through 11 display rooms and 400 years of history; an old streetcar; and a simulated shoe factory. Periodic expositions feature Montreal's past. Open daily May 11 through late September; closed Mondays late September through May 10. Admission charge. South of Rue St-Paul O. (phone: 872-3207).

ELSEWHERE IN MONTREAL

PARC ANGRIGNON A 262-acre, year-round recreational oasis, this park is at its busiest from mid-December to late March, when it becomes the city's winter wonderland, a place for all kinds of free outdoor fun, from cross-country skiing, snowshoeing, and skating on the decorated rink to thrilling slides down the icy toboggan run. 3400 Blvd. des Trinitaires. Get off at the *Angrignon Métro* station.

PARC OLYMPIQUE (OLYMPIC PARK) Having hosted the *1976 Summer Olympic Games,* Montreal is now using these spectacular facilities for all types of sporting events and exhibits. The *Expos* play at the all-weather stadium, with its tower and retractable roof. A restaurant and observation deck offer panoramic views of the city. Meets, classes, and public swimming periods are held regularly in the 50-meter pool and 50-foot diving pool. A 45-minute guided tour (conducted in English daily, except holidays) explains some of the facility's impressive, technologically advanced features—the ripple and bubble machines, for example, enable coaches to create air bubbles instantly on the surface of the pool to protect a diver from the impact of a bad dive. Admission charge. 4141 Av. Pierre-de-Coubertin; take the *Métro* to *Viau* (phone: 252-TOUR).

BIODÔME Housed in the *Parc Olympique*'s former *Velodrome* are four natural ecosystems. In the two zones representing South, Central, and North America, more than 4,600 birds, marine creatures, and other animals inhabit such settings as a tropical rain forest, a beaver lake, a salt marsh, and an Arctic snowbank. In the St. Lawrence Marine Ecosystem, fish and other ocean dwellers patrol a salty artificial sea, while scores of starfish, anemones, crabs, sea urchins, and other invertebrates make their home in a tidal pool near the salt marsh habitat of black ducks and shorebirds. The Polar Ecosystem represents the two icy worlds of the Arctic and Antarctic, which can be viewed from a glass-enclosed observation site. Bilingual tours are conducted daily. Open daily. Admission charge. 4777 Av. Pierre-de-Coubertin (phone: 872-3034).

JARDIN BOTANIQUE (BOTANICAL GARDEN) Across from the *Parc Olympique,* this noted horticultural showplace was founded by naturalist Brother Marie Victorin. Actually a complex of some 30 specialized gardens and 10 greenhouses, the garden displays more than 26,000 different species and varieties of plants, grouped according to use and habitat. The garden is said to have North America's most complete collection of bonsai trees and the country's largest and grandest exhibition greenhouse. With the highly acclaimed *Jardin Japonais* (Japanese Garden), the *Insectarium*—a giant house with thousands of live insects on display—and the addition of the traditional *Jardin de Chine* (Chinese Garden), Montreal's botanical garden is now the world's second-largest (after London's *Kew Gardens*). The visitors' reception center offers videos and bilingual guides. Open daily. Admission charge. 4101 Rue Sherbrooke E. (phone: 872-1400).

MONT-ROYAL Because it dominates the city scene, visitors can't avoid seeing Mont-Royal from one angle or another (the mountain has two peaks: Mont-Royal and Westmount). Not only is it a fine vantage point from which to view the St. Lawrence River, Montreal, and the mountains beyond; it's also a good spot from which to observe Montrealers at their leisure. For more information, see "Parc du Mont-Royal" in *Quintessential Montreal and Quebec*

City, DIVERSIONS, and *Walk 4: Parc du Mont-Royal* in DIRECTIONS—MON-TREAL. The park is bounded by Av. Park on the east and, continuing counterclockwise, Blvd. Mont-Royal, Voie Camillien-Houde, Chemin Remembrance, Chemin de la-Côte-des-Neiges, and Av. Pine.

ORATOIRE ST-JOSEPH (ST. JOSEPH'S ORATORY) For more than two million people each year, a visit to this shrine is reason enough for a trip to Montreal. The on-site museum is open daily; donations accepted. For more information, see *Historic Churches* in DIVERSIONS. 3800 Chemin Queen-Mary (phone: 733-8211).

WESTMOUNT The heights of this mountainside "city within a city" were traditionally the enclave of Montreal's well-heeled English-speaking population. Today, the residents of Upper Westmount must still be wealthy to maintain their stately homes, but the "English-only" requisite has eased somewhat as the city's cultures have blended. This is the section of town for mansion staring. *West Mount,* the palatial stone house that gave the area its name and was owned by *Beaver Steamship Line*'s William Murray, has been torn down, but a number of other impressive 19th- and early-20th-century homes (and a few even earlier landmarks) fill the gap. The sturdy of limb can take the *Métro* to *Atwater* station, which is linked to the elegant *Complexe Westmount Square* (see above), and start a walking tour of the area from there. But because of Westmount's hills, the less hearty may prefer to see it by car. The most interesting sights fall between Rues Sherbrooke and Edgehill, from Avenues Greene to Victoria.

OUTREMONT The traditional French-speaking counterpart to English-speaking Westmount is the *"ville"* of Outremont, hidden on the northeast slope of Mont-Royal. Incorporated in 1875, the village principally comprised large tracts of farmland owned and cultivated by "gentleman farmers" from Scotland and England. While the farms have long since been divided into smaller building lots, some of the original farmhouses still exist. Outremont's terrain is easily as demanding as Westmount's, so it is best explored by car. The section's main thoroughfare, Chemin de la Côte Ste-Catherine, and the parallel Avenue Maplewood display the best of Outremont's landmark mansions, and Avenue Laurier is lined with smart boutiques and cafés. Try *Café Laurier* (394 Av. Laurier O.; phone: 273-2484) for a relaxing coffee break. Bounded north and south by Av. Glendale and Blvd. Mont-Royal; east and west by Avs. Hutchison and Canterbury.

UNIVERSITÉ DE MONTRÉAL Opened in 1876 as a branch of Quebec City's *Université Laval,* the *U of M* has developed into the largest French-language university outside of Paris, with nearly 60,000 students and more than 200 undergraduate programs. The Mont-Royal campus, which opened in 1943, now accommodates 13 faculties, more than 60 research units, and affiliated schools of engineering and commerce, as well as a huge sports complex. 2900 Blvd. Edouard-Montpetit (phone: 343-6111).

PLANÉTARIUM DOW Outer space is highlighted in this giant theater of the stars, the first of Canada's planetariums, which was a gift to the city from the Dow Brewery in the mid-1960s. Its programs change throughout the year and are narrated in French and English on alternate hours (call for times). Closed Mondays during the day. Admission charge. 1000 Rue St-Jacques O. (phone: 872-4530).

MAISON DE RADIO-CANADA One of the world's largest and most modern radio and television centers, the Canadian Broadcasting Company (CBC) head-quarters of French and English broadcasting sprawls over 25 acres in downtown Montreal. The 23-story hexagonal building that houses the studios also has galleries and an extensive collection of paintings, sculptures, and graphics done mostly by artists of Quebec and the Atlantic provinces. Visitors are allowed at only a limited number of shows; call ahead for information. No admission charge. 1400 Blvd. René-Lévesque E. (phone: 597-7787).

ST. LAWRENCE SEAWAY Montreal is the starting point of this modern engineering miracle, which makes it possible for ocean-bound ships to travel all the way through to the Great Lakes. Often missed by the average visitor, the observatory at the *Ecluse de St-Lambert* (St-Lambert Lock) offers a close look at the intricate locking procedures as well as a fine view of Montreal's skyline across the river. A scenic bicycle path runs along the lock. Closed weekends and from mid-November to mid-April. No admission charge. Take the *Pont Victoria* (Victoria Bridge) from downtown across to *Ecluse de St-Lambert* on Route 132, on the south shore of the river (phone: 672-4110).

ST. LAWRENCE RIVER ISLANDS/ PARC DES ILES

The largest of Montreal's St. Lawrence River satellite islands is Ile Ste-Hélène, which Samuel de Champlain named after his wife, Hélène Boulé. It was once the site of a military installation and, somewhat more recently, part of the extensive grounds of *EXPO '67,* which also included its neighboring island, Ile Notre-Dame. There's plenty to do on these islands, which now make up an oasis of greenery called *Parc des Iles.* Access to the mid-river playground is via the Autoroute Bonaventure or Pont Jacques-Cartier by car or by the *Métro* system (*Ile Ste-Hélène* stop).

ILE NOTRE-DAME Its annual *Floralies* flower show has been so successful that the island has become a popular year-round park, with Montreal's only downtown beach. Pedal-boat rentals are an ideal way to explore the island's canals in summer, which in winter become huge ice skating rinks. Snowshoeing, cross-country skiing, and horse-drawn sleigh rides also can be enjoyed. Other sites here include the *Bassin Olympique* (Olympic Rowing Basin), which becomes a skating rink during winter, and the *Canadian Grand Prix* racetrack, *Gilles Villeneuve Circuit.* Also here is the *Casino de Montréal* (see *Nightclubs and Nightlife*).

ILE STE-HÉLÈNE *La Ronde,* a rollicking amusement park, covers 135 acres of this island. In addition to rides, the park has spirited restaurants and pubs that Montrealers frequent on warm summer evenings (especially from the end of May to mid-June, when *La Ronde* is the launching pad for a 10-day fireworks festival). *La Ronde* also is home to an aquapark with water slides and swimming and wading pools. *La Ronde* is closed September through May; admission charge (phone: 872-6222).

The *Musée David M. Stewart* in Ile Ste-Hélène's *Vieux Fort* (built in the early 1820s by order of the Duke of Wellington) houses period uniforms, military equipment, and model ships. It features special historical displays June through October (weather permitting) and also hosts several temporary exhibitions during the year. In the summer, two colorfully uniformed resident companies of colonial troops—the Compagnie Franche de la Marine (French) and the 78th Fraser Highlanders (Scottish)—perform authentic 18th-century drills and marches. The museum is closed Tuesdays; admission charge (phone: 861-6701).

The *Vieux Fort*'s *Festin du Gouverneur* restaurant (phone: 879-1141; reservations necessary) invites diners to enjoy an 18th-century banquet served by costumed performers who sing, dance, and draw patrons into the act. *Hélène de Champlain* (phone: 395-2424) is a restaurant in an attractive Norman-style building overlooking the river and rose gardens. Near the *Vieux Fort,* the *Théâtre de la Poudrière* (phone: 954-1344) stages summertime productions in a restored powder house.

Sources and Resources

TOURIST INFORMATION

INFOTOURISTE (1001 Sq. Dorchester; phone: 873-2015; 800-363-7777 in Canada and the US) has information, maps, and brochures; it's open daily. The tourist bureau kiosk at the international tourist reception center in Vieux Montréal at Place Jacques-Cartier (no phone; open daily) and at *Dorval* and *Mirabel* airports (no phone; both closed *Labour Day* through May) have similar facilities. *INFOTOURISTE*'s toll-free number (see above) also serves a central reservation system *(Centre de Réservations Touristiques du Québec,* or *CRTQ),* through which travelers can reserve rooms throughout the province and pay for them by credit card.

LOCAL COVERAGE There is one English-language newspaper, the *Montreal Gazette,* available at newsstands every morning. The free weekly English newspaper *Mirror,* available in restaurants, cafés, and bars, gives a complete listing of entertainment and cultural activities. Monthly *Scope* magazine, available at newsstands, also has entertainment and restaurant listings.

TELEPHONE The area code for Montreal is 514.

SALES TAX Quebec has a provincial sales tax of 8%, in addition to the 7% federal Goods and Services Tax (GST). In many cases, visitors can receive refunds of both the provincial and federal taxes. For details on Quebec tax rebates, call 800-567-4692.

GETTING AROUND

CAR RENTAL For information on renting a car in Montreal, see GETTING READY TO GO.

HARBOR CRUISES A scenic and restful way to see the entire island is from the St. Lawrence. *Croisières du Port de Montréal* (phone: 842-3871) offers a variety of voyages up and down the river, lasting from one to three hours, from May to October 15. Tickets are available at major hotels and kiosks on the *Quai de l'Horloge.* At least five excursions depart daily from the foot of Rue Berri; phone ahead for reservations in peak season. In addition, *Amphibustour* (phone: 386-1298) travels on both the streets and waters of the port; a ferry runs from the *Quai Jacques-Cartier* to the *Cité du Havre* island park daily from noon to 10 PM. *Les Tours St-Louis* (300 Chemin du Canal, Lachine; phone: 365-4440) schedules several two-hour cruises daily around Lac St-Louis on the *St-Louis IV,* which boards 180 passengers per voyage. Tours run from May 15 to October 15; advance reservations are advised.

HORSE-DRAWN CARRIAGE A romantic way to see the town is by calèches, which are stationed on Rues Notre-Dame and de la Commune in Vieux Montréal, at Place Jacques-Cartier, at Square Dorchester, and atop Mont-Royal. *Calèches A. Boisvert* (phone: 653-0751) operates carriages and, in winter, one-horse sleighs.

JET-BOAT TOURS Organized expeditions over the Rapides de Lachine, in large hydrofoil-like craft, leave from the *Quai de l'Horloge* at the foot of Rue Berri in Vieux Montréal. From May to late September they depart daily every other hour from 10 AM to 6 PM. Contact *Expéditions dans les Rapides de Lachine* (105 Rue de la Commune O.; phone: 284-9607).

MÉTRO AND BUS *STCUM* (phone: 288-6287), Montreal's efficient transit system, links various areas of the city with four underground lines and 150 bus lines. (The same tickets—which cost CN$1.75 at press time—are used on the *Métro* and the buses.) *Métro* trains are clean and quiet, whizzing underground on rubber-tired wheels. The price of the ride admits visitors to a veritable underground art gallery of murals, sculptures, stained glass windows, enameled steel frescoes, and ceramics built into the 65 stations of the system. *STCUM* issues a helpful map of the routes, available free at hotel desks and all *Métro* station ticket booths.

TAXI Cabs may be hailed on the street; taxi stands are located on the corners of main intersections near the railway stations and at hotels.

TOURS Some taxicab drivers are licensed tour guides; *Taxi LaSalle* (phone: 277-7552), for instance, offers tours. Sightseeing tours leaving from *INFO-TOURISTE* at Square Dorchester are provided by *Autocar Connoisseur Gray Line* (Rue du Sq.-Dorchester; phone: 934-1222) and *Murray Hill* (Rue du Sq.-Dorchester; phone: 871-4733). Other private tour companies include *Guidatour* (phone: 844-4021); *Hertz Tourist Guides* (phone: 937-6690); *Step-on-Guides* (phone: 935-5131); *Visites de Montréal* (phone: 933-6674); and *Voyages Astral* (phone: 866-1001). For more information on guided tours, call *INFOTOURISTE* (see *Tourist Information,* above). *A Walking Tour of Vieux Montréal,* available free from the tourism bureau, is a must for those who choose to go it alone. Also see *Walk 2: Vieux Montréal* in DIRECTIONS—MONTREAL. For further information on companies offering tours in and around Montreal, see GETTING READY TO GO.

LOCAL SERVICES

For information about local services not listed below, call the *Office des Congrès et du Tourisme du Grand Montreal* (Greater Montreal Convention and Tourism Bureau; phone: 844-5400).

AUDIOVISUAL EQUIPMENT *Corpav* (460 Rue St-Paul E.; phone: 842-1440) or *Inter-Cité Video* (8270 Rue Mayrand; phone: 342-4545).

BABY-SITTING *Baby Sitting Service* (367 Blvd. Henri-Bourassa E.; phone: 953-9544).

BUSINESS SERVICES *Travelex Business Center* (1253 Av. McGill College; phone: 871-8616) rents furnished offices by the hour, day, or week, and provides bilingual secretarial and telephone-answering services plus photocopying, telex, fax, and word-processing facilities.

COMPUTER RENTAL *Centre Micro Informatique CIAP* (1690 Rue Gilford; phone: 522-2427) or *Vernon Rental & Leasing* (3500 Blvd. de Maisonneuve O.; phone: 843-8888).

DRY CLEANER/TAILOR *Milton Dry Cleaning & Tailoring* (1447 Rue Drummond; phone: 843-6132; and 1001 Rue University; phone: 875-7928) or *Nettoyeur 60 Minutes* (*Gare Centrale,* 935 Rue de la Gauchetière O.; phone: 861-8003).

LIMOUSINE *Phoenix Limousine* (phone: 875-8715).

MECHANIC *Darmo Auto* (21 Av. Somerville; phone: 486-0785) or *Nelson Garage* (1100 Blvd. Décarie; phone: 481-0155).

MEDICAL EMERGENCY For information on local medical services and pharmacies, see GETTING READY TO GO.

PHOTOCOPIES *Copiemont* (1447 Rue Drummond; phone: 288-7592) or *Recan Reproductions* (2024 Rue Peel; phone: 849-3279).

PHOTOGRAPHER *The Professionals* (490 Rue Guy; phone: 933-5728) or *René Delbuguet Photo Media* (1209 Rue Guy; phone: 932-1630).

POST OFFICES For information on local branch offices, see GETTING READY TO GO.

SECRETARY/STENOGRAPHER *A & A Secretarial Services* (117 Rue Ste-Catherine O.; phone: 288-3795) or *Travelex Business Center* (see *Business Services,* above).

TELECONFERENCE FACILITIES The *Bonaventure Hilton International, Château Champlain, Du Parc, Queen Elizabeth, Ritz-Carlton Kempinski,* and *Westin–Mont Royal* hotels have teleconference facilities (see *Checking In* for all).

TELEX *Telepublic,* with many locations throughout the city, including 1015 Côte du Beaver Hall (phone: 871-8616).

TRANSLATOR *Berlitz Translation & Interpretation Service* (in the *2020 University* complex, at 2020 Rue University; phone: 288-3111).

SPECIAL EVENTS

Vieux Montréal, Ile Ste-Hélène, and Ile Notre-Dame host the *Fête des Neiges,* a 10-day pre-*Lenten* snow carnival that features costume balls on ice, skating races, sledding, and other outdoor activities, plus plentiful refreshments. Imaginative snow sculptures are part of the fun.

With over 40,000 cyclists competing, early June's *Tour de l'Ile de Montréal* (phone: 847-8356) is fast becoming one of the most popular bicycle races in North America. The route encircles the island of Montreal via city streets. The *Grand Prix du Canada* (phone: 392-0000) is a Formula One racing car event held in mid-June at the 4.41-km *Gilles Villeneuve* track on Ile Notre-Dame.

The *Fête du Vieux Port* (Vieux Port Festival) kicks off the season on the *Fête Nationale* (St-Jean-Baptiste Day; June 24), with events continuing until *Labour Day.* Daily activities include puppet shows, clowns, movies, dancing, and theater (all free); at night, the large outdoor stage facing the harbor is the site of numerous performances—from the *Orchestre Symphonique de Montréal* to various rock groups.

The 10-day *Festival International de Jazz de Montréal* (phone: 289-9472) draws music greats—and more than one million of their fans—every year in early July. Major concerts are held at the *Place des Arts* (see *Special Places*), with many more intimate events happening along Rue Ste-Catherine and in the *Théâtre St-Denis* (Rue St-Denis) and the *Spectrum* (318 Rue Ste-Catherine O.). The *Festival Juste pour Rire* (Just for Laughs Festival; phone: 845-3155) is a 10-day event in early August, attracting stand-up comics from all over the world who match wits in French and English. It is held at the *Comedy Nest* (1234 Rue Bishop), the *Théâtre St-Denis,* and *Place des Arts* (see above for the last two).

During the last week in August and the first week in September, the *Festival des Films du Monde* (World Film Festival) brings the latest movies and their stars to Montreal's *Cinéma le Parisien* (480 Rue Ste-Catherine

O.; phone: 866-3856), *Place des Arts,* and *Complexe Desjardins* (see *Special Places;* phone: 281-1870). Another film event, the *Festival International du Nouveau Cinéma et de la Vidéo de Montréal* (Montreal Festival of New Cinema and Video; phone: 843-4725), presents avant-garde films in October.

MUSEUMS

In addition to those mentioned in *Special Places,* other notable Montreal museums include the following:

CENTRE CANADIEN D'ARCHITECTURE (CANADIAN CENTRE FOR ARCHITECTURE) The world's first nonprofit institution devoted solely to the study of architecture is the brainchild of Canadian-born architect Phyllis Lambert. Available here are study and research facilities, a lecture hall, and the founder's exhaustive collection of manuscripts, folios, artwork, and archives that include 47,000 prints and drawings, 45,000 photographs, and 35,000 books spanning the history of architecture from the Renaissance to the 20th century. Works by Leonardo and Michelangelo are on display. The sculpture garden across Boulevard René-Lévesque Ouest from the museum is an enchanting spot to rest during a visit here. Closed Mondays and Tuesdays. Admission charge. 1920 Rue Baile (phone: 939-7026).

CENTRE SAIDYE-BRONFMAN Contemporary works by national and international artists. Closed Saturdays. No admission charge. 5170 Côte Ste-Catherine (phone: 739-2301).

MAISON DE SIR GEORGE-ETIENNE-CARTIER Some of the rooms in this building—the Montreal home of one of Canada's founding fathers—have been restored to their former Victorian glory; others are reserved for various exhibitions. Open daily mid-May to *Labour Day;* closed Mondays and Tuesdays the rest of the year. No admission charge. *Métro* stop *Champs-de-Mars.* 458 Rue Notre-Dame E. (phone: 283-2282).

MUSÉE D'ART CONTEMPORAIN (CONTEMPORARY ART MUSEUM) The museum features art completed since 1939 by Québécois and other Canadian and international artists. Included are pieces by Quebec-based artists Jean-Paul Riopelle, Paul-Emile Borduas, David Moore, and Alfred Pellan as well as national artists Barbara Steinman, Jack Bush, and Michael Snow. Guided tours for groups with advance reservations are available. Closed Mondays. Admission charge. 185 Rue Ste-Catherine O. (phone: 873-2878).

MUSÉE D'ART DE ST-LAURENT This arts and crafts center is housed in the old chapel that once served the *Collège St-Laurent.* Closed mornings, Saturdays, and Mondays. No admission charge. *Métro* stop *Du Collège.* 615 Blvd. Ste-Croix, St-Laurent (phone: 747-7367).

MUSÉE DES ARTS DÉCORATIFS (MUSEUM OF DECORATIVE ARTS)—CHÂTEAU DUFRESNE Built between 1915 and 1918 by the Dufresne family, this restored early-20th-century mansion is the site of the *Liliane and David M. Stewart Collection* *of International Design;* temporary exhibitions of furniture, textiles, ceramics, and graphic arts also are mounted. Closed Mondays and Tuesdays. Admission charge. 2929 Rue Jeanne-d'Arc (phone: 259-2575).

MUSÉE DE LA BANQUE DE MONTRÉAL (BANK OF MONTREAL MUSEUM) Early currency and bank memorabilia. Closed weekends and holidays. No admission charge. 129 Rue St-Jacques at Pl. d'Armes (phone: 877-6892).

MUSÉE DU COMMERCE DE LA FOURRURE (FUR TRADE MUSEUM) A warehouse within a national historic site displays memorabilia from the area's rich fur-trading past. Open daily May 15 through October 20; closed Mondays and Tuesdays February 21 through May 14 and October 21 through December 7; closed December 8 through February 20. No admission charge. 1255 Blvd. St-Joseph at Av. 12, Lachine (phone: 637-7433).

MUSÉE MARC-AURÈLE-FORTIN Works and memorabilia of the Canadian artist. Closed Mondays. Admission charge. 118 Rue St-Pierre (phone: 845-6108).

MUSÉE MARGUERITE D'YOUVILLE This is the motherhouse of the Grey Nuns (Sisters of Charity of Montreal), a religious order founded by Marguerite d'Youville. Guided tours are given of the chapel and crypt where she is buried. Closed Mondays, Tuesdays, and mornings. No admission charge. 1185 Rue St-Matthew (phone: 937-9501).

MUSÉE MCCORD D'HISTOIRE CANADIENNE (MCCORD MUSEUM OF CANADIAN HISTORY) Here is one of Canada's largest collections of aboriginal art and artifacts, plus a good selection of the works of such masters as Cornelius Kreighoff and Théophile Hamel. Located in *Université McGill's Centre Universitaire* (Union Building), a hybrid of Baroque, Gothic, and classical architecture, its galleries also contain a treasure trove of period costumes, furniture, religious art, toys, and photographs from the *Notman Archives,* a collection of some 700,000 glass negatives and prints of Montreal scenes, some dating from the 1850s. Closed Mondays and holidays. Admission charge. 690 Rue Sherbrooke O. (phone: 398-7100).

MUSÉE REDPATH An impressive anthropological collection, including Egyptian mummies and rare fossils. Closed weekends September through May; closed Fridays through Sundays the rest of the year. No admission charge. *Métro* stop *Peel* or *McGill.* 859 Rue Sherbrooke O. (phone: 398-4086).

POINTE-À-CALLIÈRE, MUSÉE D'ARCHÉOLOGIE ET D'HISTOIRE (MUSEUM OF ARCHAEOLOGY AND HISTORY) A landmark in the heart of Vieux Montréal's historic sector, it sits on the spot where the city was founded in 1642. Featured are relics collected from the archaeological exploration at Place Royale and Pointe-à-Callière, where the first settlers landed. The complex includes three historic sites: the *Edifice de l'Eperon* (Eperon Building), the *Crypte Archéologique* (Archaeological Crypt), and the *Vieille Douane* (Old Customs House). Guided tours available. Closed Mondays. Admission charge. 350 Pl. Royale (phone: 872-9150).

SHOPPING

Since the duty-free allowance for US citizens returning from Canada after a two-day or longer stay is CN$400, and the US dollar is at a premium north of the border, there are excellent bargains to be found on a shopping spree in Montreal. Canadian import tariffs are different from those in the US, so in some cases this may mean even better buys. It also usually means a wider selection of imported products.

The underground shopping areas (see *Special Places*) provide an enormous variety of shops—including branches of many Paris fashion houses—that satisfy most shopping needs. Montreal's department stores also have fine selections of clothing, china, crystal, and furniture.

For information on standard shopping hours, see GETTING READY TO GO.

ANTIQUES

Antiques Retro-Ville On Rue Notre-Dame Ouest's "attic row," a 10-block stretch of antiques and secondhand shops, this store deals mainly in nostalgia—old signs, toys, magazines, sports collectibles, and the like. 2652 Rue Notre-Dame O. (phone: 989-1307).

Antiquités Phyllis Friedman Those looking for precious pine pieces usually make their first stop here, where the blanket boxes, spinning wheels, chests, and armoires are all at least 150 years old. 5012 Rue Sherbrooke O. (phone: 483-6185).

Blue Pillow Antiques A tiny shop in the *Queen Elizabeth* hotel's underground shopping mall, it might offer such treasures as a Royal Crown Derby tea set or a diamond-encrusted platinum brooch, as its specialty is estate jewelry. 900 Blvd. René-Lévesque (phone: 871-0225).

Circa-Circa Beyond the western reaches of the city, this place stocks Québécois furniture of pine, ash, oak, and butternut in all price ranges. 68 Av. Westminster N. (phone: 481-3410).

Coach House Antiques This gallery is the place to look for a sterling silver tea service or a mahogany-framed hunting print, as well as fine antiques, art, and estate jewelry. 1325 Av. Greene, Westmount (phone: 937-6191).

Daniel J. Malynowsky Antiques Sterling silver and fine bone china stand out here, along with marble-topped Victorian tables, *étagères*, and the cracked leather seats of high-backed chairs. 1642 Rue Notre-Dame O. (phone: 937-3727).

Deuxièmement A grab-bag of secondhand furniture, household items, china, and toys. 1880 Rue Notre-Dame O. (phone: 933-8560).

Henrietta Antony Beautiful early Québécois furniture, including a few rare pieces from the late 1700s, some with traces of the original finish. Pieces range from traditional farmhouse relics to naive versions of Versailles elegance that Quebec cabinetmakers made to order for the local seigneurs 200 years ago. 4192 Rue Ste-Catherine O. (phone: 935-9116).

Petit Musée Probably one of the most intriguing and expensive of Montreal's antiques shops, it is really more of a fine arts gallery, with an eclectic collection of furniture, china, and objets d'art from Europe, the Middle East, and the Far East. 1494 Rue Sherbrooke O. (phone: 937-6161).

ART

Dominion Gallery Easily recognizable by Rodin's *Bourgeois de Calais* and Henry Moore's *Upright Motif* on the plaza in front of its limestone townhouse, it is a leader in Canada's art world, displaying and selling paintings and sculptures by international and Canadian artists. 1438 Rue Sherbrooke O. (phone: 845-7471).

Galerie d'Art A part of the *Musée des Beaux Arts,* this attractive gallery rents museum art for display; works are for sale as well. 1446 Rue Sherbrooke O. (phone: 285-1611).

Galerie Claude Lafitte A showcase for the best of Canadian art, including the work of Jean-Paul Riopelle, as well as such international masters as Chagall and Ernst. 1480 Rue Sherbrooke O. (phone: 939-9898).

Galerie Jean-Pierre Valentin Canadian and European paintings. 1434 Rue Sherbrooke O. (phone: 849-3637).

Galerie Lippel One of the few sources of pre-Columbian artwork in Montreal. 1324 Rue Sherbrooke O. (phone: 842-6369).

Galerie Tansu Japanese and Chinese antiques, bronzes, embroidered silks, lacquer works, kimonos, obis, and ancient dolls. 1460 Rue Sherbrooke O. (phone: 845-8604).

Galerie Walter Klinkhoff This family-owned gallery is among the most respected in the city. The Klinkhoffs show primarily Canadian artists, although they have international works as well. 1200 Rue Sherbrooke O. (phone: 288-7306).

BOOKS

Bibliomania Booke Shoppe A haven for browsers, its shelves are well stocked with titles old and new, in French and English, including some rare collectors' items. 4872 Av. Park (phone: 278-6401).

Coles There are outlets of this bookstore all over the city, selling a variety of French and English publications. The flagship store is at 1171 Rue Ste-Catherine O. (phone: 849-8825).

Double Hook A quaint Victorian house is the site of this bookshop specializing in Canadian authors; its cozy atmosphere welcomes browsers. 1235 Av. Greene, Westmount (phone: 932-5093).

Paragraph A bookstore-cum–coffee shop, it attracts serious bibliophiles and students from nearby *Université McGill*. The store often hosts lectures and readings by well-known Canadian authors. 2065 Rue Mansfield (phone: 845-5811).

Russell Though it's shabby and located in a run-down part of town, its shelves are well stocked with out of print and secondhand books. A must stop for collectors. 275 Rue St-Antoine O. (phone: 866-0564).

Ulysses Travel publications on Montreal, Canada, and the world plus globes and travel cases. Three locations: 1307 Rue Ste-Catherine (phone: 842-7711, ext. 362); 560 Av. President-Kennedy (phone: 843-7222); and 4176 Rue St-Denis (phone: 843-9447).

W. H. Smith Best sellers, paperbacks, magazines, and international newspapers are its stock in trade. Two downtown branches: *Place Ville-Marie* (phone: 861-1736) and *Gare Centrale* (phone: 861-5567).

CHILDREN'S CLOTHING

Gamineries This neat little boutique on the street level of a 19th-century townhouse specializes in expensive but unusual European- and US-made fashions for chic children. 1458 Rue Sherbrooke O. (phone: 843-4614).

Jacadi Sweaters and pleated skirts, knitted suits, and smart chapeaus from France are in the affordable range in this *Centre Eaton* boutique for fashion-conscious kids. 705 Rue Ste-Catherine O. (phone: 282-1933).

Oink-Oink This Westmount store for preteens also stocks a nice selection of toys. 1361 Av. Greene (phone: 939-2634).

DEPARTMENT STORES

La Baie (The Bay) Founded in 1845 as Henry Morgan and Company, it was purchased by the Hudson's Bay Company in 1969. While it's strong on new trends, French boutique styles, and campus fashions, the store no longer sells furs. Dining spots within include a cafeteria, a licensed dining room, and *Le Soupière,* which serves soup and sandwiches. 585 Rue Ste-Catherine O., at Sq. Phillips (phone: 281-4631).

Eaton This branch of the Canadian department store chain dates back to 1925. Its merchandise runs the gamut from appliances to works of art, and a personalized shopping service will do all the work for reluctant shoppers. The ninth-floor Art Deco restaurant is modeled after the dining room of the steamship *Ile de France.* 677 Rue Ste-Catherine O. (phone: 284-8484).

Holt Renfrew This firm traces its heritage to the 1837 furriers Henderson, Holt, and Renfrew. It is still known for its truly chic fur fashions as well as haute couture lines, a *Gucci* boutique, and stylish men's clothing. 1300 Rue Sherbrooke O. (phone: 842-5111).

Ogilvy This once tartan-trimmed testament to days gone by is now a glossy complex of boutiques and elegant counters. However, the columns and grand main-floor chandeliers have been retained, and traditional goods still can be found. The store's Scottish heritage manifests itself at noon, when shoppers hear the skirl of the bagpipes played by a kilted piper. Every *Christmas* since 1947, Montrealers have looked forward to *Ogilvy*'s main window display of animated Steiff toys. *Ogilvy pour Enfants,* on the fourth floor, offers a very good selection of children's clothing. 1307 Rue Ste-Catherine O. (phone: 842-7711).

FASHION

Agatha Stylish young Montreal career women swear by this boutique. 1054 Av. Laurier (phone: 272-9313).

Alfred Sung A white marble salon in *Place Montreal Trust* features haute couture for women and children by one of Canada's best-known designers. 1500 Av. McGill College (phone: 843-3539).

Aquascutum Three branches of the British fashion house offer the best in raincoats, blazers, and other classic clothing. *Ogilvy,* 1307 Rue Ste-Catherine O.: second floor for women (phone: 843-7836); main floor for men (phone: 843-8428); 1 *Place Ville-Marie* for men and women (phone: 875-7010); and *Les Cours Mont-Royal,* 1455 Rue Peel, for women (phone: 843-7319).

Brisson & Brisson Catering to the well-dressed Montreal male, it carries elegant European-style suits, vests, and designer silk ties. 1472 Rue Sherbrooke O. (phone: 937-7456).

Chakok Youthful styles incorporating riots of color distinguish the designs in this French import outlet in the *Cacharel* boutique. 1 *Complexe Westmount Square* (phone: 933-8223).

Jaeger The *Ogilvy* branch of one of Britain's top-of-the-line fashion houses carries fine English woolens, tweeds, classic suits, coats, and dresses. 1307 Rue Ste-Catherine O. (phone: 845-5834).

Marks & Spencer The Montreal outpost of Britain's venerable fashion and food chain carries a wide selection of men's, women's, and children's clothing that's both affordable and serviceable. *Place Montreal Trust,* 1500 Av. McGill College (phone: 499-8558).

Polo Ralph Lauren A townhouse has been transformed into a showcase for fashions by the internationally popular designer. 1290 Rue Sherbrooke O. (phone: 288-3988).

Rodier Paris Knits and ensembles from the exclusive French house. Two branches: *Ogilvy,* 1307 Rue Ste-Catherine O. (phone: 284-0234), and *Complexe Desjardins* (phone: 844-5010).

l'Uomo Boutique Trendsetting menswear. 1452 Rue Peel (phone: 844-1008).

FURS

Alexandor's One of the finer salons dealing in Canadian-made furs. 2055 Rue Peel (phone: 288-1119).

Birger Christensen The Danish fur fashion house has its Quebec salon in *Holt Renfrew* (see above; phone: 842-5111).

Desjardins Fourrures This large, two-story house has served generations of customers. 325 Blvd. René-Lévesque E. (phone: 288-4151).

Grizzly Fourrure Bargain-priced new and secondhand furs. 3692 Rue St-Denis (phone: 288-9959).

McComber Canadian-made coats for women plus a small selection of furs for men. 440 Blvd. de Maisonneuve O. (phone: 845-1167).

Oslo Fourrures Basically a manufacturing house, it opens its showroom to the retail market as well. 4316 Blvd. St-Laurent (phone: 499-1777).

Shuchat High-fashion designs in furs. 402 Blvd. de Maisonneuve O. (phone: 849-2113).

FURNITURE

Décors et Confort de France Elegant French furniture and decorative fixtures are featured here, all of them expensive. 1434 Rue Sherbrooke O. (phone: 281-9281).

Roche-Bobois For those who prefer the latest in leather sectionals, chrome-frame furniture, and glass-topped tables on arty pedestals. 1425 Blvd. René-Lévesque O. (phone: 871-9070).

HANDICRAFTS

Canadian Guild of Crafts, Quebec Devoted to authentic Inuit carvings, prints, and other crafts, the collection is open to viewing, while the boutique is regarded as the best place in Montreal to learn about the artists of Canada's far north. Each piece is signed by the artist. 2025 Rue Peel (phone: 849-6091).

Centre de Céramique Bon Secours Original ceramics and sculpture by Quebec artists are displayed and sold here. Closed Saturdays. 444 Rue St-Gabriel, Vieux Montréal (phone: 866-6581).

Galerie le Chariot In the heart of the historic quartier this place stocks a wide selection of signed Inuit carvings from Cape Dorset and other parts of the Canadian north. 446 Pl. Jacques-Cartier (phone: 875-4994).

Galerie Elena Lee-Verre d'Art The one-of-a-kind pieces on display in this gallery/boutique are true works of art: plates, vases, and other *objets* the artist infuses with glowing color. 1428 Rue Sherbrooke O. (phone: 844-6009).

Le Rouet Métiers d'Art A trio of boutiques features tasteful, reasonably priced, Québécois ceramics, weaving, copper and enamel jewelry, wooden toys, and carvings. 136 Rue St-Paul E., Vieux Montréal (phone: 935-8266); 1 *Place Ville-Marie* (phone: 866-4774); and 700 Rue Ste-Catherine O. (phone: 861-8401).

JEWELRY

Birks Canada's most prestigious jewelry store has also been the source of sterling silver, china, and crystal for generations. Crystal chandeliers and marble pillars set the tone. 1240 Sq. Phillips (phone: 397-2511).

Cartier This treasure chest of a boutique carries a representative selection from the famous Paris *joaillier.* 1498 Rue Sherbrooke O. (phone: 939-0000).

Kaufmann A long-established midtown company where Rolex and Piaget watches share display cases with diamond rings and things. 2195 Rue Crescent (phone: 848-0595).

Oz Bijoux Young fashionables on a budget patronize this boutique known for its original designs in chunky silver and copper. 3900 Rue St-Denis (phone: 845-9568).

LINEN

Linen Chest The largest branch of this Canadian enterprise stocks a bountiful supply of bed and bath linen, china, crystal, gift items, and home accessories. *Les Promenades de la Cathédrale,* 625 Rue Ste-Catherine O. (phone: 282-9525).

Pratesi Gift shoppers and brides buy their imported and high-fashion bed, bath, and table linen here. The store also carries an enchanting selection of imported toiletries. 1448 Rue Sherbrooke O. (phone: 285-8909).

SHOES

Bally Affordable yet stylish men's shoes and boots by *Bally of Canada. Place Montreal Trust,* 1500 Av. McGill College (phone: 499-9766).

Brown's A popular chain for high-fashion women's shoes, boots, and bags. 1 *Place Ville-Marie* (phone: 334-5512).

Pegabo For the latest in youthful footwear for women, particularly boots, this chain is a good bet. Main store at 4065 Rue St-Denis (phone: 848-0272).

Roots Canada's own health-shoe company is a big hit in this walkers' city, where men and women like to combine style with comfort. 716 Rue Ste-Catherine O. (phone: 875-4374).

SWEETS

Lenôtre Paris For chocolates and pastries with a European flair, the Montreal branches of this French *pâtisserie* are worth the trip. 1050 Av. Laurier O. (phone: 270-2702) and 1277 Av. Greene, Westmount (phone: 939-6000).

Pâtisserie Belge Fine pastries, baguettes, and extraordinary cheeses are sold here. Light lunches are served on the terrace in warm weather. 3487 Av. Park (phone: 845-1245).

Pâtisserie La Brioche Lyonnaise This distinctly Québécois pastry shop is also a restaurant where you can sip coffee and savor a cream-filled cake or two. An outdoor terrace is open in spring and summer. 1593 Rue St-Denis (phone: 842-7017).

TOBACCO

Davidoff An upmarket establishment, it stocks imported tobacco products (including Cuban cigars—it's legal to sell them here), pipes, lighters, and other smoker's accessories. 1452 Rue Sherbrooke O. (phone: 289-9118).

SPORTS

BASEBALL The *National League*'s *Expos* play at the spectacular *Stade Olympique* (Olympic Stadium) in *Parc Olympique* (see *Special Places;* phone: 253-3434).

BICYCLING The island of Montreal has 20 bike paths, 12 of them city-run. The *Métro* opens the last two doors of its tail car to cyclists and their wheels (limited to four passengers at a time) weekdays after 7 PM and weekends at all hours for transportation to trails. For biking maps, contact the *Service des Sports et Loisirs de la Ville de Montréal* (Department of Parks and Recreation; 7400 Rue St-Michel; phone: 872-6211). For information on commercial rentals, call *Vélo-Québec* (phone: 847-8356). Rentals also are available at *La Cordée* (2159 Rue Ste-Catherine E.; phone: 524-1515); *Cycle Peel* (6665 Rue St-Jacques O.; phone: 486-1148); and *Cyclo-Touriste* (in the *INFOTOURISTE* center on Rue Dorchester; see *Tourist Information,* above). Following is a list of places where you'll get a rolling, intimate view of the country in the city.

BEST BIKING

Canal de Lachine This 7.8-mile (12-km) path is lit for evening biking along the old canal, once the only way to bypass the Rapides de Lachine, but take your first ride along the historic trail by day. The gateway to the Great Lakes, the canal was once lined with shipyards and foundries, rail lines, factories, and mills. The path gets prettier as it nears *Parc René-Lévesque.* Bikers can see the Rapides de Lachine from here as they cycle along the waterfront to *Parc St-Louis,* where most travelers stop for a breather or a picnic snack under the trees before the return trip. If you are driving here and planning to rent a bike, pick up the Canal de Lachine route and follow Rue de la Commune west from the Vieux Port to Rue Mill under the Autoroute Bonaventure, and park in the lot there. 7115 Rue Peel (phone: 283-6054).

The Islands Both Ile Ste-Hélène and Ile Notre-Dame are captivating places to explore on two wheels, although neither maintains trails exclusively for bikers. Choose a sunny day, because the weather on the islands can be a few degrees colder and windier than downtown. Weekend cyclists can transport their wheels via *Métro* to the *Ile Ste-Hélène* station and spend a full day taking in the sights of Montreal's mid-river playgrounds. The islands are linked by two bridges. In the floral park on Ile Notre-Dame, *Quadricycle International* (phone: 768-9282) rents only pedal-powered, four-wheeled "vehicles" that seat up to six (no traditional two-wheelers). The service operates June 5 through August. For more information, call the *Société de l'Ile Notre-Dame* (phone: 872-6093).

Parc Angrignon Out in the southwest section of the city, the home of Montreal's winter wonderland (see *Skating*, below) reveals a 4-mile (6.5-km) cycling path when the snow melts. This cool summer retreat of little lakes and picnic groves is the last *Métro* stop from downtown on the *Angrignon-Honoré-Beaugrand* line. Bikers wheel out of the station into the north end of the park. 3400 Blvd. des Trinitaires. For information, contact the *Service des Sports et Loisirs de la Ville de Montréal* (see above).

Parc Maisonneuve This 525-acre parkland has room to spare for bikers in a vast green domain that, in addition to a well-maintained bicycle track, includes Montreal's *Jardin Botanique* and a nine-hole municipal golf course. Take the *Métro* to the *Viau* station. 4601 Rue Sherbrooke E. (phone: 872-6555).

St. Lawrence Seaway Heading west from the *Ecluse de St-Lambert* (St-Lambert Lock), cyclists can ride for miles, keeping up with slow-moving vessels as they negotiate this narrow part of the seaway. Ten miles (16 km) long, the seaway bike route begins at the locks on its south side and ends in the community of Côte Ste-Catherine, at the foot of the Rapides de Lachine. It goes as far east as Ile Notre-Dame. Take the Pont Victoria from downtown across to the *Ecluse de St-Lambert* on Rte. 15. This route is open daily, May through August; closed weekdays, September and October; closed the rest of the year (phone: 672-4110).

Vieux Port (Old Port) Vieux Montréal's ever-growing waterfront park maintains a scenic, 1½-mile (2.4-km) bike path that parallels Rue de la Commune from Rue Berri west to Rue McGill. It is well illuminated for night riders. From the port path, cyclists can continue west to join the Canal de Lachine route. Visiting bikers can rent wheels of all kinds at the port. *Accès Cible* (phone: 525-8888) rents bicycles and tandems. Open daily except Monday mornings, mid-May through *Labour Day*. *Quadricycle International* (phone: 768-

9282) rents the four-wheeled variety only. Open daily to midnight, June through August; open weekends only to midnight, May and September; closed the rest of the year. 333 Rue de la Commune O. (phone: 283-5256; 496-PORT in summer).

GOLF The nine-hole *Golf Municipal de Montréal* (phone: 872-1143) is located at Rues Sherbrooke and Viau. In addition, there are more than 50 courses on the island of Montreal and in the surrounding area. Reciprocal agreements with private clubs in the US make two nearby clubs—the *Royal Montreal* and *Beaconsfield*—available to visitors who are accompanied by a member. For more information, see *Good Golf Nearby* in DIVERSIONS.

HOCKEY From October through April, the ice is hotly contested at the *Forum* by *Les Canadiens* and their *NHL* challengers (*Métro* stop *Atwater;* 2313 Rue Ste-Catherine O.; phone: 932-2582). *Université Concordia* boasts one of the country's leading collegiate hockey teams, the *Stingers,* which play in the university's *Arena Loyola* (phone: 848-3850). Hockey dominates the skating scene, and aspiring professionals begin early. Drop into any community center/arena to see the small fry in action. Montreal boasts 150 outdoor rinks and more than 20 indoor arenas for hockey and public skating (see *Skating,* below).

HORSE RACING Harness racing takes place nightly, except Tuesdays and Thursdays, at the *Hippodrome Blue Bonnets* (7440 Blvd. Décarie; phone: 739-2741). Races begin at 7:30 PM; 1:30 PM on Sundays.

JOGGING *Parcs du Mont-Royal* and *Angrignon* have paved trails for taking a pleasant run. There is another good trail from Vieux Montréal along the Canal de Lachine.

SKATING The *Canadian Figure Skating Association* (phone: 613-748-5635) has 1,400 clubs nationwide that stage seminars for skaters and interclub competitions, sending the winners on to sectional, divisional, national, and international contests. Montreal boasts close to 200 rinks. The following are some of our favorites; all are open from freeze to thaw.

GOOD SKATES

Ile Notre-Dame Site of the city's 10-day *Fête des Neiges* from mid-January to early February, the island's summer beach area is transformed into a winter playground once the snow falls. There's skating on the lake and the mile-long *Bassin Olympique* (Olympic Basin). Be careful: It can be bitterly cold on the open river, and the wind cuts like a knife when the temperature drops; even the most bundled-up skater is not immune to a touch of frostbite. No admission charge (phone: 872-6093).

Laurentides (Laurentians) The trick here is to arrive after a spell of weather has iced over the myriad ponds, lakes, and streams of this lovely area—but before the snow. Then you can skate for miles, play hockey to your heart's content, or trace figures so large that giants might have made them. Even after snowfalls, there's no dearth of places to skate here. Almost every village has its rink—if not an oval set up in a schoolyard, then a section of a nearby lake kept plowed for the season. There are indoor rinks as well. The European flavor of après-ski likewise applies to après-skate, with long sessions at the hearths of cozy inns; the satiation of appetites in one of the many fine restaurants in the quaint villages; and lively nightlife. For information, contact the *Association Touristique des Laurentides* (14142 Rue de Lachapelle, RR1, St-Jérôme, QUE J7Z 5T4; phone: 436-8532).

Parc Angrignon The large skating rink here is particularly enchanting in the evening, when the park is fancifully illuminated. No admission charge. 3400 Blvd. des Trinitaires (phone: 872-6211 or 872-3066).

Parc du Mont-Royal and Parc Lafontaine Two of the most popular open-air rinks are at *Parc Lafontaine* and *Parc du Mont-Royal* (both lighted at night and near downtown). There's no admission charge to either. *Parc du Mont-Royal*, Chemin Remembrance; *Parc Lafontaine*, Rue Sherbrooke E. between Av. Papineau and Rue Parc-Lafontaine (phone: 872-6211 for both).

SWIMMING The Olympic-size pool at the *Parc Olympique* (see *Special Places*; phone: 252-4622) is open to the public year-round; admission charge. The city operates 50 additional indoor and outdoor pools, including the large ones on Ile Ste-Hélène (phone: 872-6093); admission charge. Two of the best indoor pools are the *Cégep du Vieux Montréal* (255 Rue Ontario E.; phone: 872-2644) and the *Centre Claude-Robillard* (1000 Rue Emile-Journault; phone: 872-6900); neither charges admission. Montreal's only downtown beach is on Ile Notre-Dame (*Métro* stop *Ile Ste-Hélène*).

TENNIS The *Internationaux Player's Limitée* (Player's Limited International) championships are held each summer at the *Stade de Tennis Jarry* (*Parc Jarry*; phone: 273-1515; men's tournaments are held in odd-numbered years; women's, in even-numbered years). Montreal's more than 200 municipal courts are open to the public, either at no charge or for a nominal fee. For information and court reservations, call 872-6763.

WINTER SPORTS In addition to skating and hockey, the city counts among its facilities 11 cross-country ski areas, each with several trails; 11 large snowshoeing areas; seven alpine slopes; and nine toboggan runs. For information, call the *Service des Sports et Loisirs de la Ville de Montréal* (phone: 872-6211). The Laurentides (Laurentian Mountains), which extend from 20 to 80 miles

(32 to 128 km) north of Montreal, boast some of the best ski and all-season resorts in eastern North America. For more information on skiing, see *Cross-Country Skiing* and *Downhill Skiing* in DIVERSIONS.

THEATER

French-language productions are presented at more than a dozen theaters around town, including such well-known stages as the *Théâtre de Quat' Sous* (100 Av. des Pins E.; phone: 845-7277); the *Théâtre du Nouveau Monde* (84 Rue Ste-Catherine O.; phone: 861-0563); and the *Théâtre du Rideau Vert* (4664 Rue St-Denis; phone: 844-1793). The *Théâtre Centaur* (453 Rue St-François-Xavier; phone: 288-3161) schedules a regular season of mainly English-language drama and musicals (see also *The Performing Arts* in DIVERSIONS). Local newspapers and in-hotel magazine guides list current attractions. The *Théâtre Biscuit* (221 Rue St-Paul O.; phone: 845-7306) is a puppet theater featuring shows on weekends and a puppet museum. When it is not on tour (usually in summer), Montreal's unique and now world-famous *Cirque du Soleil* (phone: 522-2324) performs its delightful circus antics at the Vieux Port.

CINEMA

Visitors to Montreal can see the latest film releases from Hollywood in English and from Paris, Algiers, and other French-language cities in French. Most movies are screened in multiple complexes like the five-theater hub on the top floor of the *Centre Eaton* (see *Special Places;* phone: 985-5730), where films are shown in both languages. Other centrally located cinema complexes are the *Cineplex Odéon Centre-Ville* (2001 Rue University; phone: 849-3456); *Cinéma Place Bonaventure* (901 Rue de la Gauchetière O.; phone: 861-7437); *Palace 6* (698 Rue Ste-Catherine O.; phone: 866-6991); and *Egyptian* (1455 Rue Peel; phone: 843-3112).

The *National Film Board (NFB),* Canada's main government-supported film organization, presents a regular program of made-in-Canada films, some of which have won international acclaim, at the *Cinémathèque Québécoise* (335 Blvd. de Maisonneuve E.; phone: 842-9763). Devoted chiefly to Québécois cinema, the theater presents two different films a day, not all of which originate with the *NFB.* Screenings are scheduled Tuesdays through Saturdays at 6:35 and 8:35 PM; Sundays at 3, 6:35, and 8:35 PM.

MUSIC

The *Orchestre Symphonique de Montréal* performs at the *Salle Wilfrid-Pelletier* in the *Place des Arts* (see *Special Places*), as do *Les Grand Ballets Canadiens, L'Opéra de Montréal,* and various guest companies and soloists. Programs of chamber music are held at the *Théâtre Maisonneuve* and *Théâtre Port-Royale,* also located in the *Place des Arts.* The *Salle de Concert Pollack* (555 Rue Sherbrooke O.; phone: 398-4547) regularly schedules varied musical programs. Throughout the year, rock stars perform at the *Forum* (2313 Rue Ste-Catherine O.; phone: 932-2582) and *Stade Olympique* (in the *Parc*

Olympique; phone: 252-4400). Special productions, such as a summer *Mozart Festival* and *Christmastime* performances of Handel's *Messiah,* are presented at the *Basilique Notre-Dame* (see *Special Places;* call the *Orchestre Symphonique de Montréal* office; phone: 842-3402) and at other churches. Up-to-date schedules of musical events are printed in the guides listed in *Local Coverage,* above.

NIGHTCLUBS AND NIGHTLIFE

The supper club crowd can choose from among the many hotel and restaurant dining-entertainment spots in Montreal. On weekends, the *Château Champlain*'s 36th-floor *L'Escapade* restaurant (see *Checking In*) affords a good view along with music. The *Queen Elizabeth*'s *Beaver Club* restaurant (see *Eating Out*) features a trio for dancing on Saturday nights, and there's nightly dancing at the *Radisson-Gouverneurs*'s revolving *Tour de Ville* restaurant (see *Checking In*). The *Ritz-Carlton Kempinski*'s *Café de Paris* (see *Eating Out*) has piano music. *Solmar* (111 Rue St-Paul E.; phone: 861-4562) has fado music and Portuguese cuisine. *Vieux Munich* (1170 Rue St-Denis; phone: 288-8011) features a Bavarian orchestra and dancing nightly after 6 PM, while *Sabayon* (666 Rue Sherbrooke O.; phone: 288-0373) offers a dance band and Greek music and food.

Disco and barhopping abound around Rues Crescent, de la Montagne, St-Denis, St-Laurent, Bishop, and Mackay and a number of side streets between Boulevard René-Lévesque and Rue Sherbrooke. Currently popular are *Club Soda* (5240 Av. Park; phone: 270-7848), dean of Montreal's rock rooms; the *Grand Prix Bar,* the *Ritz-Carlton Kempinski*'s rendezvous for mature singles on expense accounts (see *Checking In*); *Angel's* (3604 Blvd. St-Laurent; phone: 282-9944), offering two floors of late-night pub-club action; and *LUX* (see *Eating Out*), which stays open round-the-clock for piano bar patrons and the dawn patrol. More nightlife can be found at *Thursday's* (1449 Rue Crescent; phone: 288-5656), the city's original singles bar; *Biddles,* for great jazz and ribs (2060 Rue Aylmer; phone: 842-8656); *Cheers* (1260 Rue Mackay; phone: 932-3138); *l'Esprit* (1234 Rue de la Montagne; phone: 397-1711); *Metropolis* (59 Rue Ste-Catherine E.; phone: 288-5559), a turn-of-the-century theater with six bars and dancing on three floors; *Salsathèque* (1220 Rue Peel; phone: 875-0016), for Latin music and dancing; the *Sir Winston Churchill Pub* (1459 Rue Crescent; phone: 288-0616); and *Winnie's* (1455 Rue Crescent; phone: 288-0623).

Vieux Montréal is fast becoming a hot nightspot area. Favorite places include *Le Bijou* (417 Rue St-Pierre O.; phone: 284-6640); *La Cage aux Sports* (395 Le Moyne; phone: 288-1115), popular with sports personalities; *Chez Brandy* (25 Rue St-Paul E.; phone: 871-9178); the vintage jazz joint *l'Air du Temps* (191 Rue St-Paul O.; phone: 842-2003); and *Monte Carlo* (419 Rue St-Pierre; phone: 281-5712), an elegant, upscale disco with crystal chandeliers and private alcoves with individual sound control.

For gamblers, Ile Notre-Dame is home to the *Casino de Montréal* (phone: 392-2746; 800-665-2274 in Canada and the US), an international class venue that moved into the former French pavilion on the *EXPO '67* grounds in 1993. The casino has 65 gaming tables and 1,200 slot machines; players can try their luck at blackjack, baccarat, roulette, and keno. The complex also includes five levels of dining, shopping, and entertainment. Minimum age is 18. It's open daily from 11 to 3 AM. (Most bars are open daily and close at 3 AM.)

Best in Town

CHECKING IN

With more than 16,000 hotel rooms in the Montreal area, there is no difficulty finding suitable accommodations. Hotels in all categories dot the downtown area, close to shopping centers, restaurants, and the city's other attractions. Some luxury hotels even offer weekend packages that are real bargains, including the small extras that make a stay more pleasant. Double room rates per night will run more than $200 in the very expensive category; from $110 to $200 in the expensive category; and from $75 to $110 in the moderate category, excluding taxes. All hotels feature such amenities as air conditioning, private baths, TV sets, and telephones. Among the firms that handle bed and breakfast lodgings are *B & B Chez Antonio* (101 Av. Northview; phone: 486-6910); *Bed & Breakfast de Chez Nous* (3717 Rue Ste-Famille; phone: 845-7711); *Bed & Breakfast Downtown Network* (3458 Av. Laval; phone: 289-9749); *Bed & Breakfast Montreal* (PO Box 575, Snowdon Station, Montreal, QUE H3X 3T8; phone: 738-9410); *Relais Montréal Hospitalité* (3977 Av. Laval; phone: 287-9635); and *Welcome Bed & Breakfast* (3950 Av. Laval; phone: 844-5897).

The downtown *YMCA* (1451 Rue Stanley; phone: 849-8393) and *YWCA* (1355 Blvd. René-Lévesque O.; phone: 866-9941), as well as the youth hostel (3541 Aylmer; phone: 843-3317), offer inexpensive accommodations. In the summer, *Université McGill* and the *Université de Montréal* (see *Special Places* for both), *Collège MacDonald* (Ste-Anne de Bellevue; phone: 398-7716), and the *Collège Français* (Rue Fairmont O.; phone: 495-2581) also have inexpensive rooms to let. In addition, *KOA* runs a campground on the south shore at St-Philippe (phone: 659-8626). All telephone numbers are in the 514 area code unless otherwise indicated.

For an unforgettable experience in Montreal, we begin with our favorites—all classified as very expensive—followed by our cost and quality choices of hotels, listed by price category.

GRAND HOTELS

Bonaventure Hilton International Located at the top of *Place Bonaventure* in the heart of the city's business district is an oasis of comfort.

Guests enter the elevator at the underground level in the most commercial part of Montreal and are whisked up 17 stories to the lobby to check in. There is a heated outdoor pool, which in winter is surrounded by evergreens covered in snow (swimmers enter the pool through a narrow covered passageway). Guests with a garden-view room often wake up to the sight of a pheasant strutting across the Japanese garden, complete with babbling brooks, cascades, and tree-shaded ponds. Yet only an elevator ride away are the mall and exhibition hall, the *Métro, Place Ville-Marie,* and the *Gare Centrale,* all major gateways to the Ville Souterraine. There are 400 contemporary rooms in this penthouse location, including seven executive and 13 junior suites. Convention and business facilities are located on the floor below the hotel's lobby, where the main ballroom can accommodate 2,000, and meeting rooms and secretarial services are available on request. The main dining room, *Le Castillon,* recalls the 17th century, right down to its seigneurial decor, baronial fireplace, and the waiters' period attire. 1 *Place Bonaventure* (phone: 878-2332; 800-268-9275 in Canada; 800-HILTONS in the US; fax: 878-3881).

Inter-Continental Montreal A stunning blend of the old and new, this property is a favorite choice in Vieux Montréal. The reception area and guestrooms are located in a turret-topped, 25-story tower, a 20th-century echo of its 19th-century counterpart. The Victorian music hall, where such stars as Sarah Bernhardt and P. T. Barnum's celebrated Tom Thumb once entertained, now houses the hotel's public rooms and three restaurants. Both the foyer, with its natural wood wainscoting and stenciled frieze, and the ballroom's vast plaster ceiling are sensational. *La Cave des Voûtes* wine-tasting bar and *Les Voûtes* steak and seafood restaurant are down in the restored Nordheimer vaults, which historians believe were part of Montreal's early fortification system. In *Chez Plume,* a casual lounge-café, the upper walls are painted with friezes of stylized peacocks in full plumage. All 22 suites and 337 rooms are decorated in gentle pastel shades, with spacious marble bathrooms. A concierge and room service are available 24 hours a day; other amenities include signature toiletries and complimentary newspapers. Guests can work out in the 10th-floor health club or do laps in the 50-foot pool and then relax in the sauna, steam, and massage rooms. One of the best business centers in town offers secretarial, translation, telex, and courier services, to name a few. 360 Rue St-Antoine (phone: 987-9900; 800-361-3600 in Canada; 800-327-0200 in the US; fax: 987-9904).

Ritz-Carlton Kempinski The details matter at this 240-room, European-style hotel in the heart of Montreal. The secret is making luxury seem natural. Even the ducks in the flower-fringed pond are forever young—when they reach a certain age, they are retired to the country and replaced by more youthful birds. Opened more than 80 years ago by the legendary hotelier César Ritz, the Montreal establishment became an instant institution, catering to Canada's high and mighty, and a loyal international clientele. The *Café de Paris* restaurant here (see *Eating Out*) is consummately elegant. The hotel (now managed by the German Kempinski Group, which has not compromised an iota of comfort) sets the standard for amenities—not just the now-ubiquitous toiletries, but an umbrella in each room. Personalized service comes in the form of two staff members to each guest. Since the days of transatlantic cruises (the *Ritz* opened in 1912, the year the *Titanic* sailed and sank), the custom of unpacking and packing guests' steamer trunks (or suitcases) persists. Just ask, and your garment bag will be looked after, wrinkled suits pressed, and shoes shined. This is, after all, the *Ritz*. 1228 Rue Sherbrooke O. (phone: 842-4212; 800-363-0366 in Canada; 800-426-3135 in the US; fax: 842-3383).

Westin–Mont Royal A leader among the prime properties on Rue Sherbrooke, this is a favorite for those who choose contemporary luxury with traditional comforts. The 31-story, 300-room tower appeals to business travelers, young fashionables, and show-biz bigwigs; its two split-level suites are especially popular among Hollywood types. Those here on business can plug in a computer, have business calls routed to one of two phones, and work at a larger-than-average, well-lit desk. Fitness fanatics can stay in shape at the health club, where there is a sauna, a whirlpool bath, a steamroom, and an outdoor pool for all seasons (in winter, it's heated to a steamy 90F). There's a minimal charge for computerized Kaiser and Nautilus equipment, aerobics classes, and shiatsu massage. Joggers will find a map in their rooms with directions to the best trails in nearby *Parc du Mont-Royal,* just a sprint away up Rue Peel. In keeping with the lobby's exotic Asian decor, dinner is served Szechuan-style at *Zen,* one of the best Chinese restaurants in town (see *Eating Out*). 1050 Rue Sherbrooke O. (phone: 284-1110; 800-268-6282 in Canada; 800-228-3000 in the US; fax: 845-3025).

EXPENSIVE

Château Champlain The huge, arched picture windows covering the 36-story façade of this Canadian Pacific property make it a distinctive landmark on Montreal's skyline (it's known to locals as the cheese grater). Its 617 rooms and suites are spacious and elegantly furnished, and there also is a health club and a pool. The top-floor *L'Escapade* restaurant offers a good view. 1 Pl. du Canada (phone: 878-9000; 800-441-1414 in Canada and the US; fax: 878-6761).

Delta Here is a luxury high-rise with 453 rooms (most with balconies), a dining room, a health club, pools, and an innovative Creativity Center designed to keep young travelers occupied while their parents are sightseeing. Conveniently located downtown, on the corner of Rues Sherbrooke and City Councillors (phone: 286-1986; 800-268-1133 in Canada; 800-877-1133 in the US; fax: 284-4342).

Holiday Inn Crowne Plaza The largest and most convenient of the several *Holiday Inns* in the area, this 489-room link in the chain has an indoor pool and a restaurant. 420 Rue Sherbrooke O. (phone: 842-6111; 800-HOLIDAY in Canada and the US; fax: 842-9381).

Manoir LeMoyne Just a few blocks from the *Forum*, it has 286 rooms, most of which are apartments with fully equipped kitchens, dining alcoves, and spacious balconies. *Le Bistro de l'Hôtel* is its pretty good restaurant and piano bar. There's an indoor pool and sauna, too. 2100 Blvd. de Maisonneuve (phone: 931-8861; 800-361-7191 in Canada and the US; fax: 931-7726).

Le Méridien Montréal This 601-room property is the focal point of the enclosed commercial-business complex at *Complexe Desjardins,* adjacent to the *Place des Arts,* Montreal's performing arts center. The atmosphere is French at this local member of the *Air France* hotel chain. There also are indoor and outdoor pools and a restaurant. 4 *Complexe Desjardins;* enter at 4 Rue Jeanne-Mance (phone: 285-1450; 800-361-8234 in Canada; 800-543-4300 in the US; fax: 285-1243).

De la Montagne This 132-room hostelry is within a stone's throw of the chic boutiques and restaurants in the Rue Crescent–Rue de la Montagne area. Its rooftop pool and terrace are popular for summer rendezvous, and its dining room, *Le Lutetia,* is highly regarded. 1430 Rue de la Montagne (phone: 288-5656; 800-361-6262 in Canada and the US; fax: 288-9658).

Du Parc The hub of a major office-apartment-shopping complex at the base of Mont-Royal, this 463-room hostelry has an attractive lobby lounge and piano bar, indoor and outdoor pools, a sauna, and indoor tennis. *Puzzles* restaurant is a popular spot. 3625 Av. du Parc (phone: 288-6666; 800-363-0735 in Canada and the US; fax: 288-2469).

Queen Elizabeth With 1,046 rooms, this is the city's largest hotel. Offering direct access to underground *Place Ville-Marie*'s shops and services and *Canadian National*'s *Gare Centrale,* it is one of the most conveniently located, too. In addition to the restaurants in the hotel, including the well-known *Beaver Club* (see *Eating Out*), the building features an elegant shopping arcade in the lower lobby, separate from the shops of *Place Ville-Marie.* 900 Blvd. René-Lévesque O. (phone: 861-3511; 800-268-9420 in Canada; 800-828-7447 in the US; fax: 954-2256).

Radisson-Gouverneurs An ambitious establishment with 737 rooms, it has a 40-foot-high atrium lobby with glass-enclosed elevators, an indoor pool, a sauna, and a massage room. *Chez Antoine,* an Art Deco–style restaurant in the corridor linking the hotel to *Place Victoria,* serves an innovative menu featuring seafood and meat grilled over charcoal flavored with mesquite, apple wood, sassafras, and hickory. *Le Tour de Ville* is the city's only revolving rooftop restaurant. 777 Rue University (phone: 879-1370; 800-333-3333 in Canada and the US; fax: 879-1761).

Ramada Inn Centreville Of the three in the Montreal area, this 205-room member of the chain is the most convenient to downtown. An outdoor pool, a dining room, and complimentary parking are among its attractions. 1005 Rue Guy (phone: 938-4611; 800-228-9898 in Canada and the US; fax: 938-8718).

Le Shangrila This high-rise has 167 well-appointed rooms, an agreeable ambience, and the glass-enclosed sidewalk *Café Park Express.* 3407 Rue Peel (phone: 288-4141; 800-361-7791 in Canada and the US; fax: 288-3021).

Vogue Representing a new approach to upmarket innkeeping, this midtown establishment opposite the *Ogilvy* department store has transformed an ordinary office building into a classy little *hôtel particulier.* Although it was inspired by the discreet hotels favored by affluent European travelers, with comforting Old World touches—goosedown duvets and pillows and, in some cases, canopy beds—there's nothing turn-of-the-century about the amenities. The 126 rooms are equipped with fax machines, and the luxurious bathrooms feature whirlpool baths. Devotees admire the classical/modernist decor. There's a restaurant, and corporate pluses include three boardrooms equipped with audiovisual and computer projection systems, as well as secretarial, translation, and courier services. 1425 Rue de la Montagne (phone: 285-5555; 800-363-0363 in Canada; 800-243-1166 in the US; fax: 849-8903).

MODERATE

Château Versailles This European-style hotel with 70 deluxe rooms is a favorite with repeat visitors. It serves only breakfast, but it's located in an area abounding in good, moderately priced restaurants. 1659 Rue Sherbrooke O. (phone: 933-3611; 800-361-7199 in Canada; 800-361-3664 in the US; fax: 933-7102).

Holiday Inn Centre Ville Holiday Inn's newest Montreal property, in the financial district, has added an exotic new dimension to the small Chinese quarter with illuminated rooftop pagodas and a reflection pool and cascade in the dining area. Across the street from the *Palais des Congrès* (Convention Center), it has 235 well-appointed rooms, six suites, and an executive floor. There's also a 40-shop mini-mall and a fitness center with an indoor pool and exercise room. 99 Av. Viger O. (phone: 878-9888; 800-HOLIDAY in Canada and the US; fax: 878-6341).

Tour Versailles This 107-room hotel is located in a converted high-rise apartment building across the street from its cousin, the *Château Versailles* (see above). Rooms have Shaker-style furniture, and the bathrooms are decorated with Italian marble. The more expensive rooms have a Jacuzzi, microwave oven, and refrigerator. Next door is the elegant little French restaurant *Champs-Elysées* (phone: 939-1212), under the same management as the two hotels. 1659 Rue Sherbrooke O. (phone: 933-3611; 800-361-7199 in Canada; 800-361-3664 in the US; fax: 933-7102).

EATING OUT

For the Francophile gourmand, Montreal provides a cornucopia of delights comparable to anything available on the other side of the Atlantic. Even homegrown French Canadian cuisine takes a back seat to the French variety, although local influences show up in the form of *ragoût de pattes* (pig's feet in a garlic stew) or *ragoût de boulettes* (a stew of pork meatballs), and several metropolitan dining spots offer *oka,* a strong-smelling, soft cheese made by Trappist monks. Many of the city's ethnic restaurants, as well as its seafood spots and steakhouses, are excellent. Montrealers put a high value on ambience, too, and our choices reflect this native concern. Expect to pay from $70 to $90 for a dinner for two in a restaurant rated expensive; from $35 to $65 in a moderate restaurant; and $35 or less in an inexpensive one. Prices do not include drinks, wine, or tip. By law, all menus must be posted outside the establishment. All telephone numbers are in the 514 area code unless otherwise indicated. All restaurants are open for lunch and dinner unless otherwise noted.

For an unforgettable dining experience, we begin with our culinary favorites—all expensive—followed by our cost and quality choices, listed by price category.

INCREDIBLE EDIBLES

Beaver Club Founded in 1785 by the 19 fur-trading partners of the North West Company, the original *Beaver Club* was a private enclave that restricted membership to those hardy souls who had spent a winter in the Northwest. Following amalgamation with the Hudson's Bay Company in 1821, the club disbanded until the 1950s, when it was revived as a restaurant in the *Queen Elizabeth* hotel. Though the spirit of the traders is preserved in the restaurant's decor of buffalo hides and other furry trophies, the food is light-years beyond the banquet fare of the old Nor' Westers. Edward Merard, one of Montreal's early disciples of nouvelle cuisine, has created an à la carte menu of great sophistication and variety, featuring such specialties as medallions of deer in a *grand veneur* (master huntsman) sauce with fresh blueberry garnish, noisettes of veal with gorgonzola cheese, and pink Atlantic salmon poached in endive-scented cider. Club regulars favor the roast beef, either sliced thin, English-style, or in juicy, steak-thick slabs. Open daily. Reservations advised. Major credit cards accepted. 900 Blvd. René-Lévesque O. (phone: 861-3511).

Café de Paris This is Montreal's most beautiful restaurant, the *Ritz-Carlton Kempinski*'s main dining room. It is best described as an elegant salon, an island of blue-and-gold civility off the mainstream of Rue Sherbrooke. Its walls are covered in watered silk, and gilt-framed mirrors reflect intimate groupings of velvet banquettes and French doors that open onto the *Ritz Garden,* a warm-weather dining terrace. The cuisine is every bit as fine as the ambience, but be prepared: The golden accents in the decor are reflected in the menu's prices. (Gourmet Impérial, a selection of beluga, ossetra, and sevruga caviar, adds up to a $150 appetizer!) Chicken 21 with wild rice is a longtime favorite, as are Dover sole, Gaspé salmon, venison, and other game dishes. The traditional baron of beef is a carnivore's delight. Open daily. Reservations advised. Major credit cards accepted. 1228 Rue Sherbrooke O. (phone: 842-4212).

Les Halles The great charm of this townhouse is attributable to proprietor Jacques Landurie, whose hearty welcome sets the tone for a delightful dining experience. A nostalgic version of the bistros that once surrounded the Paris marketplace of the same name, it's decorated with murals of the erstwhile market scene, café signs salvaged from the old *quartier,* and other memorabilia of a sadly missed Parisian landmark. Chef Dominique Crevoisier's robust pot-au-feu (tender boiled beef and fresh garden vegetables) draws the lunchtime crowd; for dinner try the warm appetizer of grapefruit, lobster, and scallops dressed with mayonnaise and French mustard, or the king-size ravioli with four varieties of imported mushrooms. Marinated venison, a favorite wintertime entrée, gives way to rack of Quebec lamb in summer. Among the wicked temptations from the dessert trolley are strawberries Florentine (strawberry mousse sandwiched between two thin slices of chocolate topped with marinated strawberries and *sauce anglaise*). The *carte des vins* is an encyclopedia of fine but pricey wines. Closed Sundays and holidays. Reservations necessary. Major credit cards accepted. 1450 Rue Crescent (phone: 844-2328).

La Marée Once a private residence, this restored property is home to one of the best seafood restaurants in town. Though meals are served by formally dressed waiters in a velvet-draped dining room, the menu is shaped more by the quality and freshness of the food than by culinary flourishes. Much of the fish and seafood is imported daily from France, and the kitchen turns out such sat-isfying yet simply prepared specialties as bouillabaisse, sole meu-nière, halibut in creamy lobster sauce, and poached or grilled salmon. The chef is not averse to adding hearty old-fashioned favorites such as onion soup gratinée. Closed Sundays in winter. Reservations necessary. Major credit cards accepted. 404 Pl. Jacques-Cartier (phone: 861-8126).

Les Mignardises Host Jean-Pierre Monnet, a former executive chef at *Les Halles,* has transformed a fussy 19th-century townhouse into a complex of three serene and intimate rooms. The small entryway is simply furnished with a few choice antique pine pieces that com-plement the exposed gray stone walls and small oak bar. Beyond the bar are two petite dining parlors in an unassuming provincial setting of flower-sprigged wallpaper and oak-framed plaster. Quail sautéed in Armagnac, or lobster salad with raspberries and limes will sharpen the appetite for a main course of Atlantic salmon cut-lets sweetened with pink grapefruit, or guinea fowl in orange sauce. Other popular entrées are a robust saddle of rabbit with a rhubarb compote, and slices of venison in a delicate sauce of herbs and shal-lots. The wine list features heady choices (mostly expensive), with a few manageable offerings for customers who prefer to keep the tab in the neighborhood of CN$150 for two. Closed Sundays. Reservations necessary. Major credit cards accepted. 2037 Rue St-Denis (phone: 842-1151).

Le St-Amable Next door to *La Marée* (see above) and under the same ownership, this dining landmark in Vieux Montréal makes its home in the *Maison Benjamin-Viger,* a heritage property built more than 220 years ago. Opening off lane-width Rue St-Amable, the historic building is just large enough to accommodate a kitchen and a small street-level dining room, cozily ensconced in the orig-inal gray stone and brick walls with a warm red decor. House spe-cials include roast breast of duckling spiced with red peppercorns and tart apples served in a creamy sauce; sherry-laced filet of veal; filet mignon with truffles; and a classic chateaubriand. The dessert table is a groaning board of chocolate *gâteaux,* pastries, and cus-tard-filled *mille-feuilles* (puff pastry). There's also a memorable cherries jubilee. Feeling romantic? Ask for a table in the lamp-lit bar down in the old homestead's vaulted cellar. If it hasn't been reserved for group dining, this little hideaway is often deserted—just right for an intimate dinner. Closed *Christmas.* Reservations necessary. Major credit cards accepted. 188 Rue St-Amable (phone: 866-3471).

EXPENSIVE

Auberge le Vieux St-Gabriel Long favored for its good French Canadian food and old-time ambience, this restaurant rambles through a Vieux Montréal building that dates from fur-trading days, complete with a tunnel leading to a room (now a cozy bar) once used to hide pelts from raiding natives. For a taste of Old Quebec, this is the place. Open daily. Reservations advised. Major credit cards accepted. 426 Rue St-Gabriel (phone: 878-3561).

Bagel-Etc. Perfect for the insomniac, this jazzy, all-night rendezvous spot prepares everything from caviar dishes to beef stew. There's a terrific hamburger menu, too. Sunday brunch features the widest variety of egg dishes in town. Open weekdays to 4 AM; Fridays and Saturdays to 6 AM. Brunch reservations advised. Major credit cards accepted. 4320 Blvd. St-Laurent (phone: 845-9462).

Les Chênets At this small, intimate French place, decorated with copper pots, try the oysters from France (called *portuguese*), mussels *marinière* (prepared in white wine with herbs), fresh Pacific salmon, pheasant with mushrooms—or anything else; it's all very good. The excellent wine list also includes 60 kinds of cognac. Open daily. Reservations advised. Major credit cards accepted. 2075 Rue Bishop (phone: 844-1842).

Chez Delmo Well-prepared seafood draws locals to this restaurant in the financial district of Vieux Montréal. At lunchtime seafood also is served up at the Victorian-style mahogany bar. Closed Sundays and some holidays. Reservations advised. Major credit cards accepted. 211 Rue Notre-Dame O. (phone: 849-4061).

Chez Desjardins A favorite since 1892, it features a nautically inspired menu, yet this is not a nets-hanging-from-the-ceiling, buoys-bobbing-in-your-face kind of place. The decor is tastefully appointed in this most elegant of settings. Open daily. Reservations advised. Major credit cards accepted. 1175 Rue Mackay (phone: 866-9741).

Chez la Mère Michel In this fine old stone house converted to an attractive, dark-beamed, candlelit dining spot, French fare achieves authentic excellence. The lobster soufflé is a special treat, and don't miss having a drink in the snug downstairs bar. Closed Sundays. Reservations necessary. Major credit cards accepted. 1209 Rue Guy (phone: 934-0473).

Claude Postel One of the city's finest French restaurants (formerly *Le Petit Havre*) is located in Vieux Montréal in the old *Richelieu* hotel. Specialties include venison with raspberry sauce; salmon in a sherry, shallot, and cream sauce; smoked seafood; and homemade pastries. Open daily. Reservations advised. Major credit cards accepted. 443 Rue St-Vincent (phone: 875-5067).

Le Fadeau Seventeenth-century ambience and excellent food and service are offered at this classic Gallic restaurant in a Vieux Montréal house. Selections from an excellent wine cellar complement the cuisine. Closed Sundays. Reservations necessary. Major credit cards accepted. 423 Rue St-Claude (phone: 878-3959).

Gibby's If you are after good steaks and atmosphere, try this spot in Vieux Montréal's restored, early-18th-century *Ecuries d'Youville* (Youville Stables). While tucking into the large portions, take your time to enjoy the attractive stone-walled, beamed interior. Though most diners order a beef dish, there are other entrées as well, all accompanied by fresh, hot bread and a generous salad. Open daily. Reservations necessary. Major credit cards accepted. 298 Pl. d'Youville (phone: 282-1837).

Le Mas des Oliviers If you're gearing up for a night in Montreal's best disco area (Rues Stanley, de la Montagne, and Bishop), start off the way Montrealers do—by having dinner here. The lamb dishes are chef Jacques Muller's specialty. Open daily. Reservations necessary. Major credit cards accepted. 1216 Rue Bishop (phone: 861-6733).

Le Pavillon de l'Atlantique This seafood establishment, with its classic nautical decor, dominates the atrium of the *Maison Alcan.* Even on busy Sunday evenings, service is friendly and efficient. Among the best dishes are grilled scampi, lobster thermidor, and Arctic char. *Moby Dick's* is the lively bar section, a popular lunchtime and cocktail-hour destination, where the menus are stripped-down versions of the restaurant's seafood specials. Open daily. Reservations advised. Major credit cards accepted. 1188 Rue Sherbrooke O. *Moby Dick's* is closed Sundays. Reservations advised for lunch. Entrance at 1188 Rue Sherbrooke O. or 2121 Rue Drummond (phone: 285-1636 for both).

Vent Vert An award-winning menu boasts such specialties as quail pâté layered in *mille-feuilles,* freshly poached scallops, and watercress mousse in wine sauce. Dine on the glassed-in terrace at the front, in the small, romantic main dining room, or in the back room, designed to accommodate larger groups. Open daily. Reservations advised. Major credit cards accepted. 2105 Rue de la Montagne (phone: 842-2482).

Zen The only North American branch of the London-based restaurant, this is one of the best places in town for haute cuisine, Szechuan-style. Aromatic crispy duck is a favorite, among such specialties as lobster prepared six different ways, sesame shrimp, and whole abalone. Open daily. Reservations advised. Major credit cards accepted. In the *Westin–Mont Royal Hotel,* 1050 Rue Sherbrooke O. (phone: 284-1110).

MODERATE

Le Caveau French food is served in this cozy little house in the heart of midtown. Checkered tablecloths and candlelight add to the intimate atmosphere. The less expensive of the two menus offers good value and has almost the same selection as the other. The tournedos, house wine, and *crème caramel* are all of high quality. Open daily. Reservations advised. Major credit cards accepted. 2063 Rue Victoria (phone: 844-1624).

Les Copines de Chine This Chinese restaurant has an attractive setting in the tropical, plant-filled atrium of *Place Dupuis.* Its appetizing Szechuan dishes are served by an attentive staff. Open daily. Reservations advised. Major credit cards accepted. 870 Blvd. de Maisonneuve E. (phone: 842-8325).

Le Latini A different pasta dish is featured every day, and the veal specialties are tasty and tender. In summer, guests may dine alfresco on the terrace. Closed Sundays. Reservations necessary. Major credit cards accepted. 1130 Rue Jeanne-Mance, near *Complexe Desjardins* (phone: 861-3166).

LUX This futuristic-style bistro serves French-influenced American fare. In a converted textile mill, it has a spacious, circular main room with a steel floor and a glass-enclosed second level, reached by two spiral staircases. Open daily, 24 hours a day. Reservations necessary for parties of six or more. Major credit cards accepted. 5220 Blvd. St-Laurent (phone: 271-9272).

Le Paris Yet another fine French eatery with a truly Parisian atmosphere. Closed Sundays and holidays. Reservations necessary. Major credit cards accepted. 1812 Rue Ste-Catherine O. (phone: 937-4898).

Le Père St-Vincent Nestled in the oldest house in Vieux Montréal (1690), this eatery specializes in French dishes served beside a cozy hearth (there are three working fireplaces). The decor is rough-hewn, early Montreal, but the walls display an impressive collection of contemporary Québécois art. Open daily. Reservations advised. Major credit cards accepted. 429 Rue St-Vincent (phone: 397-9610).

La Tulipe Noire This Parisian-style café and pastry shop in the *Maison Alcan* is one of the few midtown restaurants where you can get a moderately priced bite after the theater. Also a busy spot for breakfast, lunch, and Sunday brunch, it overlooks a garden court and its own summer café terrace. Open daily. No reservations. Major credit cards accepted. 2100 Rue Stanley (phone: 285-1225).

INEXPENSIVE

Chez Vito Near the *Université de Montréal,* this popular place has fine Italian fare and a good disco upstairs. Open daily. No reservations. Major credit cards accepted. 5408-12 Côte-des-Neiges (phone: 735-3623).

Magic Pan For the best crêpes in town, head for this breezy little spot in *Place Montreal Trust.* Dessert crêpes filled with pralines are a house favorite, and chocoholics will not be disappointed with the rich chocolate crêpes. Other fillings include chicken, seafood, and cheese. Salads, sandwiches, and similarly light fare also are served in this simple place with contemporary touches. Open daily. Reservations unnecessary. Major credit cards accepted. 1500 Av. McGill College (phone: 849-4265).

La Maison Grecque A reasonable, no-frills place featuring moussaka and fish en brochette. Diners must bring their own wine. Open daily. Reservations advised. Major credit cards accepted. 450 Rue Duluth E. (phone: 842-0969).

Montreal Hebrew Delicatessen and Steak House Known locally as *Schwartz's,* this deli is famous for its smoked meat, grilled steaks, and the best French fries on this continent. See *Quintessential Montreal and Quebec City* in DIVERSIONS. Closed *Yom Kippur.* No reservations or credit cards accepted. 3895 Blvd. St-Laurent (phone: 842-4813).

Rôtisserie Laurier Chicken here is roasted Quebec-style and served with a side of barbecue sauce. Open daily. No reservations. Major credit cards accepted. 381 Av. Laurier O. (phone: 273-3671).

Stash's Café Bazaar This Vieux Montréal establishment specializes in Polish food. The decor is simple; the atmosphere, friendly. Open daily. No reservations. Major credit cards accepted. 200 Rue St-Paul O. (phone: 845-6611).

Sucrerie de la Montagne Anyone with a sweet tooth should make the trip to this spot 20 miles (32 km) southwest of the city. The maple sugar feast includes *tourtière* (meat pie) and baked beans, finished off with traditional maple syrup pie, more commonly served in Quebec City. Open from 11 AM to 8 PM. Reservations necessary for groups. Major credit cards accepted. 300 Rang St-Georges, Rigaud, off Rte. 40 (phone: 451-5204 or 451-0831).

Swensen's An outlet of the San Francisco–based chain of old-fashioned ice-cream parlors, this place serves some of the richest, creamiest ice cream in North America. Among the 27 flavors are sticky chewy chocolate, black raspberry cheesecake, butterscotch marble, and Swiss orange chocolate chip. Open daily. Reservations unnecessary. Major credit cards accepted. At the corner of Rue Ste-Catherine O. and Av. Mansfield (phone: 874-0695).

Quebec City

The key battle that determined the fate of French Canada lasted only about 20 minutes. It occurred on the morning of September 13, 1759, on the Plaines d'Abraham (Plains of Abraham) in Quebec City, the capital of New France. Under siege by the British General James Wolfe since July, the city had stood firm against the attacks. On the evening of September 12, however, Wolfe led a group of soldiers up the steep hill from Anse au Foulon and assembled the force on the Plaines d'Abraham. That is where the astonished and horrified French found them the following morning when the Marquis de Montcalm, commander of the city's defenses, rushed his troops into battle. In the ensuing struggle, both Wolfe and Montcalm were killed (Wolfe died on the battlefield, Montcalm shortly after in the city), and the French were decisively defeated. But according to legend, as smoke obscured the battlefield and the dream of New France died with its last defenders, a voice was heard across the plains crying, *"Je me souviens"*— "I remember."

Those words have become the motto of the province of Quebec, and nowhere do they resound with more conviction than in Quebec City, itself the most tangible remnant of New France in Canada. Rising on the massive cliff of Cap Diamant (Cape Diamond) some 350 feet above the St. Lawrence River, Quebec City is Canada's foundation of French culture and the rock upon which the nation's federalism often has come close to foundering. Though the English won control of Canada, Quebec City retained its French language, culture, and heritage. And through subsequent invasions by the British and Americans in the course of its history and the contemporary French-English controversy concerning the independence of Quebec, the city survives as a stronghold of French culture on an English-speaking continent.

In no other city in Canada can you see so clearly the places where the two worlds of the French and English collide. The *Monument Wolfe-Montcalm* in Lower Town, for example, commemorates both the victors and the vanquished. At the *Musée du Fort,* the guide explaining the diorama of the fateful battle in 1759 refers to the British as "the enemy." Few places have devoted so much space—250 acres of parkland at the Plaines d'Abraham—to their defeat. Even in the sports world, French and English clashes of Canadian culture reveal themselves: Quebec City nationalists charged that top hockey prospect Eric Lindros was anti-French when he turned down an offer to play for the hometown *Nordiques.*

Quebec City was the first permanent French settlement in North America, and, despite two centuries of English rule, it remains fiercely French. Most everyone here speaks French; newspapers, plays, and conversations generally are in French, though many people can and do speak English, particularly those who work in businesses catering to tourists.

Of the population of 165,000, 95% is of French stock, primarily from Normandy and Brittany on the northwest coast of France. Yet immigration to Quebec of people from French-speaking countries has not kept pace with immigration of English-speaking people to the rest of Canada, so the Québécois tend to have a deeply rooted heritage that in most cases has little to do with France. True Québécois are those who have never left the province—some actually trace their ancestry back to the 17th century. They are a family-oriented, traditional people, an attitude reflected in their city.

Many of the buildings in the city's old section are restored 17th- and 18th-century stone houses, similar to those in the villages of provincial France. The cuisine is French or hearty Québécois—thick pea soups, meat pies, and rich maple syrup pies for dessert. Even the walls surrounding Vieux (Old) Québec (Quebec City is the only walled city on the continent) seem to protect its insular culture, and they demarcate historic Quebec from the newer parts of the city, where modern hotels, shopping malls, and office buildings acknowledge the 20th century.

The history of Quebec City seems to flow from the river, where the natives inhabited the land for thousands of years, using it as their main source of transportation. And although explorer Jacques Cartier, the Breton sailor, gave Cap Diamant its name in 1535, Samuel de Champlain came to stay. Attracted by the strategically located site, Champlain founded the city in 1608 and established his first *habitation* here, a trading post comprising a store, a few houses, and surrounding fortifications. Now known as Place Royale, it became the center of a fur-trading colony—a meeting place for the merchants who governed the community as well as a commercial center and residential area where wealthy merchants built their homes. As more colonists and missionaries arrived, the settlement expanded up the hillside. In 1647, the *Château St-Louis* was built as a governor's residence at the top of the cliff (today the spectacular *Château Frontenac* hotel occupies the site).

The Canadian headquarters of the Roman Catholic church also was established in Upper Town soon after 1659, when Bishop François de Montmorency Laval settled in Quebec City. For more than three centuries, the church—initially conservative, but becoming more liberal in recent years—has acted as a cultural force in the city.

Quarrels between the church and the trading company motivated King Louis XIV to send over a royal *intendant*—an overseer of sorts—to administer the province in 1663. Jean Talon, the first *intendant,* and Comte Louis de Buade de Frontenac, the governor, dealt with this conflict and also settled problems with native tribes that had been attacking the young settlement. Together they fostered an atmosphere of security that enabled the town to develop as the center of New France.

This period was cut short by a much more significant struggle for power—between the two major colonizing forces of France and England. In 1690, Frontenac subdued an attack on the city led by Sir William Phipps, the British Governor of Massachusetts. Three years later, walls were constructed to fortify the city's defenses. In 1759, during the Seven Years' War, Quebec City fell to the British following the Battle of the Plains of Abraham. The settlement, known as the Act of Quebec (1774), guaranteed French Canadians "as much as British laws would allow" in terms of cultural and religious rights. But the battle had a profound effect on the Québécois psyche. Many members of the aristocratic class returned to France, and those who stayed taught their children what had been lost on the Plaines d'Abraham: "*Je me souviens.*"

But the British weren't the only ones with an interest in Quebec. In 1775, the Québécois resisted an invasion by American troops led by Generals Richard Montgomery and Benedict Arnold. This siege lasted a little more than a month, ending with the arrival of the British fleet and the retreat of the exhausted American troops. Concerned over further attacks, the English completed the wall surrounding the city.

Throughout the 19th century, Quebec City remained an important political center, becoming the province's capital in 1867. Peace also brought economic change. Timber and shipbuilding became the two major industries, and the city maintained its position as a significant commercial center until the mid-19th century, when Montreal and Toronto surpassed it.

But Quebec City remains the most important historical center of Canada. The restored city walls, now a historic site, surround the most interesting section of the city, Vieux Québec. More than 90% of the 17th- and 18th-century houses and buildings in the area around Place Royale have been restored and now house museums, cultural centers, and restaurants. Upper Town is a well-preserved area of narrow cobblestone streets lined with historic buildings.

Beyond the city walls, farther up the hill, lies 20th-century Quebec. Here is a concentration of all the amenities found in any other modern provincial capital—a convention center; an underground shopping gallery, *Place Québec,* connected to the *Quebec Hilton International;* several other luxurious high-rise hotels; and the stately buildings of the *Hôtel du Parlement* (National Assembly, as the legislature is called). Beyond spreads the suburb of Ste-Foy, rapidly developed in the past three decades to accommodate a growing population. Many Québécois work in Ste-Foy at the suburb's two major shopping malls or at *Université Laval.* The largest employer of all is the provincial government, with more than 53,000 civil servants.

Around Colline Parlementaire (Parliament Hill) stands further evidence that Quebec City's present is inextricably bound with its past. Sculptures of historically prominent Canadians are carved into niches in the *Hôtel du Parlement.* These figures and the nearby Plaines d'Abraham and *Citadelle*—the star-shaped fortress that won the city the sobriquet "Gibraltar of America"—record Quebec City's struggle to become what it is today.

The French-English controversy in Canada still simmers. It's often said if you scratch the surface, you will find some level of nationalism in every Québécois; that has seldom been as true as it is now. The 1980s saw the emergence of a new era, one that found Quebeckers economically confident and turning to the world at large for fresh opportunities. The province's current generation aspires to economic stability rather than political turmoil. In fact, even the fiercely separatist Parti Québécois wants to continue using the Canadian dollar and Canadian passports and to maintain trade relations with the rest of Canada. Indeed, despite warnings that sovereignty would cripple the province economically, some business leaders believe that the economy of an independent Quebec would actually improve over time. With the onset of a severe nationwide recession and high unemployment, however, the Quebec business community is suffering, and some enthusiasm for independence has cooled.

Quebec's current crisis began with its refusal to sign the Constitution. In 1987 Prime Minister Mulroney proposed the Meech Lake Accord to give all the provinces more power. Under the accord, Quebec would have been recognized as a "distinct society" and, along with the other provinces, would have been given a veto power over future constitutional changes. When Manitoba and Newfoundland refused to ratify the agreement in 1990, the accord, which required unanimous approval, failed—giving rise to a new movement toward Quebec's secession from Canada. The Meech Lake debacle was followed in 1992 by a Canada-wide referendum on a new agreement, the Charlottetown Accord. Quebec and five other provinces turned down the revised constitutional package. Quebeckers insisted the new deal failed to meet their demands, while most Canadians, weary of constitutional wrangling, felt it did not address the concerns of the country as a whole in the interest of accommodating Quebec. With the constitutional issue still in limbo, the question of sovereignty was a key issue in the 1993 federal election. Since the referendum, opinion polls have shown support for independence in Quebec running only about 50%. According to the pundits, however, the people of Quebec City are particularly supportive of independence, due to their primarily French Canadian heritage and to the fact that becoming the new nation's capital would likely mean new jobs and added prosperity for the city.

Whatever the outcome of the independence movement, Quebec City will certainly remain—as it has through almost four centuries and six invasions—authentically French. The strength of its collective memory continues to hold fast.

Quebec City At-a-Glance

SEEING THE CITY

Set on a hill, Quebec City affords a spectacular panoramic view. To the northeast is the Gaspé Peninsula, with its poor but picturesque villages; to the south, Montreal, 153 miles (245 km) away; straight up to the north are the fabulous Laurentian slopes, which the Québécois call the Laurentides. *L'Astral,* the *Loews Le Concorde* hotel's revolving rooftop restaurant-bar (see *Eating Out*), is situated on the highest point of Cap Diamant, and it commands a great panorama of Quebec City and surrounding areas, day or night. On a clear day, you can see as far as Ile d'Orléans, in summer a verdant island of fruit farms and country homes, and, some 25 miles away, a chain of mountains dominated by Mont Ste-Anne, site of the region's best ski resort. Also check out the view from the city's highest observation point, the 31st floor of *Edifice Marie-Guyart* (*Complexe G;* 1037 Rue de la Chevrotière, off the Grande Allée; phone: 643-9841). While enjoying the view, you can tour exhibitions of works by some of Quebec's best artists in the sky-high *Galerie Anima G.* The observation gallery is closed weekend mornings and December 15 to January 15; no admission charge. For more information, see *Walk 4: "New" Quebec* in DIRECTIONS—QUEBEC CITY.

Two of the best views of the river are from the *Terrasse Dufferin,* a terrace flanking the *Château Frontenac* hotel, and the *Terrasse Earl-Grey,* an observatory adjoining the Plaines d'Abraham, between Rues Wolfe and Montcalm, in *Parc des Champs-de-Bataille.*

SPECIAL PLACES

The best way to see the city is by strolling down its streets and alleys. Quebec is a people-size place where the scale of sites is that of an easy day's perambulation—quaint cobbled streets, historic houses, and the sort of secure claustrophobia conferred by a city that you can almost drape around your shoulders. But first, get a good map. The streets are laid out haphazardly, particularly in the older sections. Lower Town revolves around Place Royale at river level. To the north and west, there's a cluster of cafés, pubs, art galleries, boutiques, and antiques stores in what used to be the city's financial district. Just a few blocks north is the spruced-up port area, with old warehouses reincarnated as fashionable boutiques. Place d'Armes, at the top of the funicular next to the *Château Frontenac,* stands at the center of Upper Town. (The funicular, which links Lower and Upper Towns, operates daily from 7:30 AM to 11 PM.) Colline Parlementaire, farther up, is the site of government buildings abutting sleek high-rise hotels. Beyond them all are the suburbs. The Plaines d'Abraham have been made into a lovely park (*Parc des Champs-de-Bataille*), with miles of walking and jogging paths, picnic tables, bird-feeding stations, gardens, and great river views.

PLACE ROYALE This small, cobblestone square—a historic zone—was the site of Champlain's first *habitation* (1608), which included buildings for lodging, a store, a stockade, and gardens. During the French regime, the square was used as a marketplace, and successful merchants built their homes here. In the center of the square is a bronze bust of Louis XIV. Despite the destruction of some of the houses, the *place* and the streets leading off it are lined with the greatest concentration of 17th- and 18th-century buildings in North America. Most of the buildings clustered around the *Eglise Notre-Dame-des-Victoires* are architectural gems that began life as the houses of wealthy merchants. As the centuries slipped by, the area went downhill, and the townsfolk simply forgot its history. Then, in 1960, a fire bared some strange brick walls that eventually were discovered to be genuine historic treasures. The main floors of a number of these homes are open to the public as museums, cultural centers, art galleries, and restaurants, while the upper floors are home to modern-day Quebeckers, many of whom own businesses in the area. Off Notre-Dame at the foot of Cap Diamant near the river.

PLACE DE PARIS In 1984, France paid tribute to this city and province by inaugurating the Place au Québec in Paris. To reciprocate, a monument was erected on the exact spot where the French first set foot on Quebec soil—at the corner of today's Rues de la Place and de l'Union—and dubbed Place de Paris.

MAISONS BRUNEAU, DRAPEAU, AND RAGEOT The multimedia production "Place Royale: Centre of Trade in New France," which describes the business activities of the area during colonial times, is presented here daily from June 7 through September. No admission charge. 3A Pl. Royale (phone: 643-6631).

BATTERIE ROYALE (ROYAL BATTERY) Built in 1691, this artillery emplacement, one of the oldest in Quebec City, has been entirely restored. Corner of Rues Sous-le-Fort and St-Pierre.

MAISON FORNEL With foundations dating back to 1658 and vaulted cellars constructed in 1735, this restored house is now an exhibition center; its reconstruction in 1964 initiated the Place Royale restoration project. The exhibition "Place Royale: 400 Years of History" provides a good perspective on the area's past and ongoing restoration; a brochure (in English) is available. Open daily, June 7 through September; closed the rest of the year. No admission charge. 25 Rue St-Pierre, just south of Ruelle de la Place (phone: 643-6631).

EGLISE NOTRE-DAME-DES-VICTOIRES (OUR LADY OF VICTORIES CHURCH) This church was built in 1688 and renamed to commemorate the triumph of the French over the English during the attacks of 1690 and 1711. Mass is said Saturdays at 7 PM and Sundays (call for hours). Open daily May to October

15; closed Mondays the rest of the year. For more information, see *Historic Churches* in DIVERSIONS. Pl. Royale (phone: 692-1650).

MAISON DES VINS (HOUSE OF WINES) In this restored home is an excellent wine store with an extensive selection of imported bottles. The establishment is worth a visit for a look at its exposed brick walls, vaulted, candlelit cellars, and array of wines, ranging from a Mouton Rothschild 1879 (valued between $13,000 and $21,000) to the local favorite, *caribou,* a potent mixture of wine and alcohol. Closed Sundays and Mondays. Reservations necessary for guided tours. No admission charge. Beside *Maisons Bruneau, Drapeau,* and *Rageot* (see above), at 1 Pl. Royale (phone: 643-1214).

MAISON CHEVALIER Constructed in the 17th and 18th centuries for several merchants, including Jean-Baptiste Chevalier, these three buildings together form an interesting ethnographic museum. The changing exhibits include old toys, costumes, furniture, and folk art. Open daily, mid-May to mid-October; closed the rest of the year. No admission charge. Corner of Cul-de-Sac and Notre-Dame (phone: 643-9689).

MAISON JOLLIET This restored house was the home of explorer Louis Jolliet, who, accompanied by Jacques Marquette, discovered the Mississippi River in 1672. His house now contains the entrance to the funicular, which saves you the trouble of having to climb back to Upper Town. Opposite Sous-le-Fort at the foot of Escalier du Petit-Champlain.

VIEUX PORT (OLD PORT) Quebec's old port area today features a 6,000-seat open-air amphitheater, a tent theater seating a thousand, and a café-theater, all connected by enclosed aerial walkways. At the confluence of the St. Lawrence and St. Charles Rivers lies a lock-controlled marina big enough to accommodate several hundred pleasure craft; oceangoing merchant vessels and cruise ships moor along the wharf. The area also houses restaurants, pubs, and cafés. Easily accessible by strollers and cyclists from the waterfront promenade. 160 Rue Dalhousie.

PORT DE QUÉBEC AU 19E SIÈCLE (PORT OF QUEBEC IN THE 19TH CENTURY) INTERPRETATION CENTER Four exhibition floors in a refurbished cement factory trace the salty history of Vieux Québec when it was the center of Canada's lumber and shipbuilding trade. Run by *Parks Canada,* it displays a ship's prow, rum kegs, and a working capstan set up for visitors to try their hand. The top floor affords views of the city skyline and marina. Open daily in spring and summer; open with reservations only, December through February, except during *Carnaval,* when it is open daily. No admission charge. 100 Rue St-André (phone: 648-3300).

MUSÉE DE LA CIVILISATION All aspects of the human experience as it relates to Quebec society are explored in this stunning complex in the restored Vieux Port near Place Royale. Architect Moshe Safdie brought old and new together in 1988, joining a contemporary core to three historic properties and crowning the whole with a space-age steeple of glass and steel that covers a city block between Rues Dalhousie and St-Pierre. Summer visitors can stroll from one street to the other via a series of connecting stairways and terraces, taking in the port panorama as they go. Students of architecture consider the Safdie innovation the highlight of the museum experience, which begins in an arena-size entrance hall. The centerpiece here is a reflecting pool where Astri Reusch's *La Débacle* sculpture symbolizes the drama of the spring thaw on the ice-choked St. Lawrence. The museum takes a hands-on approach, involving children and adults in many of the exhibits through computers and video screens. Open daily, June 24 to September 7; closed Mondays the rest of the year. No admission charge Tuesdays and for children under 16. 85 Rue Dalhousie (phone: 643-2158).

UPPER TOWN

PLACE D'ARMES A small square, it served as a meeting place and parade ground during the French regime. In its center stands a Gothic fountain surmounted by the granite and bronze *Monument de la Foi* (Monument of Faith), constructed in 1916 in memory of the Récollets (Franciscan) missionaries who arrived in 1615. Today the square is a good orientation point in Upper Town, the section of Vieux Québec built above the cliff, where military, religious, and residential buildings from the 17th, 18th, and 19th centuries have been restored. One of the loveliest, *Maison Vallée* (which dates from 1732), is the home of the Tussaud-like *Musée de Cire* (see *Museums,* below). For traditional French Canadian fare and decor, check out *Aux Anciens Canadiens* (see *Eating Out*), in a house built in 1677 and named after the classic Canadian volume whose author, Philippe Aubert de Gaspé, once lived on the premises.

CHÂTEAU FRONTENAC What the *Eiffel Tower* is to Paris and the *Leaning Tower* is to Pisa, this grand hotel is to Quebec City. Everything about the present structure, built in 1893, is grand, from its broad, slanting copper roof, its turrets and towers, and its imposing red brick walls to its magnificent setting high above the St. Lawrence River. The site on which it is built has undergone numerous transitions. First a fort built by Champlain in 1620, it eventually became known as *Château St-Louis,* a regal residence of the Governors of New France. It was razed by fire in 1834. During World War II, Allied officers accompanying Roosevelt and Churchill stayed here and planned the invasion of France. In the main lobby is an interesting display tracing the château's past. Stroll around the lobby or the inner courtyard, or enjoy the majestic river view from the circular cocktail lounge. The *Terrasse Dufferin,* built in 1834, with its spectacular view of Lower Town and the Ile d'Orléans, is a favorite spot for relaxing on summer nights. At the north end of the terrace stands a statue of Samuel de Champlain, watching over the city he founded in 1608. 1 Av. des Carrières (phone: 692-3861).

JARDIN DES GOUVERNEURS (GARDEN OF THE GOVERNORS) Originally the private garden of the *Château St-Louis*, it was opened to the public in 1838. Here stands the *Monument Wolfe-Montcalm*, erected in 1828. It is one of the few monuments in the world commemorating both the triumphant and the defeated: "Their courage gave them the same lot; history, the same fame; posterity, the same monument." Open daily. No admission charge. Next to the *Château Frontenac* at Av. des Carrières and Rue Mont-Carmel.

CAVALIER DU MOULIN (WINDMILL OUTPOST) This restful little park once was an important link in the Old City's defense works. Named for the windmill that once occupied the site, the military outpost was first activated in 1693; its men had orders to destroy the Cap Diamant redoubt and the *St-Louis* bastion if they were to fall to the enemy. Closed December through April. No admission charge. At the western end of Rue Mont-Carmel.

MUSÉE DU FORT Visitors can get their historical bearings in this museum. A 30-minute sound-and-light show presented on a model of the 18th-century city re-creates the most important battles and sieges of Quebec, including the Battle of the Plains of Abraham and the attack by Arnold and Montgomery during the American Revolution. There's also a wide variety of guides and history books in English. Closed December 1 through *Christmas*. Shows alternate in English and French. Admission charge. 10 Rue Ste-Anne (phone: 692-2175).

BASILIQUE NOTRE-DAME-DE-QUÉBEC First built in 1647, this Roman Catholic church of the Cardinal Archbishop of Quebec once served the diocese of all French North America; it still serves the oldest parish north of Mexico. For more information, see *Historic Churches* in DIVERSIONS. Rue Buade and Côte de la Fabrique (phone: 692-2533).

SÉMINAIRE DE QUÉBEC (QUEBEC SEMINARY) Beyond the iron gates lies a group of 17th-century buildings that were part of a training school for Catholic priests founded in 1663 by Monseigneur François-Xavier de Montmorency-Laval, the first Bishop of Quebec. The main chapel is worth a visit for a look at its marble altars, valuable relics, and sarcophagus of Bishop Laval; the sundial over the door dates to 1773. The *Musée du Séminaire* (Seminary Museum) here has a collection of religious and secular art from both Quebec and Europe as well as some early scientific instruments. The museum (9 Rue de l'Université; phone: 692-2843) is closed Mondays; admission charge. Visits to other parts of the seminary, which must be arranged in advance, are possible June through August (phone: 692-3981).

CATHÉDRALE ANGLICANE (ANGLICAN CATHEDRAL) This stately structure was the first Church of England cathedral ever built outside of the British Isles (1804). For more information, see *Historic Churches* in DIVERSIONS. Open daily, June through August; closed Mondays and mornings the rest of the year. 31 Rue des Jardins (phone: 692-2193).

COUVENT DES URSULINES (URSULINE CONVENT) Founded in 1639, it runs the oldest school for women in North America. The convent itself was twice damaged by fire, but some original walls still stand. A few of the present buildings date from the 17th century. It is not open to the public, but the chapel, which contains a number of relics and valuable paintings, welcomes visitors. Its votive lamp, first lit in 1717, has never been extinguished, and the defeated Montcalm is buried in a tomb in the chapel. His skull is preserved under glass in the *Musée des Ursulines,* adjoining the chapel (see below). The chapel is closed Sundays and Mondays May through October; closed the rest of the year. No admission charge. 12 Rue Donnacona (phone: 694-0694).

Next door, the *Centre Marie-de-l'Incarnation* (10 Rue Donnacona; phone: 692-1569) displays a collection of objects belonging to the order's cofounder, Mother Marie-de-l'Incarnation. It also operates a bookstore and shows films tracing the Ursulines' history under French rule. The center is closed Mondays; admission charge. For more information, see *Walk 1: Vieux Québec/Upper Town* in DIRECTIONS—QUEBEC CITY.

MUSÉE DES URSULINES Fascinating and oddly touching, this repository of early Quebec memorabilia includes trappings of convent life—furniture, kitchenware, and richly embroidered altar clothes—all exhibited on three silent, dimly lighted floors. Some items date from 1639, when three intrepid members of the French teaching order arrived in the port of "Kebec." Replicas of the sisters' enclosed "cabin beds"—for warmth (they didn't install stoves in the convent until 1668)—share exhibition space with the elegant furniture of the order's wealthy cofounder, Madame de la Peltrie, and the skull (under glass) of Marquis Louis-Joseph de Montcalm, defeated commander of the French Army in the Battle of the Plains of Abraham. The general is buried in the convent chapel next door, and many of his personal effects are on display in the museum. One of the more endearing exhibits is the shirt that Murdoch Stewart, a British soldier and paymaster, the first of the "enemy" to marry a Canadian girl after the conquest of 1759, wore to his wedding to Angélique Cartier. Hand-stitched in sheer linen, with a frilled jabot, the Fraser Highlander's dress shirt is as fresh as the day it was made more than two centuries ago. Closed Mondays and December. Admission charge. 12 Rue Donnacona (phone: 694-0694).

PARC MONTMORENCY Named in honor of François de Montmorency-Laval, this park, straddling the hill between Upper and Lower Town, affords good views of Lower Town, the harbor, and the surrounding area. A monument to Sir George-Etienne-Cartier, a French Canadian political leader, and another to Louis Hébert, the first farmer to settle in Quebec City, stand in the center of the park. On the hill, off Côte de la Montagne.

MONUMENT DE LAVAL (LAVAL MONUMENT) This impressive statue honors Laval, Canada's first bishop, who arrived in 1659 and was one of the most prominent citizens of New France. He founded the *Séminaire de Québec,* the predecessor of *Université Laval.* Sculpted by Philippe Hébert, the work was unveiled in 1908. At Côte de la Montagne across from *Parc Montmorency.*

COLLINE PARLEMENTAIRE (PARLIAMENT HILL) AND THE PLAINES D'ABRAHAM (PLAINS OF ABRAHAM)

PROMENADE DES GOUVERNEURS (GOVERNORS' PROMENADE) This 2,200-foot-long walkway leads from the *Terrasse Dufferin* up Cap Diamant, beside the *Citadelle,* all the way to the Plaines d'Abraham. The walk offers excellent views of the river upstream to the Pont de Québec (Quebec Bridge) and downstream to the Ile d'Orléans. Open daily, late May through September; closed the rest of the year. No admission charge.

CITADELLE This massive star-shape fortress commands a strategic position at the highest point on Quebec's promontory, 350 feet above the St. Lawrence. The French built previous fortifications on this site, but the present citadel was constructed between 1820 and 1832 by the British government as a defense against American attack following the War of 1812. The fortress was never subjected to enemy fire. It was first occupied by British troops, then by the Royal Canadian Artillery, and since 1920 by the Royal 22nd Regiment. From mid-June to the first Monday in September, the changing of the guard is performed daily at 10 AM, and a ceremonial retreat is enacted at 7 PM on Tuesdays, Thursdays, and weekends. Closed December through February, except to groups with reservations (write to *Musée de la Citadelle,* CP 6020, Haute-Ville, Quebec City, QUE G1R 4V7); open during *Carnaval.* Admission charge. Reached by Côte de la Citadelle (phone: 648-3563).

REGIMENTAL MUSEUM This 1750 structure displays ancient weapons, uniforms, and rare documents—some dating back to the time of the French regime. Closed January and February, except to groups with reservations; open during *Carnaval.* Admission included in the entrance charge to the *Citadelle.* Côte de la Citadelle off Rue St-Louis (phone: 648-3563).

FORTIFICATIONS DE QUÉBEC The walls encircling the Old City and its four gates, now the domain of *Parks Canada,* offer a 3-mile (5-km) walk along the western section, which overlooks Vieux Québec and the surrounding area. The federal government has been actively restoring the walls since 1971. At *Porte St-Louis,* the *Poudrière de l'Esplanade* (Esplanade Powder House) is an 1810 defense site reincarnated as a reception and interpretation center, as well as the departure point for guided tours of the fortifications. The *Poudrière* is open daily, mid-May through *Labour Day;* by reservation only the rest of the year, except during *Carnaval,* when it is closed mornings. No admission charge (phone: 648-7016).

Parc de l'Artillerie, also part of the fortifications system, preserves defense works raised during the French regime, including the *Redoute Dauphine*

(Dauphine Redoubt, built from 1712 to 1748) and military structures installed by the British in the early 18th century. Visit the reception center (an old iron foundry); the redoubt, which has been converted to an interpretive center for children; and the officers' quarters. The reception and interpretive centers are closed Monday mornings, April through September; closed weekends the rest of the year. No admission charge. 2 Rue d'Auteuil (phone: 648-4205). For more information, see *Walk 1: Vieux Québec/Upper Town* in DIRECTIONS—QUEBEC CITY.

PLAINES D'ABRAHAM (PLAINS OF ABRAHAM) Named for Abraham Martin, the first St. Lawrence River pilot, this is where Canada's French-English struggle was decided in 1759. Now part of the 250-acre *Parc des Champs-de-Bataille,* the Plaines d'Abraham were the site of the battle between the British forces led by General James Wolfe and the French under the Marquis de Montcalm that sealed the fate of New France. The observation post affords excellent river views. On the grounds are various monuments and statues plus the *Musée du Québec* (see below). Open daily, June 15 to September 14; closed Mondays the rest of the year. Beyond the *Citadelle* to the west, off Grande Allée.

MUSÉE DU QUÉBEC Not many fine arts museums boast a "criminal" connection, but Quebec City is proud to claim a city jail as part of its landmark complex on the Plaines d'Abraham. Linked to the *Musée's* original neoclassical gallery in the *Parc des Champs-de-Bataille,* the jail's former cell blocks have been transformed into airy exhibition spaces, with five galleries, a library, a documentation center, and administrative offices. The *Grand Salle* (Grand Hall), the hub of the museum complex, links the old and new pavilions. With its glass walls and lofty cruciform skylight, the main entrance hall is a work of art in itself. It was built partially underground, and its connecting corridors are roofed in landscaped lawn to blend harmoniously with the natural park setting. The dramatic entry houses all the museum's public facilities, including an auditorium, a gift shop, and a restaurant with a terrace overlooking the plains and the St. Lawrence River. A sculpture garden occupies an inner court between the *Grand Salle* and the original *Pavillon Gérard-Morisset,* where six galleries are devoted to a permanent collection that traces Quebec's fine arts history from the late 1700s to the present. More than 18,000 works by artists from Quebec and other parts of the world make up the collection. Closed *New Year's Day, Christmas,* and Mondays from September 7 to May 16; open daily, May 17 to September 6 (to 9:45 PM Wednesdays). No admission charge Wednesdays. 1 Av. Wolfe-Montcalm (phone: 643-2150).

HÔTEL DU PARLEMENT (NATIONAL ASSEMBLY BUILDINGS) These imposing French Renaissance structures were built between 1877 and 1886. The 12 bronze statues in niches on the façade, commemorating people prominent in Quebec's and Canada's history, were executed by the Quebec sculptor

Hébert. Guided tours, in French and English, are available weekdays from *Labour Day* through May; daily, June 24 to *Labour Day;* no tours June 1 through June 23. The Assembly is not in session from June 24 through October or from December 22 to mid-March. No admission charge. Bounded by Rue Dufferin, Blvd. René-Lévesque E., St-Augustin, and Grande Allée (phone: 643-7239).

CHAPELLE HISTORIQUE BON-PASTEUR (HISTORIC CHAPEL OF THE GOOD SHEPHERD)
A designated historic monument, the chapel of the motherhouse of the sisters of Bon-Pasteur de Québec opened in 1868. The high altar of delicately carved wood and gold leaf dates from 1730. Many paintings displayed in the chapel were done by members of the order more than a century ago. Concerts are held here regularly, and a special Sunday mass for artists is celebrated at 11 AM, following a 15-minute musical prelude. Closed mornings and Mondays, July and August; closed mornings, Sundays, and Mondays the rest of the year; open other times by request. 1080 Rue de la Chevrotière (phone: 648-9710). For more information, see *Walk 4: "New" Quebec* in DIRECTIONS—QUEBEC CITY.

GRAND THÉÂTRE DE QUÉBEC This sleek structure built in 1970 comprises a music conservatory and two entertainment halls. 269 Blvd. René-Lévesque, at the corner of Rue Claire-Fontaine (phone: 643-8131).

SUBURBS

STE-FOY This town has grown quickly since the 1960s to become Quebec City's bedroom community of choice, a sprawling, American-style suburb of modern condominiums and apartments. In addition to its Route 175 motel strip, the town supports two large shopping malls, *Place Laurier* and *Place Ste-Foy,* and a growing number of restaurants, bars, and discos. Follow Grande Allée about 2 miles (3 km) west from the *Hôtel du Parlement*, or take bus No. 11 or 25 from downtown.

SILLERY This was estate country in the early 19th century, when wealthy lumbermen and shipping magnates built their mansions here close to the St. Lawrence River and the shipyards at the base of the cliffs. Once inhabited by mostly English speakers, today this charming residential neighborhood is decidedly more French. It's a tranquil retreat of quiet, tree-shaded streets and expensive homes, surrounded by manicured lawns and well-tended gardens. Avenue Magurie is Sillery's chic commercial zone, with several stylish restaurants. An interpretive center devoted to Sillery's past, the *Villa Bagatelle* (1563 Chemin St-Louis; phone: 688-8074), recalls the Belle Epoque of Quebec's English and Scots lumber barons and shipbuilders. In summer, the villa is the departure point for walking tours of what remains of the old baronial domain. Its popular English gardens bloom with more than 350 varieties of plants, and the adjoining studio exhibits works of promising young artists. The villa and its grounds are closed Mondays; admission charge. Nearby *Bois-de-Coulonge* is one of the prettiest parks in the area. Sillery is a 10-minute drive from the city center en route to Ste-Foy, or take bus No. 11 or 25 from downtown.

UNIVERSITÉ LAVAL An outgrowth of the *Séminaire de Québec* founded by Bishop Laval, it is the oldest French-language university on the continent. The construction of a sprawling 465-acre campus was begun in 1948 to accommodate the growing numbers of students. One of the school's 25 modern buildings is the physical education and sports complex. Its excellent facilities, including an *Olympic*-size pool, are open to the public at certain hours, mainly weekends. Off Blvd. Laurier (Rte. 175) and bounded by du Vallon, Myrand, and Chemin Ste-Foy (phone: 656-3333).

ILE D'ORLÉANS This island in the St. Lawrence River below Quebec was relatively isolated until 1935, when a suspension bridge was built to connect it with the mainland. The island retains a great deal of its 18th-century French Canadian influence. Most of the islanders are of Norman or Breton stock; like their ancestors, most are farmers. (Island apples and strawberries are especially good.) The island is only 21 miles long and about 5 miles wide. Visitors can easily make a complete driving tour in a grand circle, stopping in village after village of 17th- and 18th-century houses and churches. (Route 368 forms a 42-mile/67-km ring around the island.) Ste-Famille has the most interesting church on the island—a triple-spired structure built in 1742. On the east side of the island are some summer cottages and Ste-Pétronille, a summer resort village.

If you visit during March or April, keep an eye out for smoke coming from buildings off the main road. These are "sugar shacks," stark, wooden structures where Quebec's famous maple syrup is made. In a scene more reminiscent of a Breton landscape than of a North American village, ruddy-faced men stand around steaming metal bins, watching for just the right moment when the liquid is ready. Follow the mist: The grounds—maple trees bearing metal spigots and buckets—lead to a shack where, more often than not, the proprietor will invite you in and even give you a sample of his oh-so-sweet product. Two of the best on Ile d'Orléans are the *Sucrerie Jean-Pierre Verret* (Chemin Royal, St-Jean; phone: 522-8217 or 829-3189) and the *Cabane l'En-Tailleur* (1447 Chemin Royal, St-Pierre; phone: 828-2344 or 828-1269). Even when the sap is not running, these shacks are open for business, selling maple sugar products; both are closed November through February.

To get to Ile d'Orléans, take Autoroute Dufferin down the hill near the *Hôtel du Parlement*, then follow Route 138. *Beautemps Mauvaistemps* (phone: 828-2275) organizes personalized tours of the island.

EXTRA SPECIAL

Ste-Anne-de-Beaupré is a small village near the ski center of *Mont Ste-Anne* (see *Skiing*, below), dominated by a massive cathedral, which is an internationally renowned Catholic shrine. Millions of people have made pil-

grimages here; the piles of crutches, canes, and folding wheelchairs in the cathedral attest to healings that the faithful believe have taken place. The present building dates from 1923. The fountain of Ste-Anne in front is said to have healing powers. The sanctuary has a marble statue of Ste-Anne as well as other venerable religious items. There's an information bureau, and guides are available to lead tours (phone: 827-3781). To get to Ste-Anne-de-Beaupré, about 25 miles (40 km) northeast of Quebec City, follow Route 138. A more picturesque route leaves 138 at Beaupré and continues along Route 360. (For additional details, see *Historic Churches* in DIVERSIONS.)

Just east of *Mont Ste-Anne* is the *Réserve Nationale de la Faune du Cap Tourmente,* developed by naturalists to protect the greater snow goose, along with 250 other bird species, which stop here during their seasonal migrations. The noisy October gatherings can easily attract 100,000 screeching birds. In May, ducks, herons, swallows, and red-winged blackbirds build their nests in the many pounds of the region. The reserve also has a nature-interpretation center. To visit, head east on Route 138 from Ste-Anne-de-Beaupré and watch for signs for *Cap Tourmente* (phone: 827-4591, April through September; 827-3776, the rest of the year).

En route to Ste-Anne-de-Beaupré or on the return to Quebec City, stop off at the 274-foot-high Chute Montmorency (Montmorency Falls). In 1759, the English General Wolfe established his headquarters near the top. These old buildings have been made into a beautiful hotel, the *Manoir Montmorency* (2490 Av. Royale, Beauport; phone: 663-2877), whose dining room offers a fantastic view over Ile d'Orléans.

Sources and Resources

TOURIST INFORMATION

For maps, brochures, and the like, contact the *Office du Tourisme et des Congrès de la Communauté Urbaine de Québec* (Greater Quebec City Region Tourism and Convention Bureau; 60 Rue d'Auteuil; phone: 692-2471) or the reception office of the *Maison du Tourisme* (12 Rue Ste-Anne; phone: 873-2015; 800-363-7777 in the US, except Alaska), both open daily. The toll-free number serves a central reservation system *(Centre de Réservations Touristiques du Québec,* or *CRTQ)* through which travelers can reserve rooms throughout the province and pay for them by credit card. The Place Royale restoration has its own information center in *Entrepôt Thibodeau* (Thibodeau Warehouse; Pl. Marché-Finlay; phone: 643-6631), which is open daily June 7 through September only. Another government tourist information center is in Ste-Foy, off the Pont Pierre-Laporte (3005 Blvd. Laurier; phone: 651-2882); it's open daily year-round.

LOCAL COVERAGE *Le Soleil* and *Le Journal de Québec* are French morning dailies; *Québec Chronicle-Telegraph* is an English weekly that hits the newsstands on Wednesdays. *Voilà Québec* is a bilingual quarterly entertainment, sightseeing, and dining guide distributed free in hotels and at the various tourist information centers. For English-language television programs, tune to CKMI, Channel 5; the English radio station is CBVE at 104.7 FM.

English-language city guidebooks are hard to find. The *Librairie Garneau* (a bookstore at 47 Buade; phone: 682-3212) and the *Musée du Fort* (10 Rue Ste-Anne; phone: 692-2175) have a fair selection. One useful (and free) publication is the *Quebec City Region* tourist guide, published by the provincial government. For information on its availability, call the *Office du Tourisme et des Congrès de la Communauté Urbaine de Québec* (see above).

TELEPHONE The area code for Quebec City is 418.

SALES TAX Quebec has a provincial sales tax of 8%, depending on what is being purchased. In addition, a 7% federal tax, called the Goods and Services Tax (GST), is levied on most purchases. In many cases, visitors can receive refunds of both the provincial and federal taxes. For details on Quebec tax rebates, call 800-567-4692.

GETTING AROUND

BUS Buses serve the metropolitan area from approximately 5:30 to 1 AM. Exact change, CN$1.80 at press time, is required; tickets also can be purchased at tobacconists and convenience stores for CN$1.45. For route information, call 627-2511. During the winter, the *Skibus* serves several ski areas around Quebec daily from 7 AM to 9:30 PM. Look for the red-and-white snowflake symbol at bus stops throughout the city.

CAR RENTALS For information on renting a car, see GETTING READY TO GO.

CRUISES St. Lawrence cruises are available aboard the M/V *Louis Jolliet* from *Quai Chouinard* (10 Dalhousie; phone: 692-1159), in the Place Royale section of the city, from May to early October; children under five ride for free. Available for sailboat lovers are a variety of trips organized by *Vieux Port Yachting* (*Quai Renaud,* 80 St-André; phone: 692-0017), with cruises of up to 14 days to as far as the Saguenay River, 200 miles north of Quebec City and one of the greatest fjords in the world.

FERRY Year-round service links Quebec and its suburb of Lévis, operating every half hour from 6 AM to midnight, then less frequently. The ride affords panoramic views of both cities (phone: 644-3704).

HORSE-DRAWN CARRIAGES Calèches tour Vieux Québec, the Parliament area, and the Plaines d'Abraham year-round. A tip for the driver is customary. Calèches line up at four locations: near the main information office of the *Office du Tourisme et des Congrès de la Communauté Urbaine de Québec* (see *Tourist Information*); at the *Porte St-Louis;* at *Parc Esplanade* (west side of Rue St-Louis inside the walls); and at Place d'Armes near the *Château Frontenac* (phone: 687-9797 or 683-9222). For horse-drawn trolley tours, call 692-4566.

TAXI Most cabs cannot be hailed in the streets. Some cabbies speak French only, so have your phrasebook ready. There are cabstands at the major hotels and in Vieux Québec at Place d'Armes and at Place d'Youville. The principal cab companies are *Taxi Co-op* (phone: 525-5191; 653-7777 in Ste-Foy) and *Taxi Québec* (phone: 525-8123).

WALKING TOURS Quebec City is best seen on foot. To enrich your stroll, rent a tape-recorded tour tracing the city's history from *Sonore Tours* (open summers only; Pl. d'Armes; phone: 682-8711). Or pick up a free copy of *Quebec City Region*—which includes walking tours—at the tourist office. The *Quebec Ministry of Cultural Affairs* publishes a folder about Place Royale, which can be obtained at the Place Royale information center in *Entrepôt Thibodeau* (Pl. Marché-Finlay). *Baillairgé Cultural Tours* (phone: 658-4799) offers two-and-a-quarter-hour walking tours of the Old Town, with emphasis on history and architecture, departing from the *Musée du Fort,* across the street from the *Château Frontenac,* at 9:30 AM and 2 PM daily. The tour guides are especially interesting and knowledgeable. Tours are available from late June to mid-October. For those interested in the city's impressive religious history, the booklet "Living Stones of Old Quebec" outlines three walking tours. The free publication can be obtained through any tourist office or through the *Religion Tourism Corporation* (16 Rue Buade; phone: 694-0665). Guided tours emphasizing the city's religious background also are available. Two tours with different itineraries depart daily from the entrance of the *Basilique Notre-Dame.* Also see Quebec City walking tours in DIRECTIONS—QUEBEC CITY. For further information on companies offering tours in and around Quebec City, see GETTING READY TO GO.

LOCAL SERVICES

For additional information about local services, call the *Office du Tourisme et des Congrès de la Communauté Urbaine de Québec* (see *Tourist Information,* above).

AUDIOVISUAL EQUIPMENT *Telav Audio Visual Services* (352 St-Sacrement; phone: 687-9055).

BABY-SITTING *Service de Gardiennes d'Enfants et d'Aide Familiale de Québec* (phone: 659-3776).

BUSINESS SERVICES Try *Immeubles Gérard Bouchard* (10-20 Rue St-Jean; phone: 648-8343). *Office Plus* (215 Rue Caron; phone: 648-1431) offers time-share office space and telephone answering services.

COMPUTER RENTAL *Hamilton Computer Sales and Rentals* (3107 Rue Sasseville, Ste-Foy; phone: 651-2328).

DRY CLEANER/TAILOR *Nettoyeurs de la Capitale* (2 Pl. Québec; phone: 525-6303, and other locations).

LIMOUSINE *Les Limousines de la Capitale* (140-1400 Av. St-Jean-Baptiste; phone: 872-2664) offers 24-hour bilingual service.

MECHANIC Call *Garage L. H. Poitras* (1401 Av. 3, corner of Rue Limoilou; phone: 523-5657) for emergency service.

MEDICAL EMERGENCY For information on local medical services and pharmacies, see GETTING READY TO GO.

MESSENGER SERVICE *Loomis Courier* (3200 Rue Watt, Ste-Foy; phone: 659-6644) or *Purolator Courier* (2225 Av. Chauveau; phone: 843-3236).

PHOTOCOPIES *Jet Copie* (905 Blvd. Charest E.; phone 527-2563).

PHOTOGRAPHER *Photographes Kedl Ltée.* (336 Rue du Roi; phone: 529-0621).

POST OFFICES For information on local branch offices, see GETTING READY TO GO.

SECRETARY-STENOGRAPHER *Drake Office Overload* (203-320 Rue St-Joseph E.; phone: 529-9371).

TELECONFERENCE FACILITIES The *Château Bonne Entente* in Ste-Foy; *Le Château Frontenac; Le Germain-des-Prés; Loews Le Concorde; Quebec Hilton International;* and *Radisson Gouverneurs Quebec* (see *Checking In* for all).

TELEX *Unitel Communications* (phone: 694-9211).

TRANSLATOR *Berlitz Translation and Interpretation Services* (5 Pl. Québec; phone 529-6161).

TRAVELER'S CHECKS *Bank of America Canada, Foreign Currency Service* (24 Côte de la Fabrique; phone: 694-1937) or *American Express* (in *La Baie* department store, in *Les Galeries de la Capitale*; phone: 627-2580, and at Pl. Laurier; phone: 658-8820).

SPECIAL EVENTS

After New Orleans's *Mardi Gras,* the *Carnaval de Québec,* a 10-day affair starting on the first Saturday in February every year, is one of the biggest blowouts in North America. Over half a million people from all over Canada and the US flood the city for this winter celebration. Festivities include two parades, snow sculpture contests, fireworks, a queen's coronation and ball, a variety of theme parties, and lots of winter sports and events—hockey, skiing, and a canoe race on the frozen St. Lawrence River.

Hotels are generally booked solid during *Carnaval,* so make arrangements several months in advance. The best bet for last-minute reservations is through the *Carnaval*'s lodging committee, which can sometimes book rooms in motels or guesthouses, from December 15 to *Carnaval* time. (Note: The phone number changes every year.) For general information, contact the *Carnaval de Québec* (290 Joly, Quebec City, QUE

G1L 1N8; phone: 626-3716). Also see *Quintessential Montreal and Quebec City* in DIVERSIONS.

The critically acclaimed *Quinzaine Internationale du Théâtre de Québec* (Quebec International Fortnight of Theater) features plays performed in their original languages in theaters around the city. It's held in even-numbered years during the first two weeks in June.

For two weeks in July, between 600 and 800 artists from all parts of the world and all musical backgrounds gather in the city for the *Festival d'Eté International de Québec* (International Quebec Summer Festival; PO Box 24, Station B, Quebec City, QUE G1K 7A1; phone: 692-4540; 800-361-5405 in Canada), one of the largest cultural events in the French-speaking world. Rock, classical repertory, and jazz all can be heard in public squares and on stages around the city. Most presentations are free of charge.

MUSEUMS

In addition to those mentioned in *Special Places,* other noteworthy museums include the following:

CENTRE D'INTERPRÉTATION DE LA VIE URBAINE (URBAN LIFE INTERPRETATION CENTER) This small museum in the basement of the *Hôtel de Ville* (City Hall) concentrates on contemporary life in the provincial capital. Closed Mondays and from *Labour Day* to June 23. No admission charge. 43 Côte de la Fabrique (phone: 691-4606).

MUSÉE DES AUGUSTINES DE L'HÔTEL-DIEU DE QUÉBEC (MUSEUM OF THE AUGUSTINES OF THE HÔTEL-DIEU OF QUEBEC) Dedicated to the founders of Canada's first hospital, the small museum displays antique surgical instruments, furniture, and 17th-century memorabilia related to the order of nursing sisters. Guided tours of cellar vaults are available. Closed Mondays; call for hours. No admission charge. 32 Rue Charlevoix (phone: 692-2492).

MUSÉE DE CIRE A wax museum. Open daily. Admission charge. 22 Rue Ste-Anne (phone: 692-2289).

PARC CARTIER-BRÉBEUF A replica of Jacques Cartier's ship is moored on the St. Charles River. Open daily. No admission charge. 175 Rue de l'Espinay (phone: 648-4038).

PARKS CANADA EXHIBITION ROOM Housed on the ground floor of the *Edifice Louis-St-Laurent,* with a post office that dates from 1871, the *Parks Canada* salon presents changing exhibitions relating to Canada's national heritage. Open daily; call for hours. No admission charge. 3 Rue Buade (phone: 648-4177).

SHOPPING

Venues in Quebec City and its immediate surrounding area include 63 shopping centers, elegant boutiques, and flea markets, but the best buys are in the city's many galleries and crafts studios, where the works of local and national artists are featured. The main concentration of shopping malls is in Ste-Foy, about 2 miles (3 km) west of the *Château Frontenac.* Travelers with children should make a beeline to *Les Galeries de la Capitale,* a vast shopping center and amusement park with rides, a giant carousel, a year-round indoor skating rink, and a mini-golf course, located northwest of the city. Near the *Hôtel du Parlement, Place Québec* is a multilevel shopping promenade connected to the lobby of the *Quebec Hilton International.* For shopping in town, the best streets are Rue St-Jean, Côte de la Fabrique, Rue Ste-Anne, and Rue Buade within the walls of the Upper Town, and the Avenue Cartier neighborhood between Grande Allée Ouest (West) and Boulevard René-Lévesque Ouest.

For information on standard shopping hours, see GETTING READY TO GO.

ANTIQUES

Antique Chez Ti-Père Good reproductions of country pine as well as traditional pieces. Follow Route 20 from the Pont Pierre-Laporte (Pierre Laporte Bridge) toward Montreal and Exit 278 (about 33 miles/53 km). 128 Rue Olivier, Laurier Station (phone: 728-4031).

Antiquité Brocante A treasure trove for collectors of old silver and china, heirloom lace, antique furniture, clocks, and estate jewelry. 65 Rue St-Jean (phone: 522-2500).

Antiquités Zaor A serious collectors' rendezvous for over 30 years, it specializes in objets d'art, fine porcelain pieces, silver, and bronze. 112 Rue St-Paul (phone: 692-0581).

La Galerie 141 An eclectic gathering of furniture, ornaments, and *objets.* 97 Rue St-Paul (phone: 694-0896).

Gérard Bourguet Antiquaire Specialists in 18th-century Quebec furniture and vintage ceramics. 97 Rue St-Paul (phone: 694-0896).

Heritage Antiquité A favorite of clock collectors, it also carries a selection of furniture, oil lamps, ceramics, and pottery. 109 Rue St-Paul (phone: 692-1681).

Rendez-Vous du Collectionneur Check out a uniquely Canadian obsession: hockey-card collecting. Antique dolls and old games share the premises. 143 Rue St-Paul (phone: 692-3099).

ART

Brousseau & Brousseau An exclusive showcase of Inuit artists. Signed prints and carvings are shipped to most destinations around the world. 1 Rue des Carrières (phone: 694-1828).

Galerie Le Chien d'Or "The Golden Dog Gallery" is devoted exclusively to the works of Quebec artists. François Faucher has regular exhibitions here. 8 Rue du Fort (phone: 694-9949).

Galerie Christian Bergeron This small gallery in the *quartier* features works by artists from Quebec and other parts of Canada. 83 Rue du Petit-Champlain (phone: 694-0413).

Galerie Christin One of a dozen or more galleries along Rue St-Paul, it features works by such well-known national artists as Lemieux, Suzor-Côté, Riopelle, Cosgrove, Roberts, and Picher. 113 Rue St-Paul (phone: 692-4471).

Galerie Eliette Dufour This salon specializes in the works of such Canadian sculptors as Jordi Bonet, Donald Liardi, and Claude Dufour. 169 Rue St-Paul (phone: 692-2041).

Galerie Estampe Plus Monthly exhibitions are mounted here. Contemporary artists include Danielle April, Guy Langevin, and Paul Béliveau. 49 Rue St-Paul (phone: 694-1303).

Galerie Georgette Pihay An award-winning Belgian sculptor, Pihay exhibits works in aluminum and bronze in her studio-salesroom in the *quartier*. 53 Rue du Petit-Champlain (phone: 692-0297).

Galerie Linda Verge Avant-garde painters Michel Rivest, Guy Labbé, and Joseph Veilleux are featured here. 190 Grande Allée O. (phone: 525-8393).

Aux Multiples Collections The Brousseau family stocks the city's best collection of Inuit carvings, drawings, and prints; each piece is signed by the artist. 69 Rue Ste-Anne (phone: 692-1230) and 43 Rue Buade (phone: 692-4298).

Tirage Limité Works by Calder, Miró, and Riopelle, as well as tapestry art and original prints. 334 Blvd. René-Lévesque E. (phone: 522-1234).

Verrerie d'Art Réjean Burns This innovative Quebec artist exhibits unusual works in stained glass in his studio-salesroom. 88 Rue du Petit-Champlain (phone: 694-0013).

CRAFTS

Boutique La Corriveau Two Upper Town outlets specialize in Québécois arts and crafts—from homemade jams to hand-carved waterfowl decoys to sheepskin slippers—all from the looms, studios, and kitchens of local artists. 49 Rue St-Louis (phone: 692-3781) and 42 Rue Garneau (phone: 692-3781).

Créaly Decorative leather masks, costume jewelry in leather, and works in semiprecious stones by local artists. 16 Rue du Petit-Champlain (phone: 692-4753).

Galerie Le Fil du Temps Handmade dolls are the stock in trade at this Vieux Québec boutique. Strictly collectibles, these one-of-a-kind creations aren't for kids. 88 Rue du Petit-Champlain (phone: 692-5867).

L'Iroquois An Amerindian souvenir outlet whose best buys are moccasins, toys, baskets, jewelry, and woodcarvings. 39 Rue Sous-le-Fort (phone: 692-3366).

Le Jardin de l'Argile Canada's exclusive outlet for the popular "Lorteau" figurines, the sleepy-faced little people hand-casted in clay by the Quebec ceramist of the same name and glazed in pastel shades of pink and turquoise. Exclusive woodcarvings and ornamental duck decoys range from $300 to $6,000. Also hand-crafted toys, games, and marionettes. 51 Rue du Petit-Champlain (phone: 692-4870).

O Kwa Ri "The Sign of the Bear" sells elegant and authentic native Canadian regalia—fringed deerskin dresses and tunics, ceremonial headdresses, and jewelry. 59 Rue du Petit-Champlain (phone: 692-0009).

Petit Galerie de Pauline Pelletier Exotica from India, China, Thailand, and Bali complement works of this Quebec ceramist and other Quebec craftspeople. Look for the samurai warrior ceramics in paper robes with mini-swords. 30 Rue du Petit-Champlain (phone: 692-4871).

Pot-en-Ceil The work of more than a dozen top potters, ceramists, and wood sculptors from all over Quebec. 27 Rue du Petit-Champlain (phone: 692-1743).

Les Trois Colombes Crafts from Quebec, Atlantic Canada, Ontario, and the Canadian north in a three-story building. Fashion items include designer sweaters in handwoven mohair, decorated with leather, silk, and lace, and custom-designed coats, each an original by Quebec designer Lise Dupuis. 46 Rue St-Louis (phone: 694-1114).

NATIVE ARTISTRY

For those looking for the best in Native American crafts, there are outlets in Wendake, the Huron Village near suburban Loretteville, about 20 minutes west of the walled city on Route 358. These include *A & Artisanat OKI* (152 Blvd. Bastien; phone: 847-0574), which specializes in snowshoes, moccasins, baskets, dolls, jewelry, fringed jackets, and other hand-crafted items; *Artisanat Gros-Louis* (125 Blvd. Bastien; phone: 843-2503); *Le Huron* (25 Huron Village; phone: 842-4308); and *Artisanats Indiens du Québec* (540 Rue Max Gros-Louis; phone: 845-2150).

FASHION

Atelier Ibiza This small Lower Town salon specializes in high-fashion leatherwear, handbags, and other accessories. 47 Rue du Petit-Champlain (phone: 692-2103).

Atelier La Pomme House designers work with the finest Argentine leather, suede, and pigskin to produce a prêt-à-porter collection of clothing and accessories for men and women. 47 Rue Sous-le-Fort (phone: 692-2875).

Le Capitain d'à Bord Everything for the well-dressed sailor. 63 Rue du Petit-Champlain (phone: 694-0624).

derik et Cie. This well-established boutique in the heart of Upper Town's old business core features imported woolens from Britain. 49 Rue Buade (phone: 692-5244).

La Maison Darlington A senior member of Rue Buade's little fashion enclave, it is known for its British tweeds, Scottish cashmeres, and fine mohair shawls. There's also a good selection of Austrian sportswear and a beguiling collection of hand-smocked dresses for infants and little girls, including small sizes in Liberty-print fabrics with matching panties. 7 Rue Buade (phone: 692-2268).

La Maison Simons Established in 1840, the doyenne of Vieux Québec department stores stocks its fashion floor with designs by Anne Klein, Ralph Lauren, and Marithé and François Girbaud, plus an affordable private-label collection. 20 Côte de la Fabrique (phone: 692-3630).

Peau sur Peau This high-fashion house of leather features clothing, shoes, and accessories for men and women. Fine luggage is a specialty. Two locations: 85 Rue du Petit-Champlain (phone: 694-1921) and 70 Blvd. Champlain (phone: 692-5132).

Promenade du Vieux Québec The latest arrival on Upper Town's fashion scene has converted *Holt Renfrew*'s stately old store into a stylish complex of boutiques for young fashionables of both sexes. 43 Rue Buade (phone: 647-5964).

Les Vêteries Distinctive made-in-Quebec fashions in silk, wool, and cotton. Best buys are from an exclusive collection of high-fashion and après-ski sweaters. 31½ Rue du Petit-Champlain (phone: 694-1215).

FURS

J. B. Laliberté A leading retailer in high-fashion furs. 595 Rue St-Joseph E. (phone: 525-4841).

Joseph Lachance A long-established furrier in a city famous for top-quality pelts; a large selection of ready-to-wear, too. 634 Rue St-Jean (phone: 523-0530).

Joseph Robitaille For a hundred years this place has been the acknowledged leader of the city's huge fur-trade community. Top-quality skins at realistic prices. 700 Rue Richelieu (phone: 522-3288).

LACE

La Dentellière Lace curtains to fit all shapes and sizes of windows are a specialty. It also carries the best in handmade tablecloths and lace accessories for boudoir and bathroom, clothing, and lace trimmings. 56 Blvd. Champlain (phone: 692-2807).

MARKETS

Marché de la Place Fruit and vegetable farmers and flower sellers converge here daily from May through November. One of the best flea markets in the area, *Marché aux Puces de Ste-Foy,* is nearby. From downtown, take bus No. 14 or 15. 930 Pl. de Ville, Ste-Foy (phone: 654-4394 or 654-4070).

Marché du Vieux Port This farmers' market in the restored Vieux Port area is renowned for its flowers. Closed November through February. From downtown, take bus No. 1. 160 Rue St-André (phone: 692-2517).

SWEETS

Chocolaterie Erico Hand-dipped confections in an Upper Town candy boutique. 583 Rue St-Jean (phone: 524-2122).

Confiserie d'Epoque Madame Gigi Offering homemade chocolate of every conceivable variety, it's a crowd-stopper. In Lower Town, at 84 Rue du Petit-Champlain (phone: 692-5325).

Delicatesse Nourcy Creamy chocolate creations are featured at its two chic outlets. 1576 Chemin St-Louis, Sillery (phone: 527-2739), and 1035 Av. Cartier (phone: 523-4772).

Au Palet d'Or Hand-dipped chocolates and other custom-made bonbons share the celebrated pastry salon of Roger Geslin in the restaurant complex of chef Serge Bruyère. 60 Rue Garneau (phone: 692-2488).

TOYS

L'Echelle Hand-crafted playthings and other diversions. 1041 Rue St-Jean (phone: 694-9133).

Le Fou du Roi Wee royals will test their minds (and bodies) in this boutique of educational toys, both domestic and imported. 57 Rue du Petit-Champlain (phone: 692-4439).

SPORTS

BICYCLING Quebec City's wide green expanses of parkland, with ribbons of bike paths snaking through them, stand out as some of the most picturesque and best planned in the world. In fact, some of the most rewarding bike paths in eastern Canada can be found outside the historic quartier. For rentals, try Location Petit-Champlain (94 Rue du Petit-Champlain; phone: 692-2817). Here are our favorite two-wheel treks.

BEST BIKING

Montmorency Bikeway A challenging path of just over 6 miles (10 km) leads all the way out to Chute Montmorency (Montmorency Falls), one and a half times higher than mighty Niagara. The falls are surrounded by a park, with picnic sites, nature trails, and lookout points, all welcome rest stops before the return trip to town. The bike path starts just north of the city, off Boulevard Montmorency at *Domain Maizeret,* a small park west of Autoroute 440. Unfortunately, the busy highway is always between the cyclist and the river, but there are some fine views of the St. Lawrence and Ile d'Orléans en route. If the thought of pumping out to the falls fazes leisurely bikers, a branch trail to *Parc des Cascades* meets the Montmorency bikeway at Baie de Beauport near Avenue de la Station. It follows and crosses the Beauport River from its estuary up to a riverbank park, a distance of about a mile.

Parc des Champs-de-Bataille The most convenient trail for Sunday cyclists interested in some mild exercise in pleasant surroundings is the scenic route along Avenue George-VI in the capital's best-known park. Less than 1 mile (1.6 km) long, it stretches along the western reaches of the 18th-century battleground, from the corner of Avenue George-VI and Grande Allée, just beyond *Porte St-Louis,* to the intersection with Avenue Wolfe-Montcalm. Bikers are welcome to wheel all over historic park territory, and the return jaunt along the avenue adds up to nearly 2 miles (3 km) of peaceful parkland touring, with plenty of shady rest stops along the way. For information, contact *Parks Canada* (3 Rue Buade; phone: 648-4177).

Parc du Mont Ste-Anne Mountain biking is a favorite summer pastime at *Parc du Mont Ste-Anne,* Quebec City's all-seasons playground. The big ski domain maintains 157 trails for cyclists and mountain bikers. Explorers can rent wheels in the park at *Bicycles Marius* (phone: 827-2420 or 827-4561).

St. Charles River Bikeway Snaking along the south bank of the St. Charles River, this trail leads from Pont Samson (Samson Bridge), just northwest of the restored Vieux Port area, nearly 3 miles (5 km) to the foot of Rue Marie-de-l'Incarnation. History buffs can cycle across the bridge that spans the river at the halfway mark to visit Parc Cartier-Brébeuf, a national historic site on the north shore, where Jacques Cartier and his party spent a cruel wilderness winter in 1535–36. The park is also the site of a 17th-century mission that Jesuit Jean de Brébeuf founded in 1626; a replica of Cartier's flagship, La Grande Hermine; and a reproduction of an Iroquoian longhouse. An on-site reception and interpretive center features exhibits related to the park's history.

GOLF Though no courses exist within the city limits, there are about a dozen 18-hole and nine nine-hole courses within a 20-mile (32-km) radius. For more information, see *Good Golf Nearby* in DIVERSIONS.

HARNESS RACING They're off and running at the *Hippodrome de Québec* in the *Parc de l'Exposition* (Exhibition Grounds; phone: 524-5283). To get there, follow Boulevard Dorchester until you see the signs. Call ahead for the schedule.

HOCKEY The *National Hockey League*'s *Nordiques* face challengers at the *Colisée* in the *Parc de l'Exposition* (phone: 523-3333; 800-463-3333 in Canada; 529-8441, schedule information). Quebec winters and ice go together. From December until May, ponds, lakes, rivers, and streams turn into natural rinks that are ideal for playing hockey (see *Skating,* below).

SKATING Join the locals in *Parc d'Esplanade,* off Rue d'Auteuil (no admission charge). Other popular spots are the 2-mile (3-km) circuit on the St. Charles River (between the Ponts, or Bridges, Samson and Marie-de-l'Incarnation; phone: 691-7188) and Place d'Youville (just outside the *Porte St-Jean* in Vieux Québec; phone: 691-4685); no admission charge to either. *Village des Sports* in Valcartier (take Autoroute de la Capitale, then Rte. 371; phone: 844-3725) offers skating paths through the woods, and *l'Anneau de Glace Gaétan Boucher* (930 Rue Place-de-Ville, Ste-Foy; phone: 654-4462) is an outdoor Olympic-size skating track; there's an admission charge to both. Skating begins in mid-October and usually lasts through March.

SKIING Downhill skiing is best at *Mont Ste-Anne* (phone: 827-4561), the area's most popular winter sports center, with downhill runs, night skiing, cross-country tracks, and lift facilities. The most direct route to *Mont Ste-Anne*—located 25 miles (40 km) northeast of Quebec City—follows Route 138, but for a more scenic tour leave 138 at Beaupré and continue along Route 360. Route 440 is another alternative. *Le Relais* (phone: 849-1851) and *Mont St-Castin* (phone: 849-1893) in Lac Beauport and the *Stoneham* ski area (phone: 484-2411) also have good slopes only a short drive from the city. All of them offer good night skiing. (See *Downhill Skiing* in DIVERSIONS. For information on buses to the ski areas, see *Getting Around,* above.) For cross-country skiing and snowshoeing, try the Plaines d'Abraham or the nearby provincial parks with marked trails, or *Réserve Faunique des Laurentides,* 36 miles (58 km) northwest via Route 175. *Mont Ste-Anne,* Lac Delage, and Duchesnay also have miles of groomed cross-country trails. (See *Cross-Country Skiing* in DIVERSIONS.)

SWIMMING Some hotels have pools (see *Checking In*). The *Physical Education and Sports Pavilion* at *Université Laval* in Ste-Foy (off Rte. 175; phone: 656-2807) has an Olympic-size pool that is open to the public for a fee; the *YMCA* (835 Blvd. René-Lévesque O.; phone: 527-2518) and the *YWCA* (855 Rue Holland; phone: 683-2155) also have pools the public can use for a fee at certain hours; call ahead.

TENNIS Indoor and outdoor tennis courts (as well as squash courts) are available at the *Club de Tennis Montcalm* (901 Blvd. Champlain; phone: 687-1250). Courts are also available for rent at the *Club de Tennis Avantage* (1080

Bouvier, Charlesbourg O.; phone: 627-3343) and at *Nautilus Plus* (4230 Blvd. Hamel; phone: 872-0111).

TOBOGGANING There are toboggan runs at the *Village des Sports* (phone: 844-3725), a vast outdoor amusement park near Valcartier, 25 miles (40 km) north of the city.

THEATER

A variety of plays is offered in French, rarely in English. Major theaters include the *Grand Théâtre de Québec* (269 Blvd. René-Lévesque E.; phone: 643-8131; see also *The Performing Arts* in DIVERSIONS); *Palais Montcalm* (995 Pl. d'Youville; phone: 670-9011); *Bibliothèque Gabrielle-Roy* (350 Rue St-Joseph E.; phone: 529-0924); and *Salle Albert-Rousseau* (Cégep Ste-Foy, 2410 Chemin Ste-Foy; phone: 659-6628). The *Théâtre du Trident* (phone: 643-5873) performs French-language works at the *Grand Théâtre*. Student productions are presented at the *Conservatoire d'Art Dramatique* (13 St-Stanislas; phone: 643-9833) and at the *Théâtre de la Cité Universitaire* (on the *Laval* campus in Ste-Foy; phone: 656-2765). Summer theaters are the *Théâtre de l'Ile* (Ile d'Orléans; phone: 828-9530); *Théâtre Beaumont–St-Michel* (Rte. 2 between Beaumont and St-Michel; phone: 884-3344); and *Théâtre du Bois de Coulonge* (Blvd. Laurier; phone: 681-0088). Among the small theaters are the *Théâtre Petit-Champlain* (68 Petit-Champlain; phone: 692-2631), which often hosts folksingers; *Théâtre Périscope* (2 Rue Crémazie E.; phone: 529-2183); *Théâtre de la Fenière* (1500 de la Fenière, Ancienne Lorette; phone: 872-1424); and *Théâtre Paul-Hébert* (1451 Av. Royale, St-Jean, Ile d'Orléans; phone: 829-2202).

CINEMA

With two exceptions, Quebec City theaters screen all films in French. English-language versions of current movies are shown at the *Cinéma Place Québec* (5 Pl. Québec; phone: 656-0592) and *Cinéma Ste-Foy* (Pl. Ste-Foy, 2450 Blvd. Laurier, Ste-Foy; phone: 656-0592).

MUSIC

The *Orchestre Symphonique de Québec* performs at the *Salle Louis-Fréchette* in the *Grand Théâtre de Québec* (see above; phone: 643-6976). Touring musical groups usually play at the *Palais Montcalm* or at the *Salle Albert-Rousseau* (see above for both). The small pubs along Rue St-Jean between Rue d'Auteuil and Côte de la Fabrique, on Grande Allée, and in the Vieux Port area (see *Nightclubs and Nightlife,* below) have live music, ranging from Québécois folk to rock and blues.

NIGHTCLUBS AND NIGHTLIFE

The city's brightest lights shine along the Grande Allée, on the other side of the walls. In summer, locals and visitors alike gather here from about 5 PM to plan their evening strategy over a pre-dinner aperitif or two. The liveliest corner on this sophisticated strip is at the intersection of Rue d'Artigny and Grande

Allée. Here the entertainment complex *Vogue* (1170 Rue d'Artigny; phone: 647-2100) is hopping until 3 AM, the hour most boîtes in town call it a night. *Vogue*'s café-bar is on the main floor, its disco upstairs. *Sherlock Holmes* (phone: 529-9973), a decidedly British pub, shares the premises. Around the corner, *Brandy* (690 Grande Allée E.; phone: 648-8739), a singles' haunt and terrace café, is a popular summer rendezvous. *Chez Dagobert* (600 Grande Allée E.; phone: 522-0393) is where the capital's young congregate. There's live music for dancing downstairs and a disco for the under-30 crowd upstairs.

Disco fans—especially the younger set—favor *l'Express Minuit* (680 Grande Allée E.; phone: 529-7713). *Le Dancing* at *Loews Le Concorde* (see *Checking In*) attracts customers with its upmarket glitter. Often referred to as the "executive's disco," it's closed Mondays and Tuesdays. Confirmed discomaniacs looking for action on a grand scale converge on *Le Palladium Bar* (2327 Blvd. Versant N., Ste-Foy; phone: 682-8783), near the *Université Laval* campus. *Raspoutine* (2960 Blvd. Laurier, Ste-Foy; phone: 659-4318) attracts a more mature crowd, as does *Beaugarte* (2590 Blvd. Laurier, Ste-Foy; phone: 659-2442), an expense-account singles bar and disco for those 35 or so.

There's plenty of action in the heart of the old *Université Laval* quarter, which still attracts students. However, caution is advised when casing some of the raunchier places in the walled city's busiest entertainment zone. On the whole it's safe and laid-back, but not as geared to the tourist trade as Grande Allée. Try *Bistro Plus* (1063 Rue St-Jean; phone: 694-9252), a singles bar, or *Danse-Bar l'Arlequin* (1070 Rue St-Jean; phone: 694-1422), for hard rock. The *Bar Chez Son Père* (24 Rue St-Stanislas; phone: 692-5308) is another boîte where a house minstrel serenades night owls with sweet Québécois ballads. Another Latin Quarter boîte, *Le Petit Paris* (48 Côte de la Fabrique; phone: 694-0383), features *chansonnier* entertainment. *Le Central*, the urbane little piano bar in *A la Table de Serge Bruyère*'s restaurant complex (see *Eating Out*), attracts a more sophisticated clientele. *Zanzibar* (215 Rue St-Jean; phone: 524-3321) is a nostalgic jazz bar. Quebec City's only source of authentic contemporary jazz is *l'Emprise*, the Art Nouveau café-bar in the *Clarendon* hotel (see *Checking In*). Four-hour sessions start at 11 PM nightly.

The *Bar du Grand Hall*, the piano bar in the lobby of the *Château Frontenac* (see *Checking In*), always attracts an interesting mix of hotel guests and after-dark explorers. Many revelers choose to top off the evening romantically under the stars at the *l'Astral* bar in *Loews Le Concorde*'s revolving tower restaurant (see *Checking In*).

Best in Town

CHECKING IN

Quebec City has a wide range of hostelries, from the magnificent *Château Frontenac* and modern high-rise hotels to small, family-run guesthouses. The best bet for motoring visitors is to check into a motel in Ste-

Foy. Those planning to visit Quebec City during *Carnaval* in early February or during the summer should make reservations as far in advance as possible. During the winter, rooms generally are available, and most places even offer discount rates. Expect to pay more than $200 per night for a double room in hotels listed as very expensive; from $100 to $200 in an expensive hotel; and from $70 to $100 at those designated moderate. All telephone numbers are in the 418 area code unless otherwise indicated. All hotels feature such amenities as air conditioning, private baths, TV sets, and telephones unless otherwise noted.

For an unforgettable experience in Quebec City, we begin with our favorites—all very expensive—followed by our recommendations of cost and quality choices of hotels, listed by price category.

GRAND HOTELS

Château Bonne Entente When retired army colonel Charles Hugh Le Pailleur Jones invested his savings in a spacious frame manor house set on 120 acres around Ste-Foy more than 70 years ago, the last thing on his mind was a resort hotel. But 30 years later, the colonel's son, Mowbray, launched the *Bonne Entente*. At first a small, eight-bedroom inn, before long it was sprouting additional wings and services. Today a 170-room mini-resort, this château retains the *bonne entente* (good vibes) of the colonel's original country retreat. Its many features make it ideal for family vacationers; in fact, kids are VIP guests at *Le Village de Nathalie*, a complimentary child-care center with an outdoor playground. Guests have the run of what remains of the original estate—11 landscaped acres with tennis courts, a jogging trail, a pool, and a trout pond. The in-house business center provides secretarial and multilingual translation services, as well as audiovisual, photocopy, fax, and telex facilities. Enjoy some excellent wild game at *Le R. V.*, the *Château*'s gastronomic restaurant, or at any one of the three other less formal settings. Complimentary afternoon tea is a daily ritual at *Le Salon de Thé*. Fifteen minutes by car or No. 11 bus from the walls of Vieux Québec, at 3400 Chemin Ste-Foy (phone: 653-5221; 800-463-4390 in the US and Canada; fax: 653-3098).

Château Frontenac Atop the walled city, this railroad-built hotel is Quebec City's most recognizable landmark (see also *Special Places*). Constantly renovated, the grande dame still reigns supreme. With its imposing brick walls, turrets, towers, and copper roof, green with age, visible for miles, it was designed to resemble a 16th-century French château. Within, modern comforts have been added without compromising the hotel's Old World appeal. Many of the 620 rooms have river views. In the central tower attic are split-level "spa" units where turn-of-the-century travelers put up their maids and valets. Today the former servants' quarters are mini-suites with individual hot tubs. The fare at *Le Champlain*, where waiters wear 16th-century costume, is superb (see *Eating Out*). There's also an attractive circular cocktail lounge overlooking the St. Lawrence, an inviting inner courtyard, a café-style restaurant (see *Café de la Terrasse* in *Eating Out*), and a small gallery of shops. The *Terrasse Dufferin,* built in 1834, has a spectacular view of the historic Lower Town and the Ile d'Orléans, and is a lovely place to relax on a summer night. 1 Rue des Carrières (phone: 692-3861; 800-268-9411 in Canada; 800-282-7447 in the US; fax: 692-1751).

Loews Le Concorde The preferred choice of the city's business traveler has a stunning lobby, a golden-beige blend of marble, brass, and glass, with a hint of the exotic Orient in its delicate cherry-wood paneling and tropical greenery. Set on the edge of the Grande Allée's after-dark playground and just a 10-minute walk from *Porte St-Louis* and Vieux Québec, the geometric pyramid on the Plaines d'Abraham has a backyard as big as all outdoors in *Parc des Champs-de-Bataille*. Not surprisingly, the views are the best in town: Each of the 422 rooms looks out on the St. Lawrence River and the Plaines d'Abraham. *Club 1225* on the private-access 12th floor has its own exclusive lounge, and a full American breakfast is included. The two top-floor presidential suites feature wood-burning fireplaces in their duplex apartments, as well as saunas and whirlpool baths. Non-presidential guests will more than make do with the hotel's health club, saunas, and whirlpool bath, located next to the heated outdoor pool. Executive amenities include a business center with secretarial, photocopy, fax, and telex services. The hotel's crowning glory, *l'Astral*, a revolving rooftop restaurant-bar, offers a 360-degree view of Old Town, picturesque Ile d'Orléans, and a chain of mountains dominated by Mont Ste-Anne (see *Eating Out*). 1225 Pl. Montcalm (phone: 647-2222; 800-463-5256 in Canada; 800-223-LOEWS in the US; fax: 647-4710).

Quebec Hilton International A five-minute walk from the walled city, the 563-room terraced tower near Colline Parlementaire is conveniently close to the capital's legislative and corporate office blocks and all the shopping temptations of Grande Allée. And no other spot is as close to the chic boutiques and fine restaurants of *Place Québec*, the only underground shopping mall of its type in the downtown area—a warm, dry haven when the city's volatile weather turns mean. Business travelers like its underground link to the *Centre Municipal des Congrès* (Convention Center) and its two floors of executive-class accommodations, expansive meeting rooms, and conference halls. In addition to an outdoor pool (closed in winter), there's a health club equipped with a sauna, a whirlpool bath, massage facilities, and a big Jacuzzi. (Health-conscious guests will appreciate that seven floors are reserved for nonsmokers.) *Le Croquembroche* (see *Eating Out*) features a warm setting conducive to long, relaxed indulgences in nouvelle cuisine. 3 Pl. Québec (phone: 647-2411; 800-268-9275 in Canada; 800-HILTONS in the US; fax: 647-6488).

EXPENSIVE

Clarendon Within the Old City walls, just opposite the *Hôtel de Ville*—very convenient for sightseeing—this hotel, built in 1870, is constantly undergoing renovations. There are 89 rooms, none with air conditioning. The *Charles Baillargé* restaurant serves dinner accompanied by performances of classical music; *l'Emprise* bar, also on the premises, has the best jazz in town. 57 Rue Ste-Anne, near Rue des Jardins (phone: 692-2480; 800-361-6162 in Canada; fax: 692-4652).

Holiday Inn Ste-Foy This property has 235 spacious rooms, including VIP suites with Jacuzzis. There also is an indoor pool, a sauna, a health club, an elaborate dining room, and a cocktail lounge. Free limousine service to and from the airport is available. 3125 Blvd. Hochelaga, Ste-Foy (phone: 653-4901; 800-463-5241 in Canada; 800-HOLIDAY in the US; fax: 653-1836).

Hôtel des Gouverneurs Ste-Foy A suburban hostelry, it has 318 attractive rooms, a sophisticated restaurant, a piano bar, and a heated outdoor pool that's open only in summer. 3030 Blvd. Laurier (phone: 651-6797; 800-463-2820 in the eastern US; fax: 651-6797).

Hôtel du Théâtre The nearly-century-old former *Théâtre Capitole* has been restored to its 1920s splendor, only this incarnation of the theatrical landmark is an intimate, Parisian-style hotel. The complex also is home to a bistro, a dinner-theater, a TV studio, and boutiques. Accommodations include eight double rooms, 23 suites, and nine split-level suites. 972 Rue St-Jean (phone: 694-4040; fax: 694-9924).

Manoir Victoria The most striking aspect of this establishment in a lovely historical setting is its vast and richly decorated entry hall. It has 150 rooms, boutiques, an indoor pool, a fitness center, and valet parking. Its two restaurants serve continental and French fare. Ski packages are offered. 44 Côte-du-Palais (phone: 692-1030; 800-463-6283 in Canada and the US; fax: 692-3822).

Plaza Universel The straightforward, massive exterior of this building contrasts with the refinement of its interior, which is all marble, dark paneling, and cozy, stylish furniture. The large indoor pool and the dining room are both glass-enclosed. There are 220 rooms and 11 suites. 3031 Blvd. Laurier, Ste-Foy (phone: 657-2727; 800-463-4495 in Canada; fax: 657-2772).

Radisson Gouverneurs Quebec Adjacent to the *Quebec Hilton International,* this modern high-rise has 377 nicely appointed rooms, an elaborate dining room, a health club, and a heated outdoor pool that is open year-round. 690 Blvd. René-Lévesque E. (phone: 647-1717; 800-463-2820 in Canada; 800-333-3333 in the US; fax: 647-2146).

MODERATE

Auberge du Trésor Formerly the *Hôtel Le Homestead,* this 300-year-old building has 21 rooms, many overlooking Place d'Armes. Conveniently situated for those whose main objective is sightseeing, the hotel also has a cocktail lounge, a fine dining room with a multiethnic menu, and a café in summer. 20 Rue Ste-Anne at Rue du Trésor (phone: 694-1876).

Le Germain-des-Prés Decorated in European Art Deco, this 127-room hostelry offers personalized service. Rooms include such amenities as bathrobes and fresh fruit. The hotel has a continental breakfast room. Transportation to and from the airport is complimentary. Near shopping centers, at 1200 Germain-des-Prés, Ste-Foy (phone: 658-1224; 800-463-5253 in Canada; fax: 658-8846).

Manoir Ste-Geneviève One of the best things about this guesthouse is Marguerite Corriveau, the friendly proprietress. Built in the early 1800s, the house was one of the first in the *Jardin des Gouverneurs.* All nine rooms are individually decorated with old family pieces; three have kitchenettes (none have telephones). There's no restaurant. 13 Av. Ste-Geneviève at Rue Laporte (phone/fax: 694-1666).

EATING OUT

Even visitors who don't know the difference between flambé and soufflé will become well acquainted with Gallic fare, thanks to the myriad French restaurants in Vieux Québec. Although French nouvelle cuisine is on most menus, a few restaurants still serve typical Québécois meals of *soupe aux pois* (pea soup), *tourtière* (meat pie), and maple sugar–based desserts. The best Québécois chefs combine the wild game and succulent lamb of the countryside and farm with the sauces of their French ancestry to create an exciting cuisine. And the city's gastronomic landscape includes a variety of ethnic establishments, including Chinese and Indian. The city also boasts *salons de thé* (tearooms) where one can enjoy the traditional ritual of tea or wonderful chocolate desserts. Expect to pay $85 or more for a very expensive dinner for two; between $70 and $85 in the expensive range; $40 to $60 in the moderate range; and $40 or less in the inexpensive range. Prices do not include drinks, wine, or tip. All telephone numbers are in the 418 area code unless otherwise indicated. All restaurants are open for lunch and dinner unless otherwise noted.

For an unforgettable dining experience, we begin with our culinary favorites—all expensive—followed by our cost and quality choices, listed by price category.

INCREDIBLE EDIBLES

Aux Anciens Canadiens For travelers looking for a complete French Canadian experience, this dining spot has no equal. Even if the bill of fare were less than fine, tables here would be filled for the simple reason that the charming, white-walled *Maison Jacquet*, built about 1675, is the only example of original 17th-century architecture in Vieux Québec. Its four-foot-thick white plaster walls are crowded with corner cupboards and bolstered with hand-hewn joists. Furnished in the style of a colonial kitchen, with rustic tables covered with blue checkered cloths, it serves customers in four rooms, each decorated differently in a Vieux Québec style with antique plates, kitchen utensils, firearms, and other necessities of colonial life. Today's *table d'hôte* selections go beyond the salt pork and *soupe aux pois* that nourished generations of Québécois families to include braised goose leg with sour cream and herbs, duckling with maple syrup, and breast of pheasant in puff pastry. Traditional dishes—*fèves au lard* (pork and beans), *cretons maison* (pork pâté), *tourtière*, and *ragoût de pattes de cochon et de boulettes* (pigs' knuckles and meatball stew)—are always available. Open daily. Reservations advised. Major credit cards accepted. 34 Rue St-Louis (phone: 692-1627).

Café de la Paix This landmark started life quietly back in the 1960s, when lawyers from the old courthouse across the street discovered a new lunchtime spot that offered fine food at fair prices. Good news traveled fast: Before long, food critics from New York to Los Angeles were singing the praises of chef Jean-Marc Bass. Although genial host Benito Terzini's convivial establishment is now a Vieux Québec tourist tradition, old patrons still turn up regularly. From the outside, the café is a photographer's dream. The French *auberge* of white-plastered stone sits flush with the hillside street; an old-fashioned lantern lights a narrow doorway; and window boxes brim with flowers. Inside, it's pure back-street Paris, with lamp-lit tables, sideboards, hutches, wine racks and bar, and Desrosiers landscapes on the paneled walls—the kind of *mère-et-père* operation where locals come for lunch and linger through a lazy afternoon. Reliable and reasonably priced classics include *boeuf bourguignon*, Dover sole, frogs' legs, rack of lamb, beef Wellington, and, in season, pheasant, partridge, venison, wild boar, and moose. The dessert trolley is loaded with sherry-laced trifle, chocolate cake, custard-filled pastry, and bowls of whipped cream. Open daily. Reservations advised. Major credit cards accepted. 44 Rue des Jardins (phone: 692-1430).

Le Champlain Crossing the threshold here is like entering a time warp. Attentive waiters in formal colonial dress glide around the richly paneled room; majestic oak pillars and exposed beams support the lofty, stenciled ceiling; high-backed tapestry chairs surround damask-covered tables; a massive, hooded fireplace burns; and a harpist plucks out delicate airs. Chef Jean-François Mots oversees the preparation of such Old World favorites as rack of lamb with fresh herbs, quail in port wine and grape sauce, and beef tenderloin with a truffle and madeira sauce. But Mots pays homage to nouvelle cuisine as well. Try fresh scallops coddled in sea urchin butter, or an outstanding crayfish soufflé *à l'américaine*. The *carte des vins* is long, lavish, and priced accordingly, but wine may be ordered by the glass. This restaurant, the best (and most expensive) in the *Château Frontenac*, is closed for lunch Mondays through Saturdays. Reservations advised. Major credit cards accepted. 1 Av. des Carrières (phone: 692-3861).

Gambrinus *Quel outré*! Imagine a modern-looking restaurant in Upper Town—under the *Musée du Fort*, no less—serving nouvelle cuisine in a nouvelle setting. No exposed stone walls or colonial fireplaces here. Despite its ancient surroundings, this place has the contemporary atmosphere of a classy private club, with ceiling beams and wall panels aglow with a satiny mahogany finish; polished brass fixtures; and sheer café curtains. The chefs here are best described as food designers, innovators who combine Italian and French classics with Québécois flair. Try the seafood and veal dishes, usually coupled with pasta, or rack of lamb, duckling in madeira sauce, and several variations of beef filet. The chocolate mousse *gâteau* is one of Vieux Québec's best. The menu changes daily for lunch and weekly for dinner. Open daily. Reservations advised. Major credit cards accepted. 15 Rue du Fort (phone: 692-5144).

Le Melrose At first glance it looks like grandmother's cottage, a prim Victorian villa of rose-trimmed gray brick, rose-colored awnings, and roses growing in rose-colored window boxes, set in the charming residential enclave of nearby Sillery. It's as cozy inside as out: The small rooms are curtained in old-fashioned lace, with the original dark wood trim framing plain, pastel-painted walls. No more than 60 guests can be seated at the intimate, candlelit tables, arranged around the fireplace in the front parlor, in the dining room, and on the second floor, in what once were the bedrooms. Despite the cozy, grandmotherly feel, no gingerbread cookies bake in chef Mario Martel's ovens. Behind the country-cottage ambience, he's busy inventing house specialties: filet of caribou in a sauce of gingery peaches; pink, juicy tenderloin of lamb, seasoned with mustard and green peppercorns; and a mousse of duckling foie gras in chestnut cream. Closed Mondays. Reservations necessary. Major credit cards accepted. A ten-minute cab ride from the walled city, at 1649 Chemin St-Louis, Sillery (phone: 681-7752).

Le St-Amour Young gourmands-about-town swear by this romantic hideaway in a refurbished Victorian house within the walls of Vieux Québec. Normandy-born chef Jean-Luc Boulay and his partner Jacques Fortier have ensured that the main dining room lives up to its romantic name: It's a roseate blush of candlelight, pink table linen, and reproductions of Renoir's rose-lipped maidens. From May to November, ask for a table in the glass-enclosed terrace of greenery with a retractable roof. Specialties include tiny quail stuffed with roasted scampi, sliced into succulent rounds and served with fresh asparagus; *cornets* of escargots in a creamy herb sauce; and sautéed scallops with snow peas in lobster sauce. Calorie counters can take comfort in the chef's light sauces, which he concocts without butter or flour—but the desserts are bound to undo you. Open daily. Reservations advised. Major credit cards accepted. 48 Rue Ste-Ursule (phone: 694-0667).

A la Table de Serge Bruyère Dinner here is an essential part of the Vieux Québec experience. There's only one sitting per evening in the two small rooms of this very pricey second-floor dining room, located in a historic building. Happily, things haven't changed much since Bruyère, a Lyons-born disciple of Paul Bocuse, opened his establishment back in the 1980s. The ambience is pure Old World, with exposed walls of brick and stone, log fires crackling on the hearths, burnished antique copper reflecting the candlelight, and tables set with pastel linen, fresh flowers, and fine china. "Just a perfume" is Bruyère's definitive word on the subject of garlic and other seasonings that enhance the flavor of tender young Quebec lamb, or the way his blueberry sauce complements thin slices of rare pheasant, or the raspberry vinegar that brings out the best in roast duckling. Diners who can't choose between fresh scallops from the Iles de la Madeleine and filet of pork spiced with green peppercorns can solve their dilemma with the nightly eight-course *table d'hôte menu découverte* (tasting menu). Bruyère also boasts the best-stocked wine cellar in town, with some selections in the heady price range of $1,200. Closed Sundays and Mondays. Reservations necessary. In the same mid-19th-century house, Serge Bruyère Entreprises operates a small tearoom (inexpensive), *La Petite Table de Serge Bruyère* for light lunches (inexpensive), and the more relaxed but excellent *Le Central* (moderate). All three are closed Sundays and Mondays, and reservations are advised. Major credit cards accepted. In the heart of the old walled city, at 1200 Rue St-Jean (phone: 694-0618).

VERY EXPENSIVE

L'Atre This 1680 farmhouse-turned-fashionable-restaurant is the pride of Ile d'Orléans. The menu is Québécois. Closed early September to mid-June. Reservations necessary. Major credit cards accepted. 4403 Rue Royal (Rte. 368) near Ste-Famille, east of the island bridge (phone: 829-2474).

La Closerie One of several restaurants in the region that offer refined French fare. The menu changes every season. Chef-owner Jacques Le Pluart has been known to go so far as to import expensive ($400 per pound!) black truffles from the Périgord region of France for a special dish on the *menu dégustation*. A moderately priced menu is available at lunchtime. Closed Sundays and Mondays. Reservations advised. Major credit cards accepted. 966 Blvd. René-Lévesque O. (phone: 687-9975).

Le Croquembroche An elegant, provincial-style place, it features beautifully prepared French nouvelle cuisine and Quebec City specialties. For starters, try the snails baked in grape leaves and puff pastry or the creamed Arctic char soup with orange zest. Grilled meat and fish, roasted on a spit in the dining area and served with suave sauces, are commendable entrées. This is *the* place for the best *soupe aux pois* and *tourtière* in town. Closed weekends for lunch. Reservations advised. Major credit cards accepted. Lobby level of the *Quebec Hilton International,* 3 Pl. Quebec (phone: 674-2411).

L'Elysée Mandarin The best place in town for authentic Szechuan and other regional Chinese food. The dining room is spacious in a minimalist style; the service, courteous and discreet. Open daily. Reservations advised. Major credit cards accepted. 65 Rue d'Auteuil (phone: 692-0909).

Le Marie Clarisse A very good seafood spot near the bottom of the *funiculaire.* Closed Sundays and Mondays. Reservations necessary on weekends. Most major credit cards accepted. 12 Petit Champlain (phone: 692-0857).

Er Michelangelo For over 20 years patrons have enjoyed this restaurant's homemade pasta and seafood, as well as its other Italian specialties. It's a favorite of the area's businesspeople. Closed Sundays. Reservations advised. Major credit cards accepted. 3121 Blvd. Laurier, Ste-Foy (phone: 651-6262).

Le Paris-Brest Art Deco decor combined with stained glass windows and brass fittings creates an engaging environment in which to dine on French food, the specialty here. Open daily. Reservations necessary on weekends. Major credit cards accepted. 590 Grande Allée E. (phone: 529-2243).

EXPENSIVE

Apsara A good place for adventurous dining, it serves Thai, Cambodian, and Vietnamese fare. The plate of assorted appetizers is a wise selection for the uninitiated. Open daily. Reservations advised. Major credit cards accepted. 71 Rue d'Auteuil (phone: 694-0232).

L'Astral The only revolving rooftop restaurant in Quebec City, it's popular with buffet enthusiasts. The eatery also offers an à la carte menu at lunch and dinner. You're sure to meet plenty of capital dwellers at Sunday brunch. Open daily. Reservations advised. Major credit cards accepted. Penthouse of *Loews Le Concorde,* at 1225 Pl. Montcalm (phone: 647-2222).

Auberge Louis Hébert This restaurant offers friendly service and an attractive setting, with calico lampshades dangling above the tables. Specialties include fresh Quebec lamb and *confit d'oie,* a goose pâté. The outdoor terrace is open for summer dining. Open daily. Reservations advised. Major credit cards accepted. 668 Grande Allée E. (phone: 525-7812).

Café de Paris Robust French cuisine complements this place's romantic atmosphere. Entrées include chateaubriand, leg of lamb, and seafood dishes. A *chansonnier* serenades diners six nights a week. Open daily. Reservations advised. Major credit cards accepted. 66 Rue St-Louis (phone: 694-9626).

Café de la Terrasse Window-table diners at the *Château Frontenac*'s bistro restaurant linger here over breakfast, lunch, and dinner watching the nonstop promenade on the *Terrasse Dufferin.* The informal *Terrasse* features a bountiful prix fixe buffet and à la carte specials from the grill. Open daily. Reservations advised. Major credit cards accepted. 1 Av. des Carrières (phone: 629-3861).

La Caravelle Traditional French and Spanish dishes—including a first-rate paella—are featured in this well-respected dining establishment. A *chansonnier* enhances the 18th-century atmosphere in two rustic rooms with wood-burning fireplaces. Open daily. Reservations advised. Major credit cards accepted. 68½ Rue St-Louis (phone: 694-9022).

Le Continental The cuisine could hardly be a surprise—an extensive menu of European specialties ranging from sweetbreads *madère* to steaks *flambés au poivre.* The oak-paneled dining room is attractive and spacious and the service usually very good. For starters, try the *gaspé en crêpe* (seafood crêpe). Open daily. Reservations advised. Major credit cards accepted. 26 Rue St-Louis (phone: 694-9995).

L'Echaudé In Lower Town, this spot's Art Deco interior is cool and relaxing, its nouvelle cuisine menu intriguing, and its desserts sumptuous. Try the *bavaroise aux framboises,* a raspberry custard with a tangy sauce. Open daily. Reservations advised. Major credit cards accepted. 73 Rue Sault-au-Matelot (phone: 692-1299).

Le Graffiti Connoisseurs relish the creative *cuisine légère* menu here that feat
such artistically presented dishes as a *mille-feuilles* of three fish with fi
cucumbers and tomatoes, salmon tartare, and rabbit in a light mustard sauce.
A reasonably priced business menu is served at lunch. Open daily. Reservations
advised. Major credit cards accepted. 1191 Av. Cartier (phone: 529-4949).

Kyoto The place to go if you've got a yen for Japanese food, it's decorated in bam-
boo, with Japanese prints on the wall, and has long tables that seat eight. On
a gas burner right on your table, the chef—who loves to show off and make
people laugh—prepares chicken, steaks, shrimp, or lobster dishes, with all
the traditional accompaniments. Closed weekends for lunch. Reservations
advised. Major credit cards accepted. 560 Grande Allée E. (phone: 529-6141).

Au Parmesan For those with a taste for Italy, this is the place. Irrepressible host
Luigi Leoni presides over traditional Italian meals in a room decorated
with his collection of wine bottles. There's live Italian accordion music, too.
Open daily. Reservations advised. Major credit cards accepted. 38 Rue St-
Louis (phone: 692-0341).

MODERATE

Balico Off the usual tourist trail, this intimate little place specializes in the food
of the Provence region of France. The fish soups are delicious, the aiole
(garlic mayonnaise) unforgettable. Closed Mondays. Reservations advised.
Major credit cards accepted. 935 Rue Bourlamaque (phone: 648-1880).

Le Biarritz It's an intimate spot that can accommodate groups or twosomes for cozy
dining. The escargots are a good choice for starters, and any of the many veal
dishes will make a satisfying entrée. Open daily. Reservations advised. Major
credit cards accepted. 136 Rue Ste-Anne (phone: 692-2433).

Café du Monde Across from the *Musée de la Civilisation* (Museum of Civilization),
this funky diner-style eatery offers everything from an emperor-size Caesar
salad to a five-course dinner. The whimsical setting—featuring crystal chandeliers and hot-pink neon—is a perfect venue in which to enjoy some first-
rate fare. Open daily. Reservations advised for groups of eight or more.
Major credit cards accepted. 57 Rue Dalhousie (phone: 692-4455).

Le Chalet Suisse For a change of pace, try the fondues at this festive, multi-sto-
ried place. Some suggestions: the Chinese fondue, thinly sliced beef served
in a heated beef bouillon; raclette, a grilled cheese dish; or a traditional
Swiss cheese fondue. Since it's one of the few restaurants in town open past
11 PM, its regulars include provincial politicians when the *National Assembly*
is in session. Open daily. Reservations advised. Major credit cards accepted.
32 Rue Ste-Anne (phone: 694-1320).

Fleur de Lotus Near the *Hôtel de Ville,* this Cambodian restaurant also serves
Vietnamese and Thai food. Bring your own wine. Open daily. Reservations

advised. MasterCard and Visa accepted. 50 Rue de la Fabrique (phone: 692-4286).

Mykonos The total Greek population of Quebec City numbers about 150, so it's surprising that there's a Greek restaurant here at all, let alone such a fine one. The menu features a wide variety of Greek dishes, but lamb is the specialty. Accompanying the lamb is *briam*—fresh string beans, onions, potatoes, zucchini, and eggplant baked in layers. *Galactobouriko,* custard served in phyllo crust, tops off the meal. Open daily. Reservations advised. Major credit cards accepted. 1066 Rue St-Jean (phone: 692-2048).

Nupur This Indian spot is well worth the 15-minute drive from town. Although the decor is modest, the atmosphere is warm and the service exceptional. Try any of the tandoori or curried dishes. Open daily. Reservations advised. Major credit cards accepted. 850 Rue Myrand, Ste-Foy (phone: 683-4770).

Optimum A luxurious, two-story Victorian house with a Mediterranean deli on the first floor and a café on the second, where nouvelle cuisine is served and the desserts are sinful. Open daily. Reservations advised. Major credit cards accepted. 64 Blvd. René-Lévesque O. (phone: 648-0768).

Le d'Orsay This restaurant-pub boasts a good location and an excellent selection of European beers. Open daily. Reservations advised. Major credit cards accepted. 65 Rue Buade, across from the *Hôtel de Ville* (phone: 694-1582).

INEXPENSIVE

Café Latin A lovely place to dawdle over an espresso, sandwich, quiche, or salad to the accompaniment of taped classical music. It also has the best maple sugar pie in town. Dine outdoors on the terrace in summer. Open daily. Reservations unnecessary. No credit cards accepted. 8 1/2 Rue Ste-Ursule (phone: 692-2022).

Les Délices du Maghreb Good and inexpensive Mediterranean and Provençal food in unpretentious surroundings is the draw here. It's in a less than fashionable, but still interesting, part of downtown, surrounded by shops and cafés that seem left over from the 1960s. Bring your own wine. Open daily. Reservations unnecessary. Major credit cards accepted. 798 Rue St-Jean (phone: 529-9578).

La Garonelle A tearoom and confectionery where only a strong will can keep you away from the chocolate desserts. Pâtés, salads, and fine cheeses also are offered. Closed Mondays. Reservations advised. Major credit cards accepted. 207 Rue St-Jean (phone: 524-8154).

Le Mille-Feuilles This was the first establishment in the region to specialize in vegetarian fare. No clichés about health food hold here, however—the menu features such innovative dishes as fresh pasta with artichoke sauce, and tofu Stroganoff. Open daily. Reservations advised for lunch and weekend brunch. MasterCard and Visa accepted. Two locations: 32 Rue Ste-Angèle, inside the walls (phone: 692-2147), and 1405 Chemin Ste-Foy (phone: 681-4520).

Au Petit Coin Breton The Grande Allée branch of this small *crêperie* chain is best in summer, when the terrace café looks out on the passing parade. Crêpes, salads, onion soup, and other light fare are reasonably priced à la carte specials. Open daily. Reservations unnecessary. Major credit cards accepted. 665 Grande Allée E. (phone: 525-6904).

QUEBEC QUAFFS

Pubs, particularly those inspired by the traditional London variety, are increasingly popular in Quebec City. But unlike their British counterparts, most keep late-night hours to compete with the bar trade. *Le d'Orsay* (65 Rue Buade; phone: 694-1582), opposite the *Hôtel de Ville,* is a soigné version of the real thing, with rich cashew-wood paneling and all the requisite polished brass appointments (there's a good restaurant upstairs for those tired of pub grub). Across from the *Gare du Palais* railway station, *Thomas Dunn* (1988 Rue St-Paul; phone: 692-4693) serves imported beer to match its imported atmosphere. *L'Inox* (in the restored Vieux Port district; 37 Rue St-André; phone: 692-2877) cold-shoulders the trendy import image in favor of the home-brewed product. It's the only independent brewery in Quebec City, and pub customers can watch three exclusive brands of suds in the making before deciding on their preference. It's as notable for its king-size hot dogs as for its house potables.

Diversions

Exceptional Pleasures and Treasures

Quintessential Montreal and Quebec City

Whether it's the roaring St. Lawrence River or the craggy peak of Cap Diamant (Cape Diamond) or Mont-Royal—named by a French explorer more than 450 years ago—the past plays a major part in the life of both Montreal and Quebec City. Yet these vibrant cities are filled with new ideas, too. Once the place where the Quiet Revolution began, where the Québécois learned to stand on their feet in politics and business, French Canada is anything but quiet today. Much is shared in spirit, but visitors will delight in the differences between the two cities.

VIEUX MONTRÉAL/VIEUX QUÉBEC In few places in North America does the past live so much in the present as in Montreal and Quebec City, and nowhere do you get a better sense of the part played by the French. In Montreal it's a little harder to find those precious pockets of history, while in Quebec City a landscape brimming with the old forms a compact living museum. Although Montreal demolished its city walls, many of its most important early institutions still stand. Surrounding the memorial statue of the founder, Paul Chomedey, in the Place d'Armes are some of the oldest buildings on the continent, including the *Vieux Séminaire St-Sulpice* (Old Sulpician Seminary; 1685), which still clings to its original site next door to the Gothic Revival towers of the *Basilique Notre-Dame* (1829). Take yourself back to the days when Place Jacques-Cartier was one of the busiest farmers' markets in the New World. Lined on both sides with sidewalk cafés, bright with flower beds and poster-plastered pillars, with its old-fashioned lamp standards and rough brick paving, the rectangle of history between Rues Notre-Dame and St-Paul Est could pass for the public square of a small harbor town somewhere in France, with the river at its foot and the fussy, Second Empire *Hôtel de Ville* (City Hall) at its head.

In many ways the past is what Quebec City is all about. Entering the brick-paved market square in Lower Town, you'll suddenly feel at home in the 17th century, surrounded by a gray-stone townscape built in the late 1600s. Although it seems to have aged naturally over more than 300 centuries of careful maintenance, Place Royale, with its small parish church of *Notre-Dame-des-Victoires* (1688) and the bust of King Louis XIV at its center, has cost the provincial government millions of dollars and more than 25 years of painstaking restoration. Paving stones are replaced if they no longer look the part, and huge sums are spent on each building, ensuring the preservation of the halcyon days of French Canada. Like no other place in North America, the story of Vieux Québec unfolds in chronological sequence from its precarious 17th-century beginnings on the waterfront to its full 19th-century flowering in the walled capital on the heights.

QUEBEC À LA CARTE With so many restaurants in Montreal and Quebec City devoted to French cuisine, you would think that there would be little culinary difference between the French and Canadian cultures. But *vive la différence!* Like their forebears from France, Quebeckers in the sister cities regard their chefs with a reverence usually reserved for poets and philosophers. The best of food here—wild berries, maple syrup, fresh pork, and game birds—has been combined with nouvelle cuisine on menus throughout Montreal and Quebec City. Yet these Canadian comestibles should be enjoyed in their most traditional way, too. For almost four centuries, French Canada's menu has developed on the edge of a vast hinterland, but some establishments cling to the delicious days of yore. The *Auberge le Vieux St-Gabriel* in Vieux Montréal and *Aux Anciens Canadiens* in Quebec City have remained true to the old ways. For starters, try a little pot of *ragoût de pattes* (pigs' feet simmered with garlic, cinnamon, cloves, nutmeg, and onions), then a serving of *soupe aux pois* (pea soup) in readiness for a slice or two of *tourtière* (a spicy meat pie—Mom's apple pie to Quebeckers). For the main course, order *ragoût de boulettes* (a stew of pork meatballs). Save room for dessert: *tarte au sucre* (maple sugar pie) with a dollop of rich cream. Or order *tarte au suif* (suet pie)—a pastry collection of beef suet, maple sugar, and chopped, tart apples—and start your diet when you get home: This is no place for calorie counters.

A ONE-HORSE OPEN CALÈCHE New York has its hansom cab, Charleston its surrey with the fringe on top. And French Canada has its calèche and, at times, its one-horse open sleigh. Not that long ago, in both Montreal and Quebec City, calèche drivers exchanged the wheels of their buggies for gleaming runners when the snow flew. Sadly, that time has almost passed, as modern snow-moving equipment has conspired to keep roads clear and keep wheels on calèches throughout the year. But it's still possible to catch the feeling of a jingle-bell sleigh: On special occasions, the old-time sleighs pull passengers through *Parc du Mont-Royal* in Montreal or *Parc des Champs-de-Bataille* (Battlefields Park) in Quebec City.

To appreciate the difference between the two cities, take a calèche ride in both. In downtown Montreal, you'll select your driver from among frail-looking girls with Rapunzel-length hair and wrists of steel, portly old-timers in *Expos* baseball caps and lumberjack checks, and reedy young gallants in tank tops and tattoos. Like the best of Manhattan's old cabbies, they have a philosopher's view of big-city life, but they take off from a downtown launching pad, where Montreal motorists give no quarter. Once into the narrow streets of Vieux Montréal, where the horse has the advantage, or up on Mont-Royal's peaceful calèche road, they relax, listen, and generally are on their best behavior. By comparison, a calèche ride in Quebec City is Old World and genteel. Summer drivers for *Danny Doyle, Ltd.* (phone: 418-683-9222) favor jaunty straw boaters with green hatbands to match their green vests and green-and-white vehicles. Coachmen for *La Belle Epoque* (phone: 418-687-9797) stand out in red-and-white ensembles, harmonizing with their red-trimmed calèches. Less fashion-conscious in winter, drivers still look perky in parkas, while their steeds sport equally chic horse blankets. The horse is king of the road in Vieux Québec, setting its own speed limits on streets that become precipitous downhill turns at unexpected corners. Beyond the gates "the old reliables" let themselves go, jogging briskly along the Grande Allée to the carriageways of *Parc des Champs-de-Bataille.* In either city, it's like journeying back in time.

ICI ON PARLE FRANÇAIS Listen closely to the voices of Quebec and you're well on your way to learning something even some Canadians don't realize: Bilingual people in the province of Quebec speak two languages in the same conversation. More so in Montreal, but in Quebec City, too, listen to lunchtime chitchat among locals. A man will speak French, a woman English, each appearing to understand perfectly what the other has said, but both expressing themselves comfortably in their own mother tongue. It happens in intimate conversations between friends and lovers, parents and children, and in convivial groups, where bilingual chatter ricochets around the table. The effect is charming, and at the end of the shortest of stays even the most unilingual of English speakers will come away at least knowing when and how to say *salut, très bien,* and *mais oui.* As you decipher restaurant menus and shop where all public signs are *seulement français,* take comfort knowing that in most places you can fall back on English when the going gets tough. In the tourist areas of Quebec City, particularly, this is what people have come to expect: Old World charm with built-in communication insurance. And once outside, you'll find that *s'il vous plaît* and *merci beaucoup* will overcome a lot of linguistic barriers—especially in this predominantly French world.

English is more likely to be understood in Montreal, but then so might Turkish, Greek, Russian, or Lithuanian. Although unmistakably French, Montreal has been an international crossroads for a couple of centuries now. Multilingual skills often are taken for granted in a society where "Jean-Marc Brophy" may have an Italian grandmother and "Fiona Laberge" a Scottish grandfather. Though Quebec has always felt the need to safeguard its language and culture from within, its defiance to remain *chez eux* (at home) does not pose much of a handicap for those visitors who want to do their business or have fun in English only.

PARC DU MONT-ROYAL, Montreal From the crush of downtown Montreal, you'll see the mountain beckoning through narrow concrete canyons of high-rise towers and office complexes. In getting here, most motorists pass by the best lookout spot over the city on their first drive up the mountain along

Voie Camillien-Houde—but if you stay in the eastbound traffic lane you can't miss it. From here—the *Observatoire de l'Est*—you'll get the widest view of the landscape below, and best appreciate what Jacques Cartier must have seen more than 450 years ago, when he made his way to the top of the mountain along the St. Lawrence. Or take in the vista from the *Belvédère Mont-Royal* in front of the *Grand Chalet*—landmarks are indicated in bronze along the parapet—and think back to the time when this high spot became the New World's center of French civilization. On summer weekends, spread out a picnic blanket and basket alongside Montrealers; in winter, converge on the pine-scented trails with snowshoe enthusiasts and cross-country skiers. You'll be carried along by the spirit and speed of the skaters on Lac des Castors (Beaver Lake), which is especially pretty and romantic at night under the lights. On sunny days kids are out on the gentle toboggan slide above the natural ice rink; in fact, generations of young Montrealers have learned the rudiments of downhill skiing here on the little rope tow run. Take a whirl around the rink—it's easy to forget you're on a mountain—but don't miss a trip to the main lookout. On a clear day, you'll see the faint outline of the Green Mountains in Vermont—and realize how close the two different worlds of French Canada and the United States can be. For information about *Parc du Mont-Royal* facilities, call the park (phone: 514-872-6559) or the city's department of sports and recreation (phone: 514-872-6211).

SHOOTING THE RAPIDS, Montreal When it comes to thrill rides, the St. Lawrence River rapids are in a class by themselves. Though you can't prove it by any of the long-gone adventurers who were beaten by the turbulent waters as they set out in search of the riches of China (the rapids themselves were called "La Chine"), you can decide for yourself by riding the waves of the enterprise offered by *Expéditions dans les Rapides de Lachine* (105 Rue de la Commune O.; phone: 514-284-9607), the only company that conducts trips through these rough waters. What amounted to danger and heartache for early explorers has been transformed into derring-do for latter-day adventurers. The aluminum *saute-mouton* (leapfrogging) craft are durable, propelled by jet-pump engines, strong enough to fight the currents during a river romp, or bob through the chop when the motors idle. Before leaving port, passengers are decked out like Gloucester fisherfolk in bright yellow slickers with matching sou'westers and rubber boots—regulation life jackets complete the ensemble. Soon you're on whirlpool level, in the tradition of the Iroquois, the *coureurs de bois* (gritty fur traders who traveled by canoe into the wilderness), and the woodsmen who traversed the stormy passage on log rafts. Out where the river narrows and then descends around the green islands off Lachine's suburban shore, hundreds of standing waves crest above the flood. You bolt headlong into more than a dozen whirlpools and two hydraulics (depressions, or valleys, surrounded by walls of water) caused by the backlash of currents racing through a natural chute. Rearing up like a playful porpoise, the *saute-mouton* dives into the waves, surf crashing over the bow. Imagine yourself as one of those early travelers who, if he was lucky, emerged from an encounter with "La Chine" merely soaked to the skin and exhilarated, not battered and defeated. But leave some room for practical details: Despite the rain gear, you'll likely get wet—so wear old clothes and leave something dry to change into at the ticket office. *Saute-mouton* adventures depart the *Quai de l'Horloge* in Montreal's Vieux Port restoration every two hours daily from mid-May through *Labour Day*.

SMOKED MEAT AT SCHWARTZ'S, Montreal In a city renowned for its fine restaurants, you'd think that Montreal might lay claim to the world's best seafood or the world's finest maple syrup. But move over, Manhattan: Montrealers say they have the best pastrami (smoked meat, in Canadian parlance) sandwiches this side of heaven. Expatriate citizens dream of the *Montreal Hebrew Delicatessen and Steak House* (a.k.a. *Schwartz's*) the way displaced Viennese dream about *Demel's* café or *Sachertorte* at the *Sacher* hotel. To them it is Canada's—some even claim the world's—most satisfying source of the ultimate smoked meat on rye.

It's been more than 60 years since Ruban Schwartz introduced his home-cured "special" sandwiches and no-frills manner of service—and, as the old-timers here will tell you, little has changed. You'll either share a long counter, where the daily specials are printed large on the wall, or crowd together with regulars around arborite tables cluttering the narrow room from entrance to kitchen door. Order a *Schwartz* special, barely containing itself between slices of crusty rye; spread on extra mustard; and add a dill pickle. Then sprinkle a liberal dose of salt and white vinegar over the best French fries in a province renowned for its *frites* and enjoy. After the first bite, you'll know why the many worlds of this cosmopolitan Canadian city beat a path to this unassuming door. The *Montreal Hebrew Delicatessen and Steak House* (3895 Blvd. St-Laurent; phone: 514-842-4813) is closed *Yom Kippur*.

VILLE SOUTERRAINE (UNDERGROUND MONTREAL) Montreal's contribution to travel trade folklore records the fate of one feckless winter visitor who came to town without an overcoat. Unprepared for zero-belt temperatures, the newcomer checked into a deluxe downtown hotel, wined, dined, kept business appointments, saw a movie, attended a symphony concert, went to church—even bought a new overcoat—without venturing out into the snow-banked, traffic-jammed streets. You needn't test this tall tale, but it contains more than a grain of truth. Thanks to the amenities of Montreal's climate-controlled Ville Souterraine (a collective term for the many separate subterranean complexes), it *is* possible to spend days in coatless comfort. And while Montrealers really don't live like trolls, they do appreciate the weatherproof network of public transport and pedestrian corridors that links the shopping malls, office buildings, hotels, and other major centers in downtown Montreal. You too can escape January blizzards, July heat waves, and rush-hour gridlocks as you hustle around the bright, air conditioned "city below."

Although shopping is the prime attraction, you can travel underground to such diverse destinations as the *Université du Québec à Montréal (UQAM), Parc Olympique, Place des Arts* (the city's major performing arts center), *Cathédrale Christ Church,* and the *Bourse de Montréal* (Montreal Stock Exchange). For *the* French Canadian underground experience, try the *Complexe Desjardins.* Hardly a day goes by here without some kind of free entertainment on the lower-level concourse. Local rock musicians, school choirs, television crews doing live news spots, and puppet theaters draw big crowds during lunch hour, when office workers from the towers enclosing the multitiered atrium join in the fun. Life is especially exciting here for children at *Christmas* and *Easter.* But the light-filled central plaza, with its jungle of green plants and splashing fountains, is a favorite year-round spot for a subterranean picnic of tasty snacks from the specialty food shops on site—and when blizzards blow it's a great place to wait for the spring thaw.

BATTLES ON ICE, Montreal Hockey is *the* Canadian game, and the *Canadiens* demonstrate the best of it on their home ice at the *Forum.* Since the *National Hockey League* was established in 1924, the *Canadiens* have won more *Stanley Cup* trophies than any other team. This is the arena where Maurice and Henri Richard, Jean Béliveau, Ken Dryden, Jacques Plante, and Guy Lafleur, among others, have become legends. Accordingly, Montreal fans follow the action in noisy fervor as plays are announced, first in French, then in English. The game is fast and fierce, yet surprisingly graceful, and the excitement of the fans—Gallic and non—is infectious. You'll soon find yourself cheering along in both tongues, even if you find hockey incomprehensible in any language. During intermission, follow the rambunctious crowd as it spills out to the concession stands. For something different in between-periods snacking, try the tough-skinned Montreal hot dogs ("steamies"), served with small, spicy pickles called *cornichons.* As the venerable old house of hockey celebrates its 71st birthday this year, *Les Habs* (the *Canadiens'* nickname, short for *Les Habitants*) are about to move to a bigger arena in time for this year's season. Fans are bound to take the loss very hard. Meanwhile, come root for the *Canadiens* at the *Forum* (2313 Rue Ste-Catherine O.; phone: 514-932-2582). They're really good skates.

CARNAVAL DE QUÉBEC For a week and a half in early February, Quebec City breaks out of its winter doldrums and erupts in a northern version of New Orleans's *Mardi Gras* or Rio's *Carnaval.* Merrymakers don 18th-century costume (or at least put toques on their heads and tie *ceintures fléchées,* or traditional sashes, around their waists); menus feature such Quebec delicacies as maple sugar pie, *tourtière* (a spicy meat pie), and *caribou* (a potent mixture of wine and pure alcohol); and a dizzying array of activities presents itself at every turn. The fun begins with an opening ceremony in which the mascot, Bonhomme Carnaval (a seven-foot-tall snowman with red cap and *ceinture fléchée*), crowns the Carnival Queen at his ice palace before cheering thousands. During the next 10 days, there's much to do and see: spectacular ice sculptures and an international ice sculpture competition on Place Carnaval; tobogganing, and—for the brave—luge rides on the nearby hills; dogsled races; auto races on ice; a canoe race across the treacherous St. Lawrence; skiing; skating; hockey; and (for the more courageous still) an annual roll in the snow that attracts a surprising number of bathing suit–clad participants. At night are fireworks displays, lavish theme parties, the *Bal de Reine* (Queen's Ball), a night parade with brightly lit floats, and a torch-lit ski run. It's an exciting, invigorating experience in a dazzling wonderland of ice and snow. A half million people flock to Quebec for *Carnaval,* but the mood of the city is more festive than riotous, so, in between the parties and parades, it's possible to steal away for a romantic ride in a calèche for a private celebration of the season.

Quebec City is at its best in winter. Take a leisurely ride within the walls of the town, whose narrow streets and lanes are lined with cafés that serve coffee with steaming milk in large bowls. Listen as the words of the popular song "Mon Pays" by Gilles Vigneault stir the Québécois heart: *"Mon pays ce n'est pas un pays, c'est l'hiver"* ("My country is not a country, it is winter"). After more than 300 seasons of bone-chilling weather, Quebeckers get emotional in the cold; it is *their* time. If you notice that events have a different edge here, that cafés are more jubilant, and that even in the midst of a freezing cold snap the streets are bustling with life, don't forget that Quebeckers are proud to say they have more than a little ice flowing in their veins.

A Few of Our Favorite Things

Though Montreal and Quebec City abound with fine hotels and world class restaurants, we've singled out a few select spots. Follow our lead; we promise you won't be disappointed.

Each place listed below is described in detail in the appropriate city chapter.

GRAND HOTELS

The following are our special favorites for a stay in Montreal or Quebec City. Some are modern, resort-like havens; others, converted châteaux redolent of Old World appeal. Each in its own way offers the highest caliber of service, food, and ambience. Complete information about our choices can be found on pages 68 to 70 of the Montreal chapter and pages 108 to 109 of the Quebec City chapter in THE CITIES.

Montreal
Bonaventure Hilton International
Inter-Continental Montreal
Ritz-Carlton Kempinski
Westin–Mont Royal

Quebec City

Château Bonne Entente
Château Frontenac
Loews Le Concorde
Quebec Hilton International

INCREDIBLE EDIBLES

Both cities offer a wide variety of gastronomic experiences, from classic haute French cuisine to hearty French Canadian food. What follows is a list of restaurants in which gourmands will best enjoy the intriguing range of fare that Montreal and Quebec City boast. Complete information about our choices can be found on pages 73 to 75 of the Montreal chapter and pages 111 to 114 of the Quebec City chapter in THE CITIES.

Montreal

Beaver Club
Café de Paris
Les Halles
La Marée
Les Mignardises
Le St-Amable

Quebec City

Aux Anciens Canadiens
Café de la Paix
Le Champlain
Gambrinus
Le Melrose
Le St-Amour
A la Table de Serge Bruyère

The Performing Arts

Montreal and Quebec City offer a range of opportunities to enjoy fine concerts, plays, opera, and ballet; the *Orchestre Symphonique de Montréal* is a major force in the music world. For those nimble enough in Canada's other official language, finding professional-grade and avant-garde theater is no obstacle, but pickings tend to be slim for the English-only crowd. In Montreal, you should be able to find a play or two by Canadian-born playwrights of world class caliber or touring shows at the *Théâtre Centaur,* the only professional English-language house in the city. Music and dance offerings, particularly in Montreal, are memorable. The following is a sampling of the best venues, those that consistently present fine performances. For more information and the names of local newspapers and magazines that carry arts information, see "Sources and Resources" in *Montreal* and *Quebec City,* THE CITIES. Entries, which are given for Montreal and then for Quebec City, are arranged alphabetically within each city.

PLACE DES ARTS, Montreal A legacy of the building boom that attended *EXPO '67,* this lavish complex of stages housed in two buildings is the heart of Montreal's cultural life. The complex contains a stunning, acoustically excellent concert hall, the 3,000-seat *Salle Wilfrid-Pelletier* (the city's largest), and four smaller theaters that house another 2,000 people in a two-level, pyramid-shape building. This is the home of the *Orchestre Symphonique de Montréal, Orchestre Métropolitain de Montréal, Les Grands Ballets Canadiens, Opéra de Montréal,* and *Opéra de Québec.* It's also the setting for *Les Ballets Jazz Montréal* performances and a variety of chamber music concerts, ballet recitals, and plays. The 1,300-seat *Théâtre Maisonneuve* reserves its large, adjustable stage for drama, dance, and recitals; the smaller *Théâtre Port-Royal* and pocket-size *Café de la Place* theater complete the complex. (It's linked to Montreal's Ville Souterraine through a pedestrian corridor to the *Place des Arts Métro* station.) Tapestry murals by Quebec artists of the mythical meeting of Orpheus and Dionysus at the River Styx and the legend of Icarus adorn the main lobby. On Sunday mornings, the center lobby is the venue for "Sons et Brioche"—informal concerts and continental breakfast. Information: *Place des Arts,* 260 Blvd. de Maisonneuve O. (phone: 514-842-2112).

SALLE DE CONCERT POLLACK and SALLE CLAUDE-CHAMPAGNE, Montreal For the best in classical music outside the *Place des Arts,* the music halls at *Université McGill* and the *Université de Montréal* are the best in town. Designed by New York architect Bruce Price, the *Pollack* has been the recital hall for students from *McGill*'s faculty of music since 1899 and is now the home of the *Orchestre de Chambre McGill* (McGill Chamber Orchestra). Its concert schedule runs from September through May. Performances start at 8 PM; call for program dates. Most concerts are free of charge. Students from the *Université de Montréal*'s music faculty perform in concert and recital at *Salle Claude-Champagne* from September to July. The 1,000-seat auditorium also features folk music groups. Performances start at 8 PM; there's usually no admission charge. Information: *Salle de Concert Pollack,* 555 Rue Sherbrooke O. (phone: 514-398-4547); *Salle Claude-Champagne,* 220 Av. Vincent-d'Indy (phone: 514-343-6000).

THÉÂTRE CENTAUR, Montreal The city's only professional English-language theater has been at home in the former *Bourse de Montréal* (Stock Exchange) since 1965. The 1903 Beaux Arts temple of finance still looks like its imposing old self on the outside, but the interior has been transformed into an award-winning playhouse that includes two small theaters, one primarily a workshop stage for experimental endeavors. Works by Canadian playwrights are given priority here. French-language productions and dance companies share both stages with the English-repertory players. Information: *Théâtre Centaur,* 453 Rue St-François-Xavier (phone: 514-288-3161).

THÉÂTRE ST-DENIS, Montreal The second-largest facility after *Salle Wilfrid-Pelletier,* Montreal's grand old theater can accommodate audiences of 2,500. The theater dates from 1916; with its rebuilt Art Deco façade that traditionalists have never forgiven, it hosts the best French-language theater, many of the events of the *Festival Juste pour Rire* (Just for Laughs Festival) each July, and music and dance programs. (Also see "Special Events" in *Montreal,* THE CITIES.) Information: *Théâtre St-Denis,* 1594 Rue St-Denis (phone: 514-849-4211).

GRAND THÉÂTRE DE QUÉBEC, Quebec City The preeminent stage of French culture since it opened in 1971, this is the home of the *Orchestre Symphonique de Québec,* Canada's oldest; *Opéra Québec;* the *Théâtre du Trident* repertory company; and the *Danse-Partout* dance troupe. The symphony schedules a full concert season in the *Salle Louis-Fréchette,* one of *Le Grand's* two splendid auditoriums. From September through May, the theater company mounts productions that range from the classics to new works by Canadian, European, and American playwrights, and the opera takes over the big stage twice a year for a series of spring and fall productions. Designed by Victor Prus, the huge building is a stunning example of contemporary architecture. The interior is decorated with three massive murals in concrete by Spanish artist Jordi Bonet titled *Death, Space,* and *Liberty.* Both the building and the murals are controversial—not everyone likes Prus's bold design or Bonet's aggressive style—but they're worth seeing even if you're not staying for the concert. Information: *Grand Théâtre de Québec,* 269 Blvd. René-Lévesque E. (phone: 418-643-8131).

Historic Churches

More than any other single institution, Quebec's churches tell the tale of the land's foreign settlers. From their earliest days until the last voyageur traveled upriver in the 1820s, Montreal and Quebec City were but crude trading posts of fur and lumber barons, distinguished only by the huge churches and basilicas built by a growing Catholic church and the smaller houses of worship erected by the Protestant English. Many of these buildings survive and today serve as reminders of the determination and faith of the early settlers. Entries, which are given for Montreal and then for Quebec City, are arranged alphabetically within each city.

BASILIQUE NOTRE-DAME, Montreal This twin-towered Gothic Revival church, designed by New York architect James O'Donnell (who is buried in the church vault), was completed in 1829. Today's basilica is notable for its lavishly decorated interior, which includes a monumental altar, exquisite wood-carvings and paintings, exceptional stained glass windows depicting the history of Montreal, and a 5,772-pipe organ. There also is a museum in the sacristy. Adjacent to the main church is the restored *Chapelle du Sacré-Coeur* (Sacred Heart Chapel), with stunning bronze reredos panels by Charles Daudelin. It is a place of calm in the crush of Old Montreal. After leaving the basilica, step into Place d'Armes and glance up at the twin spires for a true perspective of the church's scale. One spire houses the *Gros Bourdon* bell, a six-foot, 12-ton monster that once taxed the muscle power of 12 burly bellringers. Powered by electricity now, Notre-Dame's massive *cloche* remains one of the world's largest and is sounded only on rare occasions. The basilica seats 5,000 and stands another 2,000, and its chapel is the scene of French Montreal's most fashionable society weddings. Guided tours are offered weekdays from mid-May to June 24 and *Labour Day* to mid-October; daily from June 24 to *Labour Day*. Museum closed weekends; no admission charge. Information: *Basilique Notre-Dame,* Pl. d'Armes (phone: 514-849-1070).

BASILIQUE ST-PATRICK, Montreal Montreal's English-speaking Catholics don't have to use a lot of imagination to find their house of worship. A bank of buttresses on the east wall of the largest English-language Catholic church in the city is as green as old Erin. Environmentalists blame a combination of acid rain and the dissolving patina from the copper roof for the verdigris stain, but whatever the cause, the color seems appropriate for a church named for the patron saint of Ireland. Opened on *St. Patrick's Day* in 1847, the church offered spiritual shelter for Irish-born Montrealers following one of the most devastating periods of the community's history. A typhus epidemic was sweeping the city at the time, and residents of "Little Dublin," those living in tenements between today's Rue de la Gauchetière and Boulevard René-Lévesque, were struck down with particular severity. Hundreds died, but the living kept the faith. In more prosperous times, parishioners learned to love the vast, brown-and-gold interior and the mighty columns, each hewn from an 80-foot pine tree. Unity was underscored by an interior decor of shamrocks, Celtic crosses, and fleurs-de-lis, a nod to the Sulpicians who'd helped them acquire the building site. The nave is splendid; its fine oak wainscoting is inset with paintings of 150 saints. The church was also the site of the 1868 funeral of Thomas D'Arcy McGee, a Father of Confederation; a silver-tongued orator, he was given one of the grandest send-offs of any Montrealer. Information: *Basilique St-Patrick,* 460 Blvd. René-Lévesque O. (phone: 514-866-7379).

CATHÉDRALE CHRIST CHURCH, Montreal Members of Montreal's Anglican community have grown accustomed to giving their cathedral a second glance these days. For years the Christ Church congregation, and most of downtown Montreal, watched with apprehension as one of the finest examples of Gothic architecture in Canada teetered over a huge canyon that shopping mall developers were burrowing beneath. The church is firmly grounded again (although the faithful still say little prayers of protection for the landmark), above *Les Promenades de la Cathédrale*'s underground retail world. Reflected in the pink glass tower of a corporate skyscraper, the cathedral's delicate spire casts a frail image. The building, which was completed in 1857, was designed to reflect the cruciform shape of 14th-century English ecclesiastical architecture; 70 years later the original spire of Canadian stone was removed because of fears of structural damage, to be replaced by an aluminum replica. The reredos at the altar is a war memorial, depicting seven scenes from the life of Christ; the monument in what's left of the cathedral grounds honors Francis Fulford, Montreal's first Anglican archbishop. The church is the venue for frequent noon-hour concerts and evening recitals; donations are suggested for concerts. Information: *Cathédrale Christ Church,* 1444 Av. Union, corner of Rue Ste-Catherine O. (phone: 514-288-6421).

CATHÉDRALE MARIE-REINE-DU-MONDE (CATHEDRAL OF MARY, QUEEN OF THE WORLD), Montreal A scaled-down replica of *St. Peter's Basilica* in Rome, complete with a row of statues depicting the patron saints of the Archdiocese of Montreal on the roof and a reproduction of Bernini's altar columns, this cathedral was under construction from 1870 to 1894. Its vast, dark interior space (architects of the time believed that the darker the church, the brighter the candles would glow and, thus, the brighter the stained glass would appear) is a symbol of the era when the Catholic church was a powerful influence on the city and the province. The domed mass is now dwarfed by the towers of modern Montreal, but it remains a monument to Quebec's Catholic heritage. Information: *Cathédrale Marie-Reine-du-Monde,* 1085 Rue Cathédrale, corner of Blvd. René-Lévesque O. (phone: 514-866-1661).

CHAPELLE NOTRE-DAME-DE-BON-SECOURS, Montreal While it doesn't pretend to the grandeur of the *Basilique Notre-Dame*, the modest little chapel at the bottom of Rue Bon Secours is much older than its neighbor on Place d'Armes. It's said that the founder himself, French career soldier Paul de Chomedey, Sieur de Maisonneuve, felled the first timber and laid the cornerstone for the tiny chapel beyond the stockades of Ville Marie in 1657. And although none of that timber remains (the present structure dates from 1772), the church has never moved from its original site. The chapel owes its beginnings to Marguerite Bourgeoys, the first Catholic saint to live and die in Canada. A pious 30-year-old French schoolteacher whom de Maisonneuve brought to New France in 1653, Bourgeoys had a dream soon after her arrival of building a shrine to the glory of the Virgin Mary in the no-man's-land beyond the settlement stockade. Later she would distinguish herself as Canada's first schoolmistress and go on to found the *Congrégation de Notre-Dame,* the first Canadian order of non-cloistered nuns, but her vision of extending the boundaries of Old Montreal was truly ahead of its time. Bourgeoys persisted in her plans, and eventually—two decades after the first cornerstone was laid—the chapel was completed, ready to enshrine an ancient wooden statue of the Virgin, donated to the cause by a bene-factor in France. Reputed to work miracles of salvation for sailors on per-ilous seas, Our Lady of Good Help was unveiled at the chapel's official opening in 1675.

Although it is the third church to occupy the site, and a new façade was added in 1895, the "Sailors' Church" retains the simple, unpretentious char-acter of early Québécois architecture. Inside, a tile mosaic of de Maisonneuve acknowledges a debt to Montreal's founder, who donated the land for the building site. A little fleet of votive lamps in the form of model ships is sus-pended above the pews; they were gifts from grateful sailors who believed in miracles. The chapel's rooftop Madonna is a familiar beacon for mariners making port in Montreal. A small chapel museum tells the story of Saint Marguerite with a collection of doll-size figurines in historically correct dress. Visitors can climb to the observation deck above the apse for a rooftop view of the port and Vieux Montréal. The museum is closed Mondays; admission charge. Information: *Chapelle Notre-Dame-de-Bon-Secours,* 400 Rue St-Paul E. (phone: 514-845-9991).

ORATOIRE ST-JOSEPH (ST. JOSEPH'S ORATORY), Montreal Founded as a tiny chapel in 1904 by Brother André, a member of the Holy Cross Order of Roman Catholic brothers, this oratory had grown into a 5,000-seat basilica by 1922. Barely literate and in poor health, Brother André purportedly had healing powers, and he had a vast following among the faithful of Quebec (he is entombed here). André is said to have cured hundreds of people, invok-ing the aid of St. Joseph, husband of Jesus's mother, Mary. The church commands the hillside on the northwest slopes of Mont-Royal, with 99 steps cut into the steep slope below the main entrance. At one time the most humble of suppliants made the ascent on their knees; today, more than two million people visit the site annually. At 860 feet above sea level, the oratory observatory is the highest point on the Montreal skyline, with a view that stretches as far west as Lake St-Louis and over the northwest section of the city. Its carillon of bells, which was designed for the *Eiffel Tower,* was judged unsuitable for the famous landmark and came to the oratory on loan in 1955; it was later purchased as a permanent fixture. Carillon concerts are held Wednesdays through Saturdays at noon and 5 PM; Sundays at noon and 2:30 PM. Organ recitals are given Wednesday evenings in the summer, and *Les Petits Chanteurs du Mont-Royal* children's choir performs on Sunday mornings. A museum houses a collection of reli-gious art and a few relics of the founder, including one of his cassocks; dur-ing the *Christmas* season exhibitions feature a collection of 200 crèches from more than 60 countries. The museum is open daily; donations are accepted. Information: *Oratoire St-Joseph,* 3800 Chemin Queen-Mary (phone: 514-733-8211).

BASILIQUE NOTRE-DAME, Quebec City Probably the finest example of Baroque architecture in Quebec, the basilica stands on the site of *Notre-Dame-de-Recouvrance,* built in 1633 by Samuel de Champlain, who probably was buried there (the actual gravesite has never been found). Destroyed by fire seven years later, it was rebuilt as *Notre-Dame-de-la-Paix,* the place where Monseigneur François-Xavier de Montmorency-Laval, first Bishop of Quebec, established the first Roman Catholic diocese in North America (outside of Mexico) in 1674. Like the *Eglise Notre-Dame-des-Victoires,* it was destroyed during the British bombardment of 1759. Repairs and additions over the next century resulted in a building that recalls the 18th-century structure. The church was restored several times due to warfare, fire, and weather. Its ornate interior (largely reconstructed after a 1922 fire) is decorated with works of art and illuminated by stained glass windows. The basilica's treasures include an Episcopal throne and a chancel lamp presented by French King Louis XIV. Three governors of New France and most of the Bishops of Quebec are buried in the crypt. Guided tours of the basilica and crypt are available from May through October. Open daily to 8 PM. Information: *Basilique Notre-Dame,* 16 Rue Buade (phone: 418-692-2533).

BASILIQUE STE-ANNE-DE-BEAUPRÉ, Quebec City Back in the 1650s, shipwrecked sailors rescued from the treacherous waters off Cap-Tourmente showed their gratitude to Saint Anne by founding a chapel in her name in the little village of Beaupré, about 25 miles (40 km) downriver from Quebec City. In part because of the good saint's reputation as a miracle worker, the faithful flocked here. The little wooden chapel was replaced after about a decade by a sturdy fieldstone church; by 1876, *Ste-Anne*'s shrine had grown to basilica size, providing a wellspring of hope for millions of cure-seeking pilgrims. Destroyed by fire in 1922, the celebrated shrine was rebuilt the following year in neo-Roman style. A vast edifice, with twin towers, lovely rose windows, and a marble statue of the saint in the sanctuary, the basilica can accommodate a congregation of 3,000. More than one and a half million suppliants come here annually, leaving behind crutches, wheelchairs, and canes as testaments to their faith in the mother of the Virgin Mary. The *Fontaine de Ste-Anne* (Ste-Anne Fountain) in front of the basilica is believed to have healing powers. An on-site information center is open daily from early May through mid-September. Information: *Basilique Ste-Anne-de-Beaupré,* 10018 Av. Royale, Ste-Anne-de-Beaupré (phone: 418-827-3781).

CATHÉDRALE ANGLICANE (HOLY TRINITY ANGLICAN CATHEDRAL), Quebec City An ecclesiastical property that has no associations with the old French regime, *Holy Trinity* is a relic of the British colonial era in Quebec. The first Church of England cathedral ever built beyond the British Isles, it has served the capital's Anglican community since 1804. Built by royal decree of King George III—who donated the silver communion set now used on royal occasions—it was inspired by London's *St. Martin in the Fields,* with pews of stalwart English oak. The cathedral still honors the monarchy with a sacrosanct royal pew reserved for the use of a visiting British sovereign or designated representative. Memorial plaques under the stained glass windows trace the history of Quebec City's English-speaking establishment in war and peace. Information: *Cathédrale Anglicane,* 31 Rue des Jardins (phone: 418-692-2193).

EGLISE NOTRE-DAME-DES-VICTOIRES, Quebec City Built over the foundations of the settlement that Samuel de Champlain founded in the early 1600s, the small, gray stone church on Place Royale has been clinging to its original Lower Town site for more than three centuries. Despite its meek appearance, *Notre-Dame* owes its name to two French victories over British aggression, one in 1690, just two years after celebrating its first mass, and another in 1711. Destroyed in the bombardment that preceded the Battle of the Plaines d'Abraham and the conquest of 1759, the church has been restored twice. Today it looks much as it did when it was the heart and soul of community life in the French colony's burgeoning port district. The pretty, pastel-tinted interior is dominated by an unusual castle-shape high altar. A scale model of a ship, suspended above the nave, recalls *Le Brezé,* the vessel that transported troops to New France in 1664. Open daily from May to October 15; closed Mondays and afternoons the rest of the year. Information: *Eglise Notre-Dame-des-Victoires,* Pl. Royale (phone: 418-692-1650).

Downhill Skiing

Canadians can be classified in two major groups: Those who ski and those who intend to learn. That's not surprising, considering the usually abundant quantities of snow north of the international border, the mountainous terrain up there, and the number of mountains developed for skiing.

Natural snowfall can be expected from late November to late March, but sometimes—particularly in eastern Canada—the "Great White North" is not quite white enough, so many major ski areas use supplementary snowmaking machinery to ensure good ski conditions even during periods of scant snowfall.

In any case, a skier in Canada is seldom far from a good run. Quebec is undoubtedly the queen of eastern Canada skiing, with *Parc du Mont Ste-Anne,* a giant area outside Quebec City; the Eastern Townships, a quartet of mountains with first class runs for all levels of ability and with a less hectic pace than at some of the older, more popular resorts; and the grand Laurentians, mountains that offer an experience notable as much for the elegant cuisine and the regional specialties served in the restaurants of the quaint villages at the lift base as for the excitement quotient of the nearly 1,000 slopes and runs of its 125-odd ski areas. The Laurentians region is one of the few ski areas in the Western Hemisphere where the chef is as esteemed as the head ski instructor, a phenomenon that more than compensates for the fact that the runs are shorter, and conditions often icier and rockier, than those in Canada's other great ski region, the ineffably beautiful Rocky Mountains. Entries, which are given for areas near Montreal and then for those near Quebec City, are arranged alphabetically.

ESTRIE (EASTERN TOWNSHIPS), Montreal Unlike the more famous Laurentides (Laurentians; see below), which were initially developed to serve as summer resorts and were then strung with lifts to help the communities make it through the winter, the mountains in this northern extension of the Appalachians, 44 miles (71 km) southeast of Montreal and just north of the Vermont border, were developed primarily for skiing, because of the suitability of the terrain. Each one is the peer of *Mont Tremblant* or any comparable Vermont resort. Mont Sutton, near Sutton, has 54 trails, nine chair lifts, a 1,509-foot vertical, and unique glade skiing. Owl's Head, near Mansonville, has a 1,770-foot vertical and 25 trails. Mont Orford, near Magog, has a 1,772-foot vertical and 32 trails. Bromont, with a 1,328-foot vertical and 26 trails, is the fourth member of the quartet of major mountains in the area. Headquarter at any one of the four mountains, ski there, and then use your interchangeable lift ticket to sample the other three. Each area has runs to suit everyone in the family, varied terrain, good lift service, and its own unique character.

The area offers accommodations to satisfy almost every taste. Owl's Head has a small lodge right at the base, plus apartment-hotels and condominiums with ski-in/ski-out access to lifts and trails. There is snowmaking equipment and a detachable quad chair lift, plus six double chair lifts. Owl's Head attracts an almost fanatically loyal crowd that returns year after year. The cozy *Auberge Bromont* (Bromont; phone: 514-534-2200) commands views of the illuminated runs. The areas around Mont Sutton and Mont Orford are livelier; they're both close to other small towns that boast restaurants and other nightspots. Among the more interesting hostelries in this area are *Village Archimèd* (phone: 819-538-3440) in Sutton; *Hovey Manor* (phone: 819-842-2421) and *Auberge Hatley* (phone: 819-842-2451) in North Hatley; and Magog's *Chéribourg* resort (phone: 819-843-3308). Although the eastern townships don't bustle with as much activity as the Laurentians, and although this is still very much the farming area that it was before the lifts went in more than 20 years ago, these mountains offer an abundance of amenities for those who've come first and foremost to ski. What's more, the quality of skiing is among the best this side of the Rockies.

Information: *Quebec Ski East,* 2883 Rue King O., Sherbrooke, QUE J1L 1C6 (phone: 819-564-8989); *Mont Orford Resort Centre,* Box 248, Magog, QUE J1X 3W8 (phone: 819-843-6548); *Owl's Head,* Mansonville, QUE J0E 1X0 (phone: 514-292-3342); *Sutton Tourist Association,* CP 418, Sutton,

QUE J0E 2K0 (phone: 514-538-2646 or 819-538-2537); and *Bromont Ski Area,* CP 29, Bromont, QUE J0E 1L0 (phone: 819-534-2200; 800-363-8920 in Canada).

LES LAURENTIDES (THE LAURENTIANS), Montreal Beginning about 35 miles (56 km) northwest of the city is a succession of ski communities—more than 20 major ones in all, each the center of a cluster of ski areas situated just minutes apart. If only for the sheer number of runs in the area—some 300 (80 lighted for night skiing) in the space of 40 square miles, a concentration greater than that of any other area of comparable size in the world—the Laurentians would be unique. But the frills of a skiing vacation here also stand out. The region's charming French villages are full of lovely inns, pleasant resorts, and small hotels so close to the skiing that it's easy to schuss right to your doorstep—or, more to the point, to your dining room, where good food is the order of the day.

Every one of the ski areas here has its special charm. At the northern end of this string of resorts is *Mont Tremblant,* the dowager queen of Canada's winter resorts, which, with a vertical drop of 2,100 feet and runs that extend up to 3.5 miles in length, offers plenty of good skiing for experts and intermediates. *Mont Tremblant* has a bubble-covered quad lift, detachable quad chair lift, and jet T-bar; restaurants at the top and the base of the mountain; a nursery; and snowmaking facilities to the very top of the mountain's southern side. Its first-rate hotels include the big *Station Mont Tremblant Lodge* (phone: 819-425-8711; 800-461-8711 in Canada and the US) and the smaller *Tremblant Club* (phone: 819-425-2731; 800-567-8341 in Canada; 800-363-2413 in the US). Some 3 miles (5 km) away in St-Jovite is the *Auberge Gray Rocks* (phone: 514-861-0187 or 819-425-2771; 800-567-6767 in Canada and the US), a friendly sprawl of a 200-room Victorian hostelry on 2,600 acres with its own ski hill, Sugar Peak, a hundred yards from the inn. The vertical here is a mere 620 feet, but it is a titan in the annals of ski history: In 1938, with war threatening, Austria's famed *Snow Eagle Ski School* was transplanted here. Since then, it has become one of the best anywhere; it's so thorough that there are even a couple of instructors whose sole job is to keep the other teachers on their toes. Graduates number among the world's best skiers. Among the lodge's outstanding features are its sports complex, indoor pool, whirlpool, saunas, nightlife (vigorous enough to make the place a good bet for the solo vacationer), and lunches (served in a dining room practically at the lift base). Other Laurentian ski areas offer similar delights. *Belle Neige* (Val-Morin; phone: 819-322-3311), offering a small hill with a vertical of only about 520 feet, two T-bars, and two chair lifts, is notable for the proximity of the *Hôtel la Sapinière* (phone: 819-322-2020), proud possessor of one of Canada's finest kitchens. In nearby Ste-Adèle is the 25-room *Hôtel l'Eau à la Bouche* (phone: 514-229-2991), which boasts some of the most haute cuisine in the Laurentians. Both are members of the prestigious Relais & Châteaux group.

If you have only one day to devote to downhill, stop at St-Sauveur, 37 miles (59 km) from Montreal. This pretty, prosperous village, tucked into its namesake valley, serves as the dining, shopping, and entertainment hub for patrons of four neighboring mountains: Mont St-Sauveur, Mont Habitant, Mont Christie, and Mont Avila, at nearby Piedmont. These four gems form one of the brightest night-skiing conglomerates in Canada, and their popularity is reflected on photogenic Rue Principale, St-Sauveur's main street, lined with fashionable restaurants, bars, and stores. King of the mountain quartet is Mont St-Sauveur, with a vertical drop of 698 feet and 26 runs, the longest of them 4,900 feet. Night skiers can choose from 23 day-bright runs. Information: *Association Touristique des Laurentides,* 14142 Rue de Lachapelle, RR1, St-Jérôme, QUE J7Z 5T4 (phone: 514-436-8532).

LE MASSIF, Quebec City This is the most unusual ski center east of the Rockies. A 2,614-foot-high escarpment that plunges toward the St. Lawrence River, it has 11 2½-mile intermediate and expert trails that boast some of the best powder snow in eastern Canada. Instead of a ski lift, eight or nine buses transport skiers from the base of the mountain to the top of the slopes. Because the center can accommodate only 350 skiers a day, reservations are a must. Information: *Le Massif,* Rte. 138, CP 68, Petite-Rivière-St-François, QUE G0A 2L0 (phone: 418-632-5879).

MONT STE-ANNE, Quebec City Quebec City skiers can't help feeling smug about *Mont Ste-Anne.* Unlike their neighbors in Montreal who can spend a traffic-logged hour creeping to a Laurentian autoroute access, piste-bashers from the provincial capital land at the base village of their local mountain within 30 minutes of a midtown takeoff.

Mountain enough to have hosted the first *Canadian Winter Games* in 1967 and now a regular stop on the *World Cup* circuit, *Mont Ste-Anne* is the biggest of the local areas and is so close to the capital that many of the city's major hotels offer ski packages. Located at Beaupré, a nondescript one-street town about half an hour's drive east of the city, it boasted terrain that was already considerable before development of its north and west sides back in the 1970s doubled the skiable area. Today, 50 slopes and 12 lifts of varying types allow for an uphill capacity of nearly 18,000 an hour. Consequently, skiers can now enjoy the sunny conditions on the southern slopes (the top three-quarters of them as challenging as any of Vermont's steepest and hairiest), or the intermediate and novice north-facing runs, or even the intermediate and expert trails of the mountain's western exposure. Every year, more runs are backed up by an elaborate snowmaking system; well over 85% of the skiable terrain is currently covered. With the addition of 13 lighted trails, *Mont Ste-Anne* claims to have Canada's highest vertical night skiing. The base village provides 140 condo units in two five-story buildings, plus an assortment of boutiques and restaurants, a children's center, and—one of the most popular features—a three-story day lodge adjacent to the existing base chalet with a 550-seat cafeteria and a bar with multilevel sun decks. The park is a year-round resort, with two 18-hole golf courses, camping facilities, and 157 miles of cycling and mountain bike trails. On clear days, year-round, a gondola climbs 2,640 feet to the summit, affording a breathtaking view of the St. Lawrence River, Quebec City, and Ile d'Orléans.

Information: *Office du Tourisme et des Congrès de la Communauté Urbaine de Québec,* 60 Rue d'Auteuil, Quebec City, QUE G1R 4C4 (phone: 418-692-2471), and *Parc du Mont Ste-Anne,* CP 400, Beaupré, QUE G0A 1E0 (phone: 418-827-4561).

STONEHAM, Quebec City The region's next most extensive skiing, even closer to the city than *Mont Ste-Anne* (20 miles/32 km north), has a respectable 1,380-foot vertical drop. Nestled in a valley, the area is protected from strong winds. Twenty-three of Stoneham's 25 runs are covered by snowmaking equipment; 15 of them are lighted. The lifts can accommodate more than 14,000 skiers an hour, and those who want to be on the slopes when they open can choose from among 50 condos and two hotels at the base of the mountain. In addition, it's possible to ski *Le Relais* and *Mont St-Castin*—two areas whose verticals measure 750 and 550 feet, respectively—at *Lac Beauport,* a popular vacation center. These areas are so close to the city that each is busy during the week and busier still on weekends. But the attractions of Quebec City make it preferable to lodge in the city and commute to the ski area, rather than the other way around. Ski bus service is available from six Quebec City hotels (phone: 418-627-2511). By car, take the Autoroute Laurentienne (Rte. 73) to Route 175.

Information: *Stoneham,* 1420 du Hibou, Stoneham, QUE G0A 4P8 (phone: 418-848-2411); *Le Relais,* 1084 Blvd. du Lac-Beauport, QUE G0A 2C0 (phone: 418-849-1851); and *Mont St-Castin,* 82 Chemin le Tour-du-Lac, Lac Beauport, QUE G0A 2C0 (phone: 418-849-1893).

Cross-Country Skiing

It's not necessary to be an *Olympic*-caliber athlete to enjoy cross-country skiing. Nor does one have to seek out hidden spots in Quebec to enjoy the sport. You can ski in city ravines, in suburban vest-pocket parks, in farmers' fields, and on frozen lakes. But with a long weekend or a week to spare, you'll want to head for the more attractive trails within easy driving distance of Montreal and Quebec City. There, given some wisdom in the ways of the winter wilderness, breaking trails through the powder makes for a great adventure. Or tackle one of the many areas where cross-country trails are marked, groomed, and patrolled. Most provincial and municipal parks have at least one trail, and most try to keep campgrounds open for die-hard winter lovers. Others can be found at a variety of hostelries: downhill ski resorts; luxury properties (where après-ski means swimming in a big pool and relaxing in a sauna); simple housekeeping cottages in the woods; cozy country inns; and rustic mountain lodges heated by wood stoves and lit by kerosene lanterns. Or try a lodge-to-lodge or tent-to-tent tour with accommodations located a day of skiing apart, on an interconnecting trail (luggage is transported separately by road).

LES LAURENTIDES (THE LAURENTIANS), Montreal Twenty-five years ago, cross-country skiing here was the exclusive domain of kamikaze types. Trails were severe, with frequent cliff-like descents. Today, most of the trails have been redesigned, upgraded, and mechanically tracked. This vast sweep of mountains may well be the ultimate cross-country ski resort area, the Aspen of cross-country skiing. Besides the skiing, the main attraction is the abundance of wonderful restaurants and lodging places. But when you consider their diversity and the variety of terrain, putting together a Laurentians ski vacation can be terribly confusing. A few basic facts about the area may be helpful: The northern Laurentians' trails are not quite so well marked as those in the south; and the farther east or west you travel from the Laurentians Autoroute, which bisects the region from north to south, the wilder and less well marked the ski routes. The trails at the better-known hostelries of the more northerly *St-Jovite–Mont Tremblant* area—the *Tremblant Club, Station Mont Tremblant Lodge*, and the *Auberge Gray Rocks*—are enjoyable (see *Downhill Skiing*, above, for phone numbers). Most people make their headquarters at one establishment, then spend their vacations exploring its trails and those of its neighbors, accessible via interregional trails. But the concentration of inns and proliferation of long-distance trails also suggest the possibility of inn-to-inn touring. In the south, where the hostelries are situated practically on top of each other, innkeepers are generally obliging about transporting your luggage via hotel bus or taxi to your next overnight stop.

Regional trail maps and the interregional trail map published by the Laurentian Ski Zone are available from local hotels and ski shops. Information: *Association Touristique des Laurentides* (see *Downhill Skiing, above*).

MONT STE-ANNE and "LES AUTRES," Quebec City One of the great charms of Quebec City in the winter is its proximity to the great outdoors. Visitors can spend days pursuing their favorite cold-weather sports (Quebec City is markedly more wintry than Montreal)—and nights in the comfort of the city's splendid hotels, sleeping off the effects of a bountiful French Canadian repast eaten in one of its cozy restaurants. Cross-country skiers will find some of the province's best trails within an hour's drive of the city. Québécois themselves take to the Plaines d'Abraham to keep in shape; though the skiing isn't the best, the views are outstanding. Quebec's best ski terrain—offering more than what's possible to explore in two weeks (let alone two weeks that leave time to enjoy the capital's delights)—is at *Mont Ste-Anne,* 25 miles (40 km) to the east; at the *Station Forestière Duchesnay* (Duchesnay

Forestry Station), 25 miles (40 km) northwest; and at *Camp Mercier,* just inside *Parc des Laurentides* (Laurentian Park), 36 miles (58 km) north of downtown. Located in the picturesque village of St-Férreol-les-Neiges, 5 miles (8 km) east of the alpine ski center, *Mont Ste-Anne*'s cross-country ski complex has over 110 miles of double-track, groomed, and patrolled trails. The trails were designed to meet the needs of beginner and intermediate skiers; expert trails are found at the competition center of *Parc du Mont Ste-Anne. Duchesnay*'s more varied forest trails, through mixed hardwood and fir, are suited to beginners, while the trails at *Camp Mercier,* far less windy than at either of the other areas, are flatter still; the snow is also better there. Inexpensive group overnight trips are available.

For those looking to escape the crowds at the three popular locations listed above, the following five centers are devoted exclusively to cross-country skiing and often leave the skier free to wander in the wide-open spaces. Each is within easy driving distance of Quebec City. *Camping Municipal de Beauport* (95 Av. Sérénité, Beauport; access via Rte. 369; phone: 418-666-2228 or 418-666-2155) has five trails of up to 9 miles of touring; a waxing room (closed weekdays); a heated relay station; restaurant facilities; and night skiing. It's open daily to 10 PM; no admission charge. The *Centre de Ski de Fond de Cap-Rouge* (4600 Rue St-Félix, Cap-Rouge; access via Rte. 440; phone: 418-659-6015) boasts eight trails of more than 23 miles; a waxing room; and a heated relay station. It's open daily to 6 PM; no admission charge. At the *Centre de Ski de Fond Charlesbourg* (Rue St-Alexandre, Charlesbourg; access via Rte. 175; phone: 418-849-9054) are 22 trails covering 120 miles; waxing and restaurant facilities; equipment rental; and a heated relay station. It's open daily to 4 PM; admission charge. Three trails of 28 miles; waxing and restaurant facilities; and a heated relay station are the draws at the *Club de Golf de Lorette* (12986 Rue Monseigneur-Cooke, Loretteville; access via Rte. 573 or 369; phone: 418-842-8441). It's open daily to 4 PM; no admission charge. And *Base de Plein Air de Val-Bélair* (1560 Av. de la Montagne O.; access via Rte. 369; phone: 418-842-7184; 418-842-7769, weekends) offers 10 trails of 37 miles; waxing and equipment rental; and a restaurant. It's open daily to 4 PM; admission charge Information: *Office du Tourisme et des Congrès de la Communauté Urbaine de Québec,* 60 Rue d'Auteuil, Quebec City, QUE G1R 4C4 (phone: 418-692-2471).

SKI-A-THON

The *Canadian Ski Marathon,* a mammoth, anyone-can-enter, two-day cross-country ski event, takes place in the Outaouais region, in the south of Quebec. Usually held in mid-February, the marathon ranks among the biggest events of its kind in the world. The starting point and finish line alternate each year between *Lac Beauchamp Lodge* in the Quebec zone of the Ottawa-Hull suburbs, and Lachute, 105 miles (168 km) to the east of Ottawa-Hull. Information: *Canadian Ski Marathon*, PO Box 98, Montebello, QUE J0V 1L0 (phone: 819-423-5157), and *Association Touristique de l'Outaouais*, 25 Rue Laurier, CP 2000, Hull, QUE J8Z 3Z2 (phone: 819-778-2222).

Good Golf Nearby

In summer, Quebeckers trade in the primary colors of their skiwear for the pastels of golf clothes, but they don't switch their destinations. The playgrounds of the Laurentians and Mont Ste-Anne provide some public golf courses, and low handicappers and duffers alike will want to spend at least a day on the links during their visit. Golfers teeing off in the foothills of Quebec City will find the weather cool, breezy, and rarely humid, and the courses challenging, pristinely kept, and with less expensive greens fees than at layouts surrounding large US cities. Golfers need not go very far afield, either.

There are 50 courses within a 30-mile (48-km) radius of Montreal, half of them public. Quebec City boasts about a dozen 18-hole spreads and nine sporty nine-hole courses within 20 miles (32 km) of town. It may be hard in peak season to fit into a tee-off schedule at the following exclusive courses without reservations, and some links restrict weekend play to members, but if you reserve a couple of days in advance, you usually can find a weekday time slot. Entries, which are given for the Montreal area and then for the Quebec City area, are arranged alphabetically within each area.

CARLING LAKE, Montreal Designed by Harold Watson, this challenging course in the Laurentian foothills has lakeside fairways and greens that test the skill of even the lowest handicapper. At 6,650 yards, it's not Canada's longest course, but the par 72 tantalizer draws a lot of top tournament events. Reserve well in advance for a tee-off time on weekends. Take the Laurentian Autoroute north to Route 158 West and Brownsburg, then Route 327 to Pine Hill. Information: *Club de Golf Carling Lake,* Rte. 327 (phone: 514-476-1212).

LE CHANTECLER, Montreal environs One of the best of the 25 Laurentian layouts that welcome greens-fee players by the day, this course spreads its 6,200-yard, par 70 field around two mountain lakes. The more-than-40-year-old course is next door to *Le Chantecler* hotel's resort complex, 28 miles (45 km) north of Montreal, about an hour's drive. To complement the beautiful mountain scenery and the challenge of its well-kept alpine fairways, the course has a clubhouse. Weekend golfers first tee up at 7 AM on a shotgun schedule. Take the Laurentian Autoroute to exit 67 at Ste-Adèle, then Route 15. Information: *Club de Golf Chantecler Ste-Adèle,* 2520 Chemin de Golf, Ste-Adèle (phone: 514-229-3742).

DORVAL, Montreal This 36-hole complex was laid out in 1982 over hilly, wooded terrain with plenty of water hazards. The par 72 *Oakville* course, at 6,359 yards, features narrow fairways and rolling greens; *Gentilly*'s broader, less challenging fairways were designed for tournament action. It's shorter by about 400 yards and carries a par of 70. Like most public courses in the area, the *Dorval* complex extends full clubhouse privileges—including pro shop facilities and club rental—to day players. Reservations are necessary for Friday, Saturday, and Sunday morning tee-off. Take Autoroute 20 west to the Sources Boulevard exit north; it's about a 15-minute drive from downtown. Information: *Golf Dorval,* 2000 Rue Reverchon, Dorval (phone: 514-631-6624).

LAC ST-JOSEPH, Quebec City This compact, 18-hole testing ground never seems to play the same from one day to the next, and some of the par 5 holes are extremely difficult. The first nine holes were laid out on hilly, wooded terrain in 1948; another nine completed the par 72 teaser in the mid-1970s. The club is open to visitors during the week, but weekends are reserved for members and their guests. Take Autoroute Charest (Rte. 440) to exit 295, then Route 367 north to Ste-Catherine-de-la-Jacques-Cartier, 23 miles (37 km) from Quebec City. Information: *Club de Golf Lac St-Joseph,* 5292 Blvd. Fossambault, Ste-Catherine-de-la-Jacques-Cartier (phone: 418-875-2074).

PARC DU MONT STE-ANNE, Quebec City The 18-hole, 6,713-yard *Beaupré* course in *Parc du Mont Ste-Anne* ranks among the best in the area. Far less challenging is the park's 6,135-yard executive course. Both demand par 72 play and offer greens-fee visitors a full range of club facilities. Reserve well in advance for weekend starting times. From town, take Autoroute Dufferin-Montmorency to Route 138 and Beaupré, then Route 360 to the park, 25 miles (40 km) from the city. Information: *Golf du Parc du Mont Ste-Anne,* Beaupré (phone: 418-827-3778).

ST-LAURENT, Quebec City One of the most scenic layouts in the region, this breezy, 18-hole, par 72 site on Ile d'Orléans is known locally as an early bird—or birdie—course. Because of its location high on the southeast shore of the island, it's the area's first course in condition for early spring play. It's the closest thing to a traditional windblown links west of the famous resort area of La Malbaie (Murray Bay). You'll shoot uphill for nine holes and downhill for the rest, always into a stiff wind. Spread out in 6,942 yards of long, wide-open fairways above the Chenal des Grands Voiliers (Big Ship Channel), the course commands a wonderful view of the St. Lawrence River traffic lanes of oceangoing vessels. Reserve well ahead. Take Autoroute Dufferin-Montmorency to exit 325 and the island bridge, then Route 367 clockwise to the village of St-Laurent, 12 miles (19 km) from Quebec City. Information: *Club de Golf St-Laurent,* 758 Chemin Royal, Ile d'Orléans (phone: 418-829-3896).

OTHER NEARBY GREENS

In addition to those listed above, noteworthy courses near Quebec City include *Golf Club Lorette* (Rue Cooke, Loretteville; phone: 418-842-8441) and *Club de Golf Mont Tourbillon* (Lac Beauport, 12 miles/19 km north of the city; phone: 418-849-4418). Avid tee-timers should check with their home club about playing the *Club de Golf Royal Montreal* (25 Rue Southridge, Ile Bizard; phone: 514-626-3977) or the *Royal Quebec* golf course (65 Rue Bedard, St-Jean-de-Boischatel; phone: 418-822-0331), the two oldest country clubs in North America, or the *Club de Golf Beaconsfield* (49 Av. Golf, Beaconsfield; phone: 514-695-2661), a regular host of *LPGA* championships. Some private clubs in the US have reciprocal agreements with the *Royal Montreal,* where members first drove the green in 1873, just six months before the *Royal Quebec* opened for business. Visitors to both clubs must be guests of an active member.

Smooth Sailing and Boating

Montreal's and Quebec City's very beginnings are rooted in sailing. The first French sailors to arrive at the base of Cap Diamant in Quebec and near Mont-Royal in Montreal weren't in it for kicks (they had a trade route to China to find, after all). They employed the best of their skills to negotiate the rolling waves, tricky winds, and cold of the St. Lawrence. Today, serious sailors can relive that challenge for the thrill of it all. The St. Lawrence River offers some of the best and hardiest river sailing anywhere in the world, and both cities have well-serviced ports that accommodate sailors of all kinds and abilities. In Montreal, the river is a little less wild, because the city's islands slow down the current; sailing is smoother on Lac St-Louis (where the river widens west of the city) and the Lake of Two Mountains. Visiting sailors can crew up for a day if their home club has a reciprocal arrangement with a port of call near Montreal. In the Quebec City region, downstream past Ile d'Orléans, where the surge of fresh water meets the first hint of salt, sailors can sense the pulse of the distant Atlantic. Although it's 650 miles from the Cabot Strait, the island has recorded tides as high as 19 feet. But never fear: If you've done most of your sailing on summer cottage lakes, the following ports of call and recreation centers will test and hone your skills—all on a safe course. Entries, which are given for Montreal and then for Quebec City, are arranged alphabetically within each area.

CLUB NAUTIQUE and PARC DE RÉCRÉATION DES ILES-DE-BOUCHERVILLE, Montreal

Those without club connections and seeking a low-key sailing experience make tracks for little Lac des Regates (Regatta Lake) on Ile Notre-Dame, where *Club Nautique,* a sailing club, rents sailboats and sailboards, or *Parc de Récréation des Iles-de-Boucherville* (Boucherville Islands Recreation Park), a few miles downstream from Montreal's Vieux Port, just east of the

Lafontaine Bridge and Tunnel. The water sports center on the island is closed from September to mid-June; *Boucherville* is open year-round. Call ahead to check out the sailing schedule. Take Route 25 south to exit 89, Iles de Boucherville. Information: *Club Nautique,* Ile Notre-Dame (phone: 514-872-6093), and *Parc de Récréation des Iles-de-Boucherville*, Ile Ste-Marguerite, Boucherville (phone: 514-873-2843).

ECOLE DE VOILE DE LACHINE, Montreal The best port near the city for serious sailors, the sailing-school marina is a gateway to Lac St-Louis, where the St. Lawrence widens into a lake. Private and group lessons have the approval of the *Quebec Sailing Federation,* and you can rent light sailboats and lasers, as well as windsurfing equipment, by the hour or the day. Closed October to May 15. Take Autoroute 20 west for 9 miles (14 km) to the Lachine exit. Information: *Ecole de Voile de Lachine,* 2105 Blvd. St-Joseph, Lachine (phone: 514-634-4326).

ROYAL ST. LAWRENCE YACHT CLUB, Montreal One of Canada's oldest private nautical clubs, this place has occupied a breezy site on the shores of Lac St-Louis since 1888, when the busy suburb of Dorval was still summer-cottage territory. A 15-minute drive from midtown Montreal, it's a hospitable harbor for visitors with courtesy privileges. Members of any "Royal" club in the world rate automatic entrée, and many other clubs have reciprocal ties with this fine old establishment. Open year-round. Information: *Royal St. Lawrence Yacht Club,* 1350 Chemin Lakeshore, Dorval (phone: 514-631-2720).

BAIE DE BEAUPORT, Quebec City A 10-minute drive from the Vieux Port of Quebec, this sheltered bay opposite the southern tip of Ile d'Orléans is a popular playground for sailors and windsurfers. Here, beginners can take lessons and rent catamarans and storm sails. Bay facilities are closed from mid-October through April. Admission charge. Information: *Baie de Beauport,* access off Blvd. Henri-Bourassa, Quebec City (phone: 418-666-8368).

LAC ST-JOSEPH, Quebec City Sailors who want to work up to the challenge of the Great River are within a half-hour drive of this sizable lake, which has two outdoor recreation centers in the *Station Forestière Duchesnay,* about 30 miles (48 km) northwest of the city. A campsite at Plage Germain offers facilities for sailing, canoeing, and windsurfing. *La Vigie,* a small inn that accommodates 120, rents sailboats, catamarans, and windsurfing equipment by the hour. Follow Autoroute Charest (Rte. 440) west to the intersection with Route 367 north, which leads directly to the forest reception center. The park is open year-round, but call for information about the summer sailing schedule before heading out. Information: *Camping Plage Germain,* 7001 Blvd. Fossambault N. (phone: 418-875-2242), and *La Vigie,* 550 Blvd. Thomas-Maher (phone: 418-875-2727).

PARC NAUTIQUE DU CAP-ROUGE, Quebec City Nautical types can rent sailboats and get professional guidance to the St. Lawrence in this water sports park at the mouth of the Cap-Rouge River. Located upstream from Ste-Foy, the center is near the site where explorer Jacques Cartier made an unsuccessful attempt to establish a colony in 1541. In addition to offering sailing, windsurfing, and other river recreations, the park is the scene of concerts and picnics in the summer. Equipment rental is available, and a landing ramp, a bar, and a terrace café are on grounds. Visiting sailors without their own wheels can make the half-hour voyage from town aboard buses Nos. 14 and 15. Admission charge. Open daily June through *Labour Day;* closed weekdays, May and September. Information: *Parc Nautique du Cap-Rouge,* 4155 Chemin de la Plage Jacques-Cartier (phone: 418-650-7770).

A Shutterbug's View

Photographers have just about everything going for them in photogenic Montreal and Quebec City: 20th-century skylines towering over well-preserved 17th-century birthplaces; river ports alive with dockyard activity; colorful Latin Quarters; and acres of public green space and landscaped gardens. Montreal has its towering peak (Mont-Royal), Quebec City its rugged cliff (Cap Diamant), and the contrast of old and new—the sight of a horse-drawn calèche wheeling nonchalantly through high-rise condo territory in Montreal or riding merrily along near the expanse of the Plaines d'Abraham in Quebec City—makes for a fertile stomping ground for shutterbugs. Even a beginner can achieve remarkable results with a surprisingly basic set of lenses and filters, for equipment is only as valuable as the imagination that puts it into use.

LANDSCAPES, RIVERSCAPES, AND CITYSCAPES Vieux Montréal and Vieux Québec are most often visiting photographers' favorite subjects. But the cities' green spaces and waterways provide numerous photo possibilities as well. In addition to the *Château Frontenac* and Place Royale in Quebec City and Place Jacques-Cartier and the *Basilique Notre-Dame* in Montreal, seek out natural beauty: seabirds while on a boat tour, the flowers and vegetables of the farmers' markets, the towering stands of trees on Mont-Royal, or the squirrels and chipmunks in *Parc des Champs-de-Bataille* (Battlefields Park).

Although a standard 50mm to 55mm lens may work well for some landscapes, most will benefit from a 20mm to 28mm wide-angle. Quebec City's Place Royale, with Cap Diamant and the *Château* looming in the background, is the type of panorama that fits beautifully into a wide-angle format, allowing not only an overview but the opportunity to include people or other points of interest in the foreground. A pedestrian, for instance, may set off a view of *Cathédrale Christ Church;* overhanging branches can provide a sense of perspective in a shot of *Parc du Mont-Royal.*

To isolate specific elements of any scene, use your telephoto lens. Perhaps there's a particular carving in a historic church that would make a lovely shot, or it might be the interplay of light and shadow on a Vieux Montréal street. The successful use of a telephoto means developing your eye for detail.

PEOPLE When photographing people, there are times when a camera is an intrusion. Consider your own reaction under similar circumstances to get an idea of what would make others comfortable enough to be willing subjects. People are often sensitive to having a camera suddenly pointed at them, and a polite request, while netting you a share of refusals, will also provide a chance to shoot some wonderful portraits that capture the spirit of the city as surely as the scenery does. For candids, a zoom telephoto lens in the 70mm to 210mm range is perfect; it allows you to remain unobtrusive while the telephoto lens draws the subject closer. For portraits, a telephoto can be used effectively as close as two or three feet.

For authenticity and variety, select a place likely to yield interesting subjects. Place Jacques-Cartier is an obvious spot for visitors in Montreal, as is the *Citadelle* in Quebec City, but if it's local color you're after, try the *Complexe Desjardins* in Montreal or the St-Charles River in snowy Quebec City; sit at a café on Rue St-Denis or Grande Allée and watch the fashion parade; or walk around the central *places,* where everyone from elderly Québécois to college students to street people flock to enjoy a sunny day. Aim for shots that tell what's different about Quebec City and Montreal.

In portraiture, keep in mind several factors. Morning and afternoon light add richness to skin tones, emphasizing tans. To avoid the harsh facial shadows cast by direct sunlight, shoot in the shade or in an area where the light is diffused.

SUNSETS When shooting sunsets, keep in mind that the brightness will distort meter readings. When composing a shot directly into the sun, frame the picture in the viewfinder so that only half of the sun is included. Read the meter, set, and shoot. Whenever there is this kind of unusual lighting, shoot a few frames in half-step increments, both over and under the meter reading. Bracketing, as this is called, can provide a range of images, the best of which may well be other than the one shot at the meter's recommended setting.

Use any lens for sunsets. A wide-angle is good when the sky is filled with color-streaked clouds, when the sun is partially hidden, or when you're close to an object that silhouettes dramatically against the sky.

Telephotos also produce wonderful silhouettes, either with the sun as a backdrop or against the palette of a brilliant sunset sky. Bracket again here. For the best silhouettes, wait 10 to 15 minutes after sunset. Unless using a very fast film, a tripod is recommended.

Red and orange filters are often used to accentuate a sunset's picture potential. Orange will help turn even a gray sky into something approaching a photogenic finale to the day, and can provide particularly beautiful shots linking the sky with the sun reflected on the ocean. If the sunset is already bold in hue, however, the orange will overwhelm the natural colors. A red filter will produce dramatic, highly unrealistic results.

NIGHT If you think that picture possibilities end at sunset, you're presuming that night photography is the exclusive domain of the professional. If you've got a tripod, all you'll need is a cable release to attach to your camera to assure a steady exposure (which often is timed in minutes rather than fractions of a second).

For evening concerts or nighttime harbor cruises, a strobe does the trick, but beware: Flash units are often used improperly. You can't take a view of the skyline with a flash. It may reach out as far as 30 feet, but that's it. On the other hand, a flash used too close to a subject may result in overexposure, resulting in a "blown out" effect. With most cameras, strobes will work with a maximum shutter speed of 1/125 or 1/250 of a second. If you set the exposure properly and shoot within range, you should come up with pretty sharp results.

CLOSE-UPS Whether of people or of objects such as antique door knockers, close-ups can add another dimension to your photography. There are a number of shooting options, one of which is to use a 70mm or 210mm lens at its closest focusable distance. Unless you're working in bright sunlight, a tripod will be worthwhile. If you are very near your subject and there is a good deal of reflective light, it may pay to underexpose a bit in relation to the meter reading.

If you do not have a telephoto lens, you can still shoot close-ups using a set of magnification filters. Filter packs of one-, two-, and three-time magnification are available, converting your lens into a close-up lens. Even better is a special macro lens designed for close-up photography.

A SHORT PHOTOGRAPHIC TOUR

The following are some of Montreal and Quebec City's truly great pictorial perspectives.

MONTREAL

JARDIN BOTANIQUE With 30 gardens to choose from, it's hard to miss a flowery photo opportunity within this 180-acre *Parc Maisonneuve* preserve. For exotic scenes, focus on the *Jardin Japonais* (Japanese Garden), a beguiling transplant from the Far East, with an iris-banked reflecting pool, a tea house, graceful little bridges, and whimsical rock formations. Move to the *Jardin de Chine* (Chinese Garden) and shoot across the *Dream Lake* and pagoda rooftops to the spaceship roof of the *Stade Olympique* (Olympic Stadium) and its inclining tower. This reproduction of a Ming Dynasty garden is a joy to capture on film, with its flowering trees, brooks, cascades, and such poetically named pagodas as the "Where Purple Clouds Hang in the Sky" pavilion. Schedule your shooting session on a weekday morning or late afternoon, when there won't be too many people around to disturb the serenity.

PLACE D'ARMES No self-respecting photographer leaves Montreal without capturing its founder on film. A dramatic statue of Paul de Chomedey, Sieur de Maisonneuve, stands with drawn sword and flaring banner atop his fountain monument, flanked by historic figures from the early days of the Ville Marie settlement. Approached from almost any angle on Place d'Armes, the statue photographs well. A stirring view of the *Basilique Notre-Dame* can be had from the north side of the square, with the monument in the foreground. From another angle you'll register the full effect of the basilica's neo-Gothic towers.

CITY CENTER Set aside Sunday morning to patrol the midtown blocks between Boulevard René-Lévesque Ouest and Rue Sherbrooke Ouest and from Avenue University to Rue Peel, where the city's towers of power glitter in the sun. One of the most memorable contrasts between old and new Montreal is the sight of *Cathédrale Christ Church*'s 19th-century steeple reflected in the pink glass shimmer of a soaring skyscraper. On a quiet Sunday morning you'll be able to focus on the reflection from the best positions on Avenue University without getting crowded off the sidewalk. A good spot for a wide-angle shot is the corner of University and Rue Ste-Catherine Ouest.

The *Tour* (Tower) *CIBC* (Blvd. René-Lévesque and Rue Peel), with its 45 stories covered in gleaming green slate, is Montreal's most sensational vertical shot. For a close-up, few subjects parallel Henry Moore's *Reclining Figure in Three Pieces* nearby.

VOIE PIÉTONNIÈRE PRINCE-ARTHUR (PRINCE ARTHUR PEDESTRIAN MALL) On fair-weather weekends this is *the* people place. Find a vacant table on a café terrace and focus on the world strolling by. The mall is lined on both sides with small cafés, so feel free to snap away, capturing clowns, street magicians, and fellow tourists on Montreal's most colorful pedestrian strip.

RUE ST-DENIS The home address of the city's largest concentration of bars, restaurants, antiques shops, art galleries, and handicraft studios, this street is a fertile field for capturing the spirit of young French Canada at play. If your visit coincides with the *Festival International de Jazz de Montréal* in June, when part of the street is closed off for open-air performances, you probably won't have enough film to record the action.

QUEBEC CITY

THE SKYLINE The famous urban landscape of the old capital presents photographers with a classic dilemma: How do you get a picture of one of Canada's best-known views without making it look like just another postcard? Try working from the bottom up. For instance, while most people head straight for the waterfront or the deck of the Quebec-Lévis ferry, the most unusual shooting site, and one newcomers often miss, is from Rue St-Paul's antiques row. Here the turrets and towers of the seemingly ubiquitous *Château Frontenac* present themselves in a unique and captivating angle across the colorful rooftops of a row of centuries-old buildings huddled under the cliff.

LOWER TOWN The crowds and the narrow streets where old buildings lean close together in the Place Royal *quartier* just don't cooperate. (Try early morning for a relatively people-free shot.) Close-ups of architectural details and people are easy, however, and there's a fine view up Rue du Petit-Champlain at its junction with Boulevard Champlain. But you'll snap some of your best shots en route between the Upper and Lower Towns. The landings on the *Escalier Casse-Cou* (Break-Neck Staircase) overlook some good views of the town at the foot of the stairs; on top, in *Parc Montmorency,* are some great spots to take overviews.

UPPER TOWN A favorite postcard composition takes in the monument to Champlain, with the city's founder on top and street performers attracting a crowd at the bottom. The horse-drawn calèche queue, waiting at the top of Rue St-Louis near the *Château Frontenac,* is always a distinctive summer subject. Try different angles of the old square area itself, with the graceful Gothic fountain of the *Monument de la Foi* (Recollet Memorial) in the foreground. For café-society studies, move down to the colorful sidewalk terraces on Rue Ste-Anne. Be quick about framing a mood piece of the artists and browsers on little Rue du Trésor before moving on. Here is where a zoom lens will come in handy, because crowds can converge at any time to spoil a shot. Walking the walls of Upper Town will open new perspectives, too, as shutterbugs look down on the spires and domes of Vieux Québec's upper level from the footpath on top of the wall's western section, between *Porte St-Louis* and *Parc d'Artillerie,* as well as of the "new" city beyond the walls.

"NEW" QUEBEC Just beyond the gates, but still the vital core of the city's old defense network, the *Citadelle* sets the stage for some exciting film footage. Time your visit to catch the daily changing of the guard, when the Royal 22nd Regiment—complete with furry busbies and regal red coats—puts on a show at 10 AM, mid-June to *Labour Day.* The *Hôtel du Parlement* (National Assembly) building is photogenic from any angle, an imposing Second Empire presence on Colline Parlementaire (Parliament Hill) since 1886. And don't miss the constant, colorful parade of pedestrians on Grande Allée, where the action goes on from noon to midnight.

Directions

Montreal Directions

Don't let Montreal's size as the number two city in Canada (behind Toronto) fool you; this city is made for walking. Caught between river and mountain, old Ville Marie (the city's original name, bestowed by the founders in honor of the Virgin Mary) has many modern and historic attractions that are within easy strolling distance of the midtown hotel area. So it's easy to walk from one century to another in less than half an hour—about the time it takes to wander downhill from the contemporary crossroads at Rue Ste-Catherine Ouest (West) and Avenue McGill College to the threshold of the 17th century on Place d'Armes.

"Down" is the operative word. You'll climb plenty of hillside streets between the historic *quartier* of Old Montreal and the heights of *Parc du Mont-Royal*—unless you follow resident pedestrians to the underground escalator and elevator services that link the old financial district to the new. The Ville Souterraine (Underground City), separate subterranean commercial areas that Montrealers refer to as if they were all interconnected, and its speedy, efficient *Métro* afford convenient connections to more widely separated walking zones. It's a long hike between the Rue Sherbrooke hotel strip, the *Jardin Botanique* (Botanical Garden), a 180-acre complex of exhibition greenhouses and outdoor gardens, and *Parc Olympique,* the site of the 1976 *Summer Olympic Games*—about 70 city blocks—but the subway ride takes less than 20 minutes.

When you're not following parkland paths or wandering the narrow streets of Vieux Montréal, be sure to keep your wits about you and your eyes on the intersections. Many Montreal drivers enter the traffic fray in a combative mood, girded for the daily battle of wills with fellow motorists, buses, cruising patrol cars, cyclists, calèche drivers, and pedestrians. Jumping traffic lights is a point of honor, and the native habit of cutting corners around slower senior citizens adds a certain zest to the conflict.

Montrealers are also accomplished jaywalkers. Some inner voice urges them into the path of oncoming traffic, against the light, against all reason. Don't even think about plunging into the stream after them. Keep an eye out for cyclists even when navigating an intersection *with* the light; rules of the road don't mean much to them, either. But *pas de problème.* Once you understand the system, walking in downtown Montreal can be safe and satisfying. Just keep your head up—and *bonne chance!*

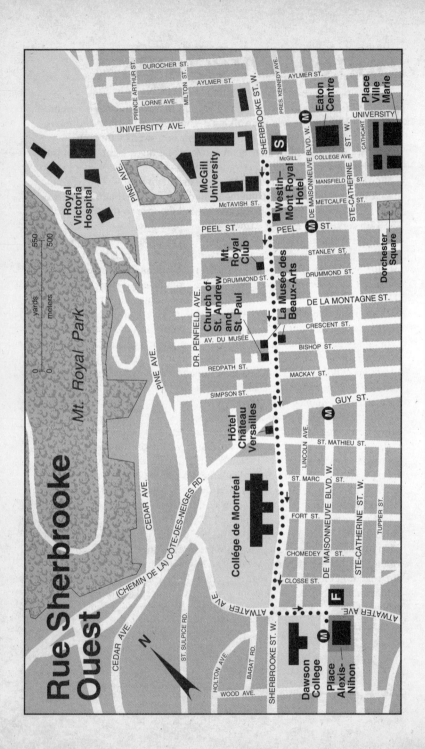

Walk 1:
Rue Sherbrooke Ouest
(Sherbrooke Street West)

Back in the glory days when Montreal's merchant princes and financial power brokers controlled two-thirds of Canada's wealth, midtown Rue Sherbrooke ranked as the city's most prestigious residential neighborhood. Lined with baronial Victorian and Edwardian mansions, it was the elm-shaded main drag of the Square Mile, a precinct of privilege and influence on the southwest slopes of Mont-Royal that stretched north from Boulevard René-Lévesque (then Boulevard Dorchester) to Avenue Pine, with Rue Guy and Chemin de la Côte-des-Neiges marking its western border, and the campus of *Université McGill* to the east.

Within this tightly controlled enclave, descendants of the North West Company's Scottish and English fur traders and the frontier entrepreneurs who flocked into Montreal after the British conquest of 1759–60 reigned supreme over the city's—indeed Canada's—social, economic, and political scene. Their forebears, primarily canny Scots from the threadbare Highlands, had pretty well cornered the market in British North America by the early 19th century, founding banks, industrial empires, and shipping lines and amassing fortunes in an age when land was cheap and income taxes an unconscionable affront.

Early Square Milers, like Nor' Wester Simon McTavish and his fur-trading contemporaries James McGill and William McGillivray, staked out lordly estates on the mountainside and along the western stretches of a country road that became Boulevard Dorchester. But their woodland domains shrank as the old walled city by the river burst its bounds, and "uptown" real estate values soared. Wealthy newcomers from town soon enhanced the fast-growing suburb with Victorian versions of Renaissance châteaux and medieval castles, surrounded by acres of lawns, orchards, and landscaped gardens. Despite the influx of French gentry who began to move up the western slope of the mountain and join in business and marriage with the self-made Scots, English, and Irish, the Square Mile flourished as a proud outpost of Britain's empire.

At the height of their exuberant heyday, from the 1840s until the 1880s, those residing in the Square Mile (a term later upgraded to Golden Square Mile by over enthusiastic travel writers) enjoyed a winter social season that reminded international visitors of czarist St. Petersburg. Montreal's close-knit aristocracy claimed knighthoods and baronies, hosted royalty, and imported their butlers and hunting pinks from London, their governesses and gowns from Paris. Their ballrooms, bloodstock stables, and vintage wine cellars lived up to the highest British standards. The mile-long stretch of Montreal's longest street, patriotically named for Governor-General Sir John Sherbrooke, was the ultimate carriage trade route to social and financial standing in Canada.

As the 1920s roared in, a new generation of first families abandoned the cumbersome Gothic fortresses their grandfathers had built to last forever in favor of a more contemporary lifestyle, unhampered by the armies of servants required to maintain a 50-room family seat. In 1925, the razing of *Rokeby*, the intimidating limestone stronghold of Andrew Frederick Gault, Canada's "Cotton King," to make way for an apartment block marked the beginning of the end of Rue Sherbrooke as an avenue of stately homes. But it was the stock market collapse of 1929 that hastened the decline of the Square Mile. One by one the Tuscan villas, Tudor manors, and Second Empire châteaux crumbled under the wrecker's ball. In time they would give way to hotels, apartment complexes, and office towers that changed the street's residential character forever. Tall terrace houses turned into high-fashion boutiques and art galleries. Finally, the last of the great family-occupied mansions, the 52-room, century-old bailiwick of *Canadian Pacific Railway* czar Sir William Van Horne, was demolished in 1973—gold-leaf wallpaper, Art Nouveau fireplaces, and all.

Today, only a few ghosts of the Square Mile's Belle Epoque cling to their Rue Sherbrooke roots. But while the empire builders and the merchant princes have departed along with the triumphal arch of elms, Sir John's namesake avenue is still gentry row, its period-piece lamp standards reminiscent of Europe's gaslight era, its sidewalk planters blooming with summer flowers. This is still Montreal's most elegant strolling strip.

A long walk through yesterday and today takes about 90 minutes, not counting stops for browsing and snacking. It begins at the *Portail Roddick* (Roddick Gates) to the *Université McGill* campus (see *Walk 5: Université McGill/Rue Prince-Arthur*), where Avenue McGill College meets Rue Sherbrooke Ouest. (*Métro* passengers should disembark at the *McGill* station and take the *McGill College* exit.)

Today's campus was the home of the original Montrealers, residents of the pallisaded Iroquois village of Hochelaga, who encountered their first foreign visitors in 1535, when Jacques Cartier and his crew dropped anchor. Before turning west to see the *Stele Hochelaga*, a small plaque commemorating that meeting, through the fence on the north side of Sherbrooke, look back down the length of city blocks that links *Place Ville-Marie* to the campus—this is a vista of downtown Montreal at its most dramatic. This mini–Champs-Elysées, with its flowery boulevard and ranks of soaring glass towers, still stops Montrealers in their tracks—especially when they recall what Avenue McGill College was as recently as the early 1980s: a common strip of retail shops, undistinguished restaurants, and lackluster bookshops.

Cross Sherbrooke at Avenue McGill College to the south side and proceed west to the *International Civil Aviation Organization (ICAO),* established in 1976 at No. 1000, the site of Sir George Drummond's turreted brownstone mansion. The only United Nations organization with headquarters in Montreal, the *ICAO* promotes the orderly development of civil aviation and sets international standards for air safety. *McGill's Bibliothèque McLennan-Redpath* (McLennan-Redpath Library) faces Place de l'Aviation Internationale (International Aviation Square) from the north side of Sherbrooke (enter the library at 3495 McTavish; phone: 514-398-4698).

The flamboyant rose granite *Tour Scotia,* the Bank of Nova Scotia's controversial contribution to Montreal's carriage-trade route, is located at the southeast corner of Rues Sherbrooke and Metcalfe. Pause for a moment here and look up to the mountain. To the north, Rue McTavish (Metcalfe changes names north of Sherbrooke) opens onto the much-photographed view of Mont-Royal and its *Eiffel*-esque cross, and the *Institute Allan* (Allan Memorial Institute), the psychiatric center of the *Hôpital Royal Victoria* (Royal Victoria Hospital). Once the stateliest of the Square Mile homes, the *Allan* started life as *Ravenscrag,* a lofty limestone perch carved into the mountainside above Pine Avenue in the 1860s by transatlantic shipping magnate Sir Hugh Allan. Newspaper accounts of the day claimed Sir Hugh's castle excelled "in size and cost any dwelling house in Canada."

Back on space-age Rue Sherbrooke, the *Westin–Mont Royal* hotel (see "Checking In" in *Montreal,* THE CITIES) dominates the block between Rues Metcalfe and Peel. The hotel—formerly the *Four Seasons*—is popular with visiting stars of stage, film, and videos. Its *Le Circle* restaurant is a pleasant lunchtime retreat for strollers who start their walk around midday. Across the traffic stream at the northeast corner of this busy intersection is *Le Shangrila* (see "Checking In" in *Montreal,* THE CITIES).

Across Peel at 1115 Sherbrooke, *Le Cartier* complex, with its posh apartments, offices, and boutiques-filled mall, towers over the northwest corner. Some of Montreal's most fashionable heads are groomed here by the trend-setting hair stylists at *La Coupe* (phone: 514-288-6131). *Le Cantlie,* an upscale apartment-hotel (1110 Sherbrooke), shares the south side of the block between Peel and Stanley with *Tour Central Guaranty*'s corporate space and *Paradis Maternité* (also at No. 1110; phone: 514-845-4350), a chic specialty store for shoppers with great expectations. Across the street, the head office of Air Liquide (No. 1155) now occupies the site of the former *Maison Van Horne* at the corner of Stanley.

Continue along Sherbrooke to its southwest juncture with Stanley to one of the city's most imaginative urban renewal projects, *Maison Alcan* (main entrance at 1188 Sherbrooke). What other developers knocked down on millionaires' mile, Alcan Aluminum conserved in its world headquarters, opened in 1983. The *Maison's* conservation includes the century-old cut-stone townhouse of the late Lord Atholstan, founder of the *Montreal Star,* the city's largest English-language daily newspaper until its demise in

1979. Alcan incorporated the press lord's corner property and some of its Rue Sherbrooke neighbors into a stunning complex that features a skylit atrium, hung with brilliant banners and decorated with modern tapestries, sculptures, and works of art. The main entrance leads through the triple archway of the abandoned *Berkeley* hotel's Art Deco façade into a light-filled interior plaza where free noontime concerts are staged twice a month from March through December (check for notices in the window for details). From concert-stage level, music lovers can see how the shell of the *Berkeley*'s gracious old lobby and the rear walls of Lord Atholstan's neighbors were used to enclose the lower levels of the eight-story atrium.

Le Pavillon de l'Atlantique restaurant opens off the atrium. *Alcan*'s Rue Stanley entrance (No. 2100) leads to *La Tulipe Noire,* a Parisian-style café and pastry shop, and to *Moby Dick's,* a hip, wood-paneled bar that's a popular after-work watering hole for uptown singles and a restful spot to enjoy lunch with a garden view. (For details on all three restaurants, see "Eating Out" in *Montreal,* THE CITIES.) Rear entrances to *Giorgeo of Montreal*'s haberdashery (phone: 514-287-1928) and the *Giorgeo Donna Boutique* (phone: 514-287-1570) at 1176 Sherbrooke open off the atrium. So does a door to the *Walter Klinkhoff Gallery* (1200 Sherbrooke; phone: 514-288-7806), a long-established showcase for Canadian artists. *Alcan* (phone: 514-848-8487) offers guided tours of its headquarters on request.

Opposite *Maison Alcan,* a trio of Square Mile monuments takes up the north side of the block between Rues Stanley and Drummond. The *Club de Mount Royal* (1175 Sherbrooke) was founded in 1899 by refugees from the *St. James's Club,* who decided their old clubhouse on Boulevard Dorchester (now Boulevard René-Lévesque) was getting too crowded. They moved into the home of former Prime Minister Sir John Abbot (1891–92) and flourished there until 1904, when the mansion went up in smoke. The present structure was raised on the same site. The work of American architect Stanford White, it offers a cool, uncluttered contrast to the overwrought Second Empire home of the *United Services Club (USC)* next door, at No. 1195. The *USC* has occupied the imposing gray stone building since 1927; its previous occupant was the former Senator Louis-Joseph Forget, the onetime President of the *Montreal Stock Exchange* and founder of the most powerful brokerage house in Canada.

On the club's western flank is *Maison Corby* (No. 1201), an 1882 relic that fell on hard times. Degraded to rooming-house depths during the Second World War, it regained its stately status in 1952, when Corby's Distilleries reclaimed the red sandstone centenarian and its coach house for executive office space.

If you're here during the summer, rally round to the *Ritz-Carlton Kempinski* (see "Checking In" in *Montreal,* THE CITIES) for tea in the hotel's duck pond garden, one of Montreal's most enchanting fair-weather interludes. The faithful have always considered the landmark hotel the *only* place to stay in town.

Once beyond the *Ritz* entrance, you're in high-fashion territory, with *Polo Ralph Lauren* (No. 1290, next door to the *Ritz*; phone: 514-288-3988) and *Holt Renfrew* (1300 Rue Sherbrooke O.; phone: 514-842-5111), the prestigious emporium for designer furs and imported couture collections.

Across Sherbrooke, the *Château Apartments* (No. 1321), with their towers and turrets, gargoyles, and courtyard arches, maintain a high feudal profile next door to the stolid, stone, more-than-century-old *Erskine and American United Church.* The three-section luxury apartment compound didn't make the Sherbrooke scene until 1925, when its battlements rose over the site of vanquished *Rokeby.* The row of tall, gray townhouses on the opposite side of the block, between Rues de la Montagne and Crescent, are older, but their upstairs/downstairs boutiques are stocked with the styles of the 1990s. The *Lippel Gallery* (No. 1324; phone: 514-842-6369) is Montreal's foremost showcase for pre-Columbian art.

West of Crescent, the *Musée des Beaux-Arts de Montréal* (Montreal Museum of Fine Arts) dominates both sides of Sherbrooke. The classic Vermont marble home of the "old" fine-arts museum (1379 Sherbrooke, on the west corner of Av. du Musée) dates from 1912, when the oldest established museum in Canada moved west from Square Phillips. Across the street and linked to the older building by an underground tunnel is Moshe Safdie's striking addition. The gleaming white companion piece to the Greek temple across the street adjoins a neo-Renaissance apartment block that the museum restored to accommodate its archives, library, and offices. The *Beaux-Arts* boasts several important collections of Canadian and international paintings and sculpture. The museum is closed Mondays; admission charge (phone: 514-285-1600).

While in the neighborhood, visit the historic *Eglise Saint Andrew and Saint Paul* (3415 Rue Redpath; enter on Sherbrooke; phone: 514-842-3431), the Presbyterian regimental church of the Black Watch (Royal Highland Regiment) of Canada. Tapestries by Sir Edward Burne-Jones decorate the chapel, and Louis Comfort Tiffany created the stained glass windows.

Don't look for any traces of Calvinism on Sherbrooke's worldly little rialto across the street. The stretch of big spenders' shopping blocks between Rues Crescent and Guy is a sophisticated, exclusive enclave of designer boutiques, art galleries, and antiques shops, great for browsing if not for buying. At Number 1438, a Rodin casting of *Jean d'Aire, Bourgeois de Calais* stares grimly past the window shoppers from his pavement stand outside the *Dominion Gallery,* an unlikely medieval figure in the company of Henry Moore's *Upright Motive.* The gallery (phone: 514-845-7474) takes credit for having introduced Moore to Canadian collectors. *Les Créateurs* (No. 1440; phone: 514-284-2101) is a salon outlet for such high-profile prêt-à-porter designers as Claude Montana.

Shopped-out strollers can take a break here and turn into the *Passage du Musée,* a mini-mall of shops and services, for a pick-me-up at *Café Il Cortile* (1442 Sherbrooke; phone 514-843-8230) before moving on toward

Rue Guy. En route, stop by *Pratesi* (No. 1448; phone: 514-285-8909), if only to admire the window display of this boudoir of pricey designer linens and bath accessories. *Davidoff* (No. 1452; phone: 514-289-9118) is the haunt of smokers in search of imported tobacco products, pipes, lighters, and other expensive necessities. *Les Gamineries* (No. 1458; phone: 514-843-4614) caters to style-conscious children with well-heeled parents, while *Brisson et Brisson* (No. 1472; phone: 514-937-7456) dresses style-conscious men.

On the north side of Sherbrooke, the *Galerie de l'Isle* (No. 1451; phone: 514-935-9885) shares its address with the handsome white *Port Royal* complex of offices and apartments. Back on the south side, the *Galerie Claude Lafitte* (No. 1480; phone: 514-939-9898) showcases Canadian, especially Québécois, art. *Le Petit Musée* (No. 1494; phone: 514-937-6161) is an Aladdin's cave of rare collectibles that has served generations of local antiques browsers. *Cartier* (No. 1498; phone: 514-939-0000) is a sumptuous little green marble *bijouterie* of costly gems and signature handbags.

Facing shoppers' row across Sherbrooke is the *Linton* (No. 1509), the grande dame of Square Mile apartment houses. *Maison Mountain View,* a separate building constructed by James Linton—the Victorian-era owner of the property—still stands behind the Beaux Arts apartment landmark on the west corner of hillside Rue Simpson. For a view of *Maison Mountain View* (which, alas, hasn't much of a view of anything now), detour around the corner of Simpson, where the forlorn ghost of this 1862 edifice waits for some form of restoration. Used over the years as casual apartment and office space, it once ranked among the loveliest properties on Sherbrooke.

Continuing west on the north side to the traffic-clogged intersection where Rue Guy becomes Chemin de la Côte-des-Neiges, you'll see at the northwest corner of Sherbrooke the last of the Square Mile's Romanesque houses raised on the neighborhood's western limits. Built in 1891 for the son of one of Montreal's biggest property owners, it came down in the world to trade and commerce after Robert Stanley Bagg died in 1911.

The Rue Guy–Côte-des-Neiges intersection marks the official western boundary of the Square Mile, but Sherbrooke follows a graceful course west under its distinctive, Parisian-style lampposts. The *Château Versailles* hotel (see "Checking In" in *Montreal,* THE CITIES), the city's best-publicized "European" property, occupies four ample, gray stone townhouses built by venturesome developers between 1911 and 1913 outside the Square Mile on the north side of the street.

The charming hotel puts up its overflow clientele in the *Tour Versailles* (see "Checking In" in *Montreal,* THE CITIES), its more contemporary property across the street. Both are close neighbors to one of the city's oldest historic landmarks: the *Grand Séminaire de Montréal.* Five years after moving into their newly built Ville Marie seminary in 1685 (see *Walk 2: Vieux Montréal*), the missionaries of St-Sulpice opened a mission about 2 miles northwest of the walled town. By 1694 the outpost was securely enclosed within fortified walls, with four stone Martello towers defending a community of native villagers, a farm, a school, and the *Château des Messieurs,* a large limestone structure on the north side of today's Rue Sherbrooke. Two of the towers were razed in the 1850s to make room for an imposing entrance to the *Grand Séminaire de Montréal,* a college for the sons of Montreal's French-speaking élite. But two towers remain on their original site, facing Rue Fort, still guarding the walled seminary (now the faculty of theology of the *Université de Montréal*), the *Collège de Montréal* at 1931 Sherbrooke, and what's left of the Sulpicians' vast seigneurial estates. Marguerite Bourgeoys, Canada's first saint, held classes in both towers. A sad little urban myth connects with one of the dank stone classrooms where she taught native girls hymns, prayers, and useful needlework. According to local legend, in the first tower on the west is the tomb of a young indigenous convert who lived within the Sulpician fortress from early childhood. Dying shortly after taking the veil, the little nun was buried in the tower, far from the forest freedom she craved all her short life.

On the northeast corner of Avenue Atwater, one of the "Priests' Farm" properties, as the vast Sulpician domain is called, has been adapted to the condominium era, its stern granite walls merged with an airy, hillside high-rise on the slopes of Atwater. Cross Atwater here to its southwest corner and stroll past the elm-shaded campus of *Collège Dawson* (3040 Rue Sherbrooke O.), where Quebec's largest junior college for English-speaking students got its start in the former *Maison Mère des Soeurs de la Congrégation de Notre-Dame* (Mother House of the Sisters of the Congregation of Notre Dame). Classified now as a historic site, the *Maison Mère* was the order's headquarters, retirement home, and hospital, as well as a private school for girls, until the collegian contingent took over the huge Beaux Arts building and its beautiful grounds in 1988.

The eastern boundary of the *Dawson College* campus follows Atwater south to Boulevard de Maisonneuve; if weary strollers take the same route, they'll arrive at *Place Alexis-Nihon,* the *Atwater Métro* station—and a speedy trip back to midtown Montreal on line No. 1.

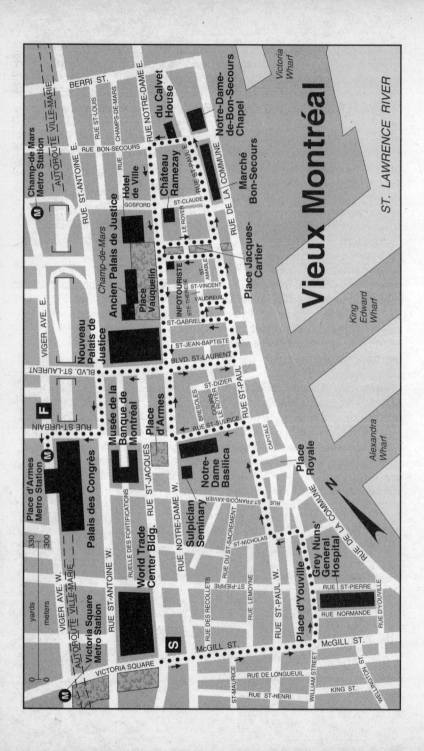

Walk 2: Vieux Montréal

Exploring the birthplace of Canada's second-largest city can add up to an hour or a lifetime. In fact, some resident historians have made Vieux Montréal a lifelong career, charting the latest restoration projects in the once-neglected waterfront neighborhood. Self-appointed watchdogs of their hometown's deepest roots, they distrust a 20th-century approach to 17th-century territory. A missing wall plaque, an archaeological dig, a builder's crane still inspire a spate of concerned letters to the editor from Vieux Montréal's undeclared sidewalk superintendents.

Visitors should set aside at least three hours to visit the area's dominant landmarks and museums and relax over lunch or dinner in one of the fine restaurants or terrace cafés of the protected historic preserve.

Take the *Henri-Bourassa* (No. 2) *Métro* line to *Square Victoria* station, leaving via the square's southern exit at the corner of Rues McGill and St-Jacques Ouest. Follow McGill south toward the waterfront to trace the course of the stone wall that once guarded the city's western approaches from the Iroquois, the English, and the American colonists (not at the same time).

Look back now to the *Centre du Commerce Mondial* (World Trade Center), on the east side of McGill between Rues St-Jacques and St-Antoine. The center straddles Ruelle des Fortifications (Fortifications Lane), where, in 1716, urban planners began construction of the town's northern ramparts. Within 20 years they'd enclosed some 95 acres of the continent's fur-trading capital with an 18-foot-high fortification that commanded the waterfront from McGill to a point just east of present-day Rue Berri. The walls and their gates were leveled less than a century later, when the port city outgrew its defense system.

Where the southwest corner of the wall once stood, the *Ancien Edifice du Grand Tronc* (Old Grand Trunk Building; 360 Rue McGill) faces Place d'Youville. Turn east here; one block farther is a broad, brick-paved pedestrian island, surrounded by historic buildings. Pass them by for the moment, proceeding to the granite obelisk at the eastern point of the wedge-shape plaza. Bronze plaques at the obelisk's base commemorate the arrival of Montreal's first settlers; on May 18, 1642, some three dozen pioneers and their leader, Paul de Chomedy, Sieur de Maisonneuve, took their first hopeful steps into a primeval wilderness. Caught up in the religious revival that blazed through 17th-century France, the landing party's leading lights had come to found a mission and spread the gospel among Canada's first citizens. Protégés of wealthy sponsors of the *Société de Notre-Dame* in Paris, they'd spent a sheltered winter in the Quebec settlement before sailing upstream with de Maisonneuve, a career soldier the society had hired to direct them in what was to be a "glorious enterprise." Few had any conception of the sacrifice that lay ahead.

Try to imagine that springtime landing at the riverbank site Samuel de Champlain had explored and approved three decades earlier. At Pointe-à-Callière, the grassy meadow where the devout little mission band knelt in the firefly light to celebrate its first mass of thanksgiving, stands the *Musée d'Archéologie et d'Histoire* (Museum of Archaeology and History), where visitors can look down into the archaeological digs that recount the centuries. Historians believe they've discovered the site of the stockade the founders erected around their vulnerable mission outpost before the first ghastly winter set in. The museum covers the site of the small fort that de Maisonneuve garrisoned near the meeting of the Little St-Pierre and St. Lawrence Rivers, centuries before landfill and harbor construction pushed the waterfront far beyond the lush, green common where the colonists' cattle once grazed. The museum is closed Mondays; admission charge (phone: 514-872-9150). The paved stretches of Rue de la Commune were a village green in the 17th century; today, parklands of the Vieux Port restoration cover the riverbank with bike paths and decorative planting.

Before leaving the cradle of Vieux Montréal, stroll around one of the city's early market squares, opened in the 19th century over the dried-up riverbed of the Little St-Pierre. At 335 Place d'Youville, the *Centre d'Histoire* (History Center; phone: 514-872-3207) occupies a nearly-century-old fire station (see "Special Places" in *Montreal,* THE CITIES). On the square's south side, the weathered stone walls of the *Hôpital Général des Soeurs Grises* (Grey Nuns' General Hospital; 138 Rue St-Pierre; phone: 514-842-9411, guided tours) still dominate the block between Rues St-Pierre and Normand. One of the original wings of the 1694 refuge for the ailing, elderly, and orphaned has been restored (Mother Marie-Marguerite d'Youville, founder of the Congrégation des Soeurs de la Charité—Grey Nuns—and North America's first home for abandoned children, died in this wing in 1771). Still on the south side of the square (296-316 Pl. d'Youville) are the old warehouses of the *Ecuries d'Youville* (Youville Stables). Parts of the complex, which dates from the 1700s, surround a tranquil garden courtyard. The erstwhile storage depot for 19th-century grain merchants and soap manufacturers is one of the historic quarter's most attractive restorations, with office space and artisans' studios sharing a picturesque location with *Gibby's,* a popular steakhouse (see "Eating Out" in *Montreal,* THE CITIES).

From Place d'Youville, follow Rue St-Nicolas uphill to Rue St-Paul and turn east. Before it had a name or a street sign, St-Paul was a narrow path through the woods linking the fort to Montreal's first hospital. It was a dangerous route to follow once Iroquois scouts discovered the new settlement. Mortal enemies of the Algonquian and Huron—whom the French had befriended—the Iroquois were ill disposed to the settlers' expansion of their river colony, and for the next 50 years villagers and their forest-dwelling allies lived in a virtual state of war with the Iroquois. Happily, this thoroughfare is a safer path today.

Some walkers interrupt their rovings at this point for coffee at *Le Pot aux Roses Café* (No. 184; phone: 514-282-1509). If you don't crave caffeine, continue east along the settlers' Main Street to Place Royale. Within three years of their 1642 arrival, the mission's first families were settling into new housing here, at their first public square. Place Royale was where de Maisonneuve drilled his defense forces and punished the colony's law-breakers. Appropriately, the parade ground was called Place d'Armes; later it served as a public market and fur-trading center, with the requisite gallows and pillory, a town crier's corner, a fountain—and plenty of dueling space for the hotheaded. The neoclassical *Vieille Douane* (Old Customs House) in the center of the square, dating from 1837, marks the rough midpoint of Montreal's long history.

Nearly two centuries earlier, de Maisonneuve's home faced the square from the north side of his namesake street. Nothing remains of the founder's household today, but if you turn into the open courtyard at 147 St-Paul you'll see a wall plaque marking the spot.

A few yards to the east, another wall plaque marks the birthplace of Charles Le Moyne, eldest of a remarkable brood of 11 brothers and three sisters sired by a Dieppe innkeeper who emigrated to Ville Marie during the early de Maisonneuve regime. A linguist who soon learned the Iroquois dialect, Le Moyne served as the colony's interpreter in its rare cease-fires with the enemy; eventually, he found his place among the frontier town's leading citizens, first as Baron of Longueuil and later as Governor of Montreal. The Le Moyne household covered an area bordered by today's Rues St-Paul and St-Sulpice, in the northwest corner. A family compound, Le Moyne *père*'s property extended north on St-Sulpice, where a wall plaque honors Montreal's first Canadian-born hero. Charles's brother Pierre Le Moyne d'Iberville (1661–1706), was a leading figure in the Anglo-French power struggle for New World supremacy. Admiral of the Sun King's fleet, he won the decisive naval confrontation with the British in the Battle at Hudson Bay. He then went on to found Biloxi, Mississippi, and Mobile, Alabama, and add all Louisiana to the North American empire of French King Louis XIV. His younger brother, Jean-Baptiste Le Moyne de Bienville, founded New Orleans and was three times Governor of Louisiana.

Jeanne Mance was a hero who marched to a different drummer. One of the original founding group, she opened Ville Marie's first hospital at the northeast corner of St-Paul and St-Sulpice two years after the Pointe-à-Callière landing. North America's first secular nurse, Mance kept a small farm here to support her fortified compound of hospital wards and chapel, commuting daily from the fort when the Iroquois threat was at its worst. Her *Hôtel Dieu* stockade once enclosed part of what is now the stylish *Cours Le Royer* condo development, which strollers can admire today as they climb up St-Sulpice to Place d'Armes. Double rows of massive stone warehouses that once belonged to *Hôtel Dieu*'s Soeurs Hospitalières de St-Joseph now house offices, shops, and condominiums. They line both sides of a long pedestrian courtyard where fountains play in geranium garden plots and old-fashioned lamp standards light a brick-paved promenade.

St-Sulpice follows the east walls of the *Chapelle du Sacré-Coeur* and *Basilique Notre-Dame* (see "Special Places" in *Montreal,* THE CITIES) to Place d'Armes and the oldest building in Montreal. Next door to the basilica (a relative newcomer to the *place*), the venerable *Vieux Séminaire St-Sulpice* (Old Sulpician Seminary) still stands on the plot the gentlemen of St-Sulpice staked out for it in 1685. The Sulpicians were the first parish priests; by the time they built their administrative center, however, they'd acquired full seigneurial rights over the entire island of Montreal, giving them the power to administer the courts and appoint governors.

The west section of the seminary (130 Rue Notre-Dame O.) has been standing, unchanged, behind its rough fieldstone walls for 310 years. The clock over the façade is the oldest public timepiece in North America. Rue Notre-Dame, the first street the Sulpicians laid out, forms the south side of Place d'Armes, the flower-banked stage for Montreal's famous memorial to de Maisonneuve and his fellow colonists. The founder's bold soldierly figure tops the fountain monument, drawn sword in one hand, the banner of France in the other, marking a near-fatal encounter with the Iroquois when Place d'Armes was still a forest clearing. Forewarned of an attack, de Maisonneuve led his outnumbered garrison out beyond the palisades to confront a force of 200 foes. Legend has it that de Maisonneuve covered a successful retreat with pistols blazing in both hands. He suffered a serious wound before the Iroquois chief fell under fire and the warriors fled.

Statues at the base of the monument represent Jeanne Mance tending an indigenous child; Charles Le Moyne; Major Lambert Closse, commanding officer of Ville Marie's militia; a subdued Iroquois brave; and Pilote, the mission's one-dog early-warning system. As resident historians will tell you, Pilote and her uncanny knack of sensing approaching danger saved the day for embattled Ville Marie on more than one occasion.

Follow Rue Notre-Dame east to the corner of Boulevard St-Laurent (or St. Lawrence), the division between old west end Ville Marie and "new" 18th- and 19th-century Montreal. Walk down St-Laurent toward the river and the boulevard entrance to *Cours Le Royer.* Just inside the court on the north wall, a window display shows the plan of the original *Hôtel Dieu.* Continue down St-Laurent to its intersection with St-Paul and a shopping spree along the north side of Montreal's first commercial street.

Near the corner of Rue St-Jean-Baptiste, *Sonja Rémy*'s little boutique (1-A Rue St-Paul E.; phone: 514-393-9023) vibrates with the latest fashion trends. On the east corner, *Chez Brandy* (25 St-Paul; phone: 514-871-9178) moves to a different beat after dark, when its regular barhopping clientele shows up. At midday it's a reasonably priced lunch stop. Next door, at the same address, *The Keg* (phone: 514-871-9093) caters to steak and seafood enthusiasts after 5 PM and to party animals late into the night.

At the corner of Rue St-Gabriel, *Restaurant du Vieux Port* (39 Rue St-Paul E.; phone: 514-866-3175) features a lunch and dinner *brochetterie* menu at modest *table d'hôte* prices. If you have something more festive in mind, turn north on St-Gabriel to the *Auberge le Vieux St-Gabriel,* at No. 426. The *Auberge* has been on this spot since 1754, keeping fresh its claim as the oldest continuously operated inn in North America. A sprawling conglomerate of cavernous, stone-walled dining rooms in the old Québécois style, it also boasts intimate café corners and a historic beer-and-sausage snack bar, all combined under one oak-beamed roof (see "Eating Out" in *Montreal,* THE CITIES).

You're in the heart of 18th-century fur-trading territory now. The inn's cellar bar and its access tunnel were storage vaults for beaver pelts and other products of the trap. Across St-Gabriel on the east side, Rue Ste-Thérèse leads to a rakish-looking condo dwelling at the corner of Rue Vaudreuil. Built in 1759, this was the warehouse trader John Jacob Astor operated when he was building the power base for one of America's wealthiest families.

Rue Vaudreuil leads back to St-Paul and the birthplace of Canadian banking: The Bank of Montreal was founded in 1817 at 32 St-Paul, at the corner of Vaudreuil. A wall plaque marks the site of the bank's first office, where Canada's first currency was issued. Head east to the corner of Rue St-Vincent and then north to *Maison Beaudoin* (427 St-Vincent), one of Vieux Montréal's oldest examples of domestic architecture. The historic monument was built in 1690 while Louis XIV still ruled New France, reconstructed in 1750, and restored in 1972. Today, it's the home of *Le Père St-Vincent* restaurant (see "Eating Out" in *Montreal,* THE CITIES).

Genial hosts at the *Hôtel Richelieu* used to refresh their guests with noggins of punch and ale in the ornamental gallery of their 1861 hostelry. It's now home to *Claude Postel,* whose genial host serves a distinctive brand of Canadian cuisine (for details, see "Eating Out" in *Montreal,* THE CITIES).

Backtrack to the north side of Rue St-Paul to the western frontier of Place Jacques-Cartier, the thoroughly quaint Old World town square travelers expect to see when they visit Vieux Montréal (see *Quintessential Montreal and Quebec City* in DIVERSIONS). Coming upon this broad hillside plaza from the crowded confines of Rue St-Paul is like walking onto a stage set for a historic film. Only the cast of characters, in seemingly anachronistic 20th-century costume, seems out of place on Montreal's 19th-century market square. Still, the *place* itself lives up to every expectation, suitably bricked with ankle-wrenching paving stones, its center mall bright with flowers, its terrace cafés shaded by colorful awnings and umbrellas.

Turn to the river to find the calèche queue waiting for weary explorers who decide to finish their tour under horsepower. Beyond the horse-and-carriage line at the south end of the long, rectangular *place,* Vieux Port's promenades and small parks open on breezy views of the St. Lawrence, the *EXPO '67* islands, and the south shore skyline. Turn to the plaza's northern limit to see Admiral Horatio Nelson in an uncharacteristic pose. Back turned to the waterfront, he gazes inland across Rue Notre-Dame from the top of his 1809 column. In summer a flower market blooms around the base of this, Montreal's oldest remaining monument.

There's a wide choice of restaurant options on either side of the *place*. Walk north from St-Paul up the west side to the house Pierre del Vecchio built in 1807 at 404 Place Jacques-Cartier. In family hands until 1946, the handsome old home now houses *La Marée,* an expensive seafood restaurant that many local connoisseurs consider the best in Montreal (see "Eating Out" in *Montreal,* THE CITIES). Next door is the *Maison Benjamin-Viger,* built in 1772. A radical lawyer and publisher, Viger was jailed for 18 months for his part in the rebellion of 1837, under Louis Joseph Papineau (see below). The home of the former rebel now harbors *Le St-Amable,* a lamp-lit French dining establishment with stone walls and plenty of atmosphere (see "Eating Out" in *Montreal,* THE CITIES). Wandering down quaint lane-width Rue St-Amable to find the front door of its namesake restaurant, you'll pass a street gallery of artists and craftspeople displaying their wares.

At the corner of Rue Notre-Dame, *INFOTOURISTE* (No. 174), Montreal's tourist information center, occupies the house built in 1811 by master mason Nicolas Morin. At its most notorious, the *Maison Morin* once was the home of the *Silver Dollar Saloon,* where patrons could boast they "walked on a fortune" when they bellied up to the bar: The floor was inlaid with 350 US silver dollars.

Cross to the east side of Place Jacques-Cartier for a corner view of the *Hôtel de Ville* (City Hall), a majestic Second Empire fixture at 275 Notre-Dame East dating from 1878. Only the exterior walls of the original building were salvaged from the ashes of a 1922 fire, and much of its early elegance has been diminished by additions and alterations.

Meander down the east side of the *place* to No. 421 and the old *Nelson* hotel, once the folksy rendezvous for farmers who set up their wagons and stalls when the area was a working marketplace. The last stalls disappeared in the 1960s; after many attempts to revive the hotel—which was completed in 1866—its facilities have disappeared as well (the building is now a government-owned property). But here, tucked away in one of Vieux Montréal's secret gardens, is a delightful outdoor restaurant, the *Terrasse Nelson* (phone: 861-5731). A wrought-iron archway opens off the street, and in summer the courtyard becomes a cool oasis under the trees, where reasonably priced meals are served to the sounds of live chamber music. Crêpes, salads, and sandwiches are specialties.

On a lazy summer afternoon, it's a temptation to linger in the shade of the *Terrasse Nelson,* but those caught in the spirit of Vieux Montréal will find that treasures await: Most of the best restorations in Montreal line both sides of Rue St-Paul's last few blocks. Turn toward the river again to head for St-Paul, past the corner house (No. 401) that Amable Amyot added to the Place Jacques-Cartier scene in 1812. On the north side of the block

(281 St-Paul E.), facing little Rue du Marché-Bon-Secours, is a sturdy survivor of Victorian Montreal's tourist boom. Back then, *Rasco's* hotel was one of North America's finest. Among its more celebrated guests was Charles Dickens, who lodged here in splendid style in 1842, when he made his debut as an actor, winning a rave review for his role in a farce called *High Life below Stairs. Rasco's* was almost brand-new at the time, a classic-revival extravagance of salons, concert hall, and ballroom that Italian hotelier Franco Rasco introduced to Montreal's beau monde in 1836. Neglected for years at the end of its golden era, it was restored by the city in 1990 as municipal office space.

Now note the silvery white dome of *Marché Bon-Secours* (330 St-Paul E.), another city-owned landmark. The neoclassical building has dominated the waterfront skyline since 1864, when it was erected over a public building that stretched over three city blocks. Built in 1845 to accommodate Montreal's *Hôtel de Ville* (City Hall), the original complex also housed reception rooms, council chambers, and the police headquarters. A city market was once installed in the basement and around the exterior walls, on the site of the 17th-century *Marché Neuf,* which replaced Ville Marie's first shopping mall on Place Royale. The mayor and his councilors moved up to the Rue Notre-Dame palace in 1878, but the market prospered under its graceful Renaissance dome for more than a century. The city renovated the interior in 1992; current plans call for the building to house a civic museum.

East of the market at the corner of Rue Bon-Secours, the *Chapelle Notre-Dame-de-Bon-Secours* (400 St-Paul E.; phone: 514-845-9991) stands out as Montreal's most appealing historic property. Still the spiritual sanctuary Marguerite Bourgeoys dreamed it would be in 1675, when she chose the site for a tiny chapel beyond the safety of Ville Marie's stockades, today's edifice is the third incarnation of the original. But while the building has changed, the spirit within remains. Enshrined is an ancient wooden image of the Virgin, reputed to work miracles for sailors on dangerous seas. The chapel still is referred to as the *Sailors' Church,* and its rooftop Madonna, arms outstretched to the harbor, presents a welcoming, nostalgic sight to homebound Montreal mariners. Visit the chapel's upstairs museum, dedicated to the life of one of Canada's truly great women—the country's first schoolmistress, its first saint, and the founder of the first Canadian order of non-cloistered nuns, the Congrégation Notre-Dame (see "Special Places" in *Montreal,* THE CITIES). For a spire-high view of Vieux Montréal and the port, climb up to the observation deck above the apse.

Follow Rue Bon-Secours to admire a block of impeccably restored 18th- and 19th-century houses. US history buffs should visit *Maison Pierre-du-Calvet* (on the east corner, at 401 St-Paul E.), the former home of an enthusiastic supporter of the War for Independence. For seven months in 1775, American soldiers invaded and held Montreal, in the hopes of persuading French Canada to renounce the British crown and join the fledgling republic. They did not have to convince du Calvet, a Huguenot merchant who during the occupation supported the revolutionary cause with goods and services. But when the effort failed and the Americans withdrew, he was tried for treason, served a long prison term, and was eventually banished. Ponder the tragic fate of the patriot of American causes over a ham and cheese on rye or a smoked meat sandwich at the deli counter on the ground floor of the current building.

In 1785, local architect Jean-Baptiste Cérat built a fine four-story house (440 Rue Bon-Secours) with walls four feet thick and a noble carriage entrance to an inner courtyard and garden. Louis-Joseph Papineau, a member of the legislative assembly and leader of the 1837 rebellion in Lower Canada, bought the house 10 years after the ill-fated uprising. The fashionable property, which remained in the Papineau family for six generations, declined with the neighborhood, neglected and defaced with ugly additions. In the early 1960s, music critic Eric McLean, an urban-restoration pioneer, bought and restored the deteriorating property, marking the beginning of the revitalization of Old Montreal.

Turn west onto Rue Notre-Dame at the corner and walk back toward Place Jacques-Cartier. Opposite the *Hôtel de Ville* is *Château Ramezay* (280 Notre-Dame E.; phone: 514-861-3708), one of the best-preserved relics of the French colonial regime. Built in 1705, it served as the official residence of Claude de Ramezay, 11th Governor of Montreal. The château's museum has been restored to reflect its original role as combined colonial office and family home of 13 children, and it is furnished in the period—from governor's office to basement kitchen. It's open daily, June through August; closed Mondays, September through May. There's an admission charge. (For additional details, see "Special Places" in *Montreal,* THE CITIES.)

Cross Notre-Dame to Place Vauquelin on the north side, where a statue of a French naval hero stares across the traffic stream—and the centuries— at the victor of Trafalgar. Lieutenant Jean Vauquelin, who defended New France to the last in the 1759 battle for Quebec, faces Admiral Nelson from a statue base above the *place* fountain.

Pause here for a moment for a sweeping view of the *Champ-de-Mars,* once a spiffy military parade ground where crack regiments from the British garrison put on a daily show of regulation drill and promenading Montrealers gathered to listen to the bands. The raised terrace has been restored to its original use as a public promenade. Back on the north side of the street, just west of Place Vauquelin, the *Vieux Palais de Justice* is one of three courthouses you'll pass on Notre-Dame, each built at a different period in the city's history. The old *Palais* (No. 155) was raised in 1856 on the site of an older courthouse, designed in the popular classic-revival style. The dome was added later, at a cost that generated the kind of public outcry that attended the construction of the controversial retractable roof on today's *Stade Olympique* (Olympic Stadium).

Across Allée des Huissiers is the 1926 *Nouveau Palais de Justice,* whose magnificent copper doors and Art Deco lamp standards were designed by Montreal architects Amos, Saxe, and Cormier. The *Edifice Ernest-Cormier,* on the other side of Rue Notre-Dame (100 Notre-Dame E.), is devoted more to culture than to criminal cases; Quebec's *Ministère des Affaires Culturelles* (Ministry of Cultural Affairs) maintains a conservatory of music and dramatic arts here.

On the northwest corner of Notre-Dame, a link in the *McDonald's* golden-arched chain occupies a site the founder of Detroit once called home. Antoine Laumet, also known as de Lamothe Cadillac, Seigneur of Port-Royal and Governor of Louisiana, built a corner house here in 1694. Walk north down the slope of St-Laurent past Ruelle des Fortifications to Rue St-Antoine, where a stream of the same name once ran below the north wall of Vieux Montréal. Two blocks west is Rue St-Urbain, the nearest entrance to the *Place d'Armes Métro* station and a convenient underground route back to home base from the birthplace of Montreal.

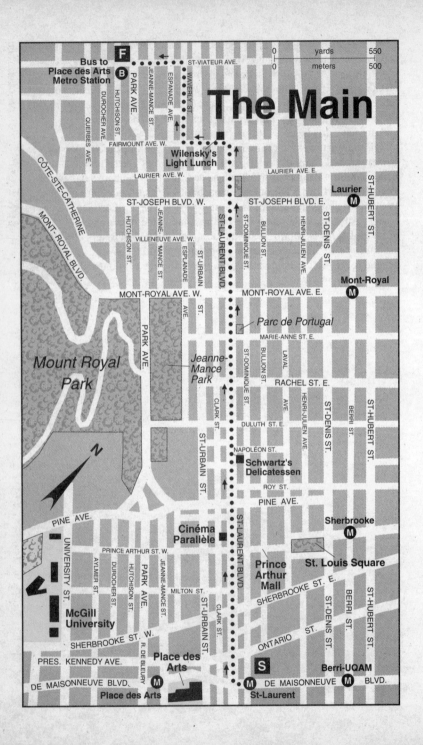

Walk 3: The Main

It may be a concrete jungle now, but The Main was not always this way. Try to imagine bustling Boulevard St-Laurent (St. Lawrence) as a pleasant country road through apple orchard farms and hillside meadows. It was this thoroughfare that pushed the city beyond its walls, linked the picturesque Rivière-des-Prairies on the island's north shore, and divided east and west Montreal.

By the 1830s it had become the road to the country retreats that well-heeled townspeople staked out among the habitant farms below the eastern slopes of Mont-Royal. But Boulevard St-Laurent is better known among today's locals as Main Street or The Main, the great divide between east and west—from its ox-cart beginnings to its traffic-jammed present.

Once the shopping preserve of the horse-and-carriage trade, The Main and its east-west tributaries opened up to the average-income citizen when the first horse-drawn trams struggled up the hill to Plateau Mont-Royal in the gaslight era. In the 1880s, a new surge of settlers, refugees from Russian and Polish pogroms, built new lives on or around Boulevard St-Laurent. As the Jewish community moved north, successive waves of newcomers from Greece, Eastern Europe, Portugal, Spain, Latin America, and the Middle East settled into the neighborhood's old cold-water flats and cramped Victorian cottages.

Waves of immigrants have changed the face of Old St-Laurent, in modern times transforming a once-dingy, abandoned industrial strip into a crucible of ethnic vitality—from its Ukrainian bakeries and Polish sausage shops to its Mexican coffee bars. The latest migratory trend, led by a young pioneer force of artists, designers, and architects, spruced up upper Main not that long ago when they established studios and apartments in abandoned factory lofts. Entrepreneurs joined the trend, opening bars, boutiques, restaurants, and other public places and reshaping nondescript buildings with glass tubing, suspended sheet metal, and halogen spot runners. The urban revival has not extended to lower Main, however: After dark, the Rue Ste-Catherine intersection is a place strollers can definitely afford to miss.

By day, however, avid explorers along lower Main will find a civic monument. Built in 1894, two years after tracks for electric streetcars were laid along The Main, the old *Monument-National Building* (1182 Blvd. St-Laurent) displays little of its old glory; at one time its theater provided the stage for first-rate drama and rousing political meetings. The *National Theater School,* which moved in back in the 1970s, still mounts student productions on the original stage.

The *St-Laurent* station on the No. 1 *Métro* line is the best place to start a sunny-day Saturday stroll up The Main. Allow about three hours for the tour if you're into serious window shopping, snacking, and detours along some of the more intriguing side streets. From the *Métro* exit, walk up to Rue Sherbrooke and continue north to the *Shed Café* (No. 3515; phone: 514-842-0220), the current "in" spot where bright, young, French-speaking party people gather to see and be seen, hopefully in the vicinity of network television stars.

Pause at the Rue Prince-Arthur intersection, where the pedestrian mall of the same name begins. Look down this colorful restaurant row to Square St-Louis, but don't venture in if you've reserved the day for The Main. Save the *Voie Piétonnière Prince-Arthur* (Prince Arthur Pedestrian Mall), with its strolling minstrels, moderately priced ethnic restaurants, and terrace cafés, for another day (see *Walk 5: Université McGill/Rue Prince-Arthur*).

Opposite the mall entrance, note the trees among the lampposts and, proceeding north, the benches and sidewalk planters—all part of a beautification project for "Village St-Laurent." North of Rue Prince-Arthur on The Main's west side is the *Cinéma Parallèle* (No. 3682; phone: 514-845-6001), the driving force behind the annual October *Festival International du Nouveau Cinéma et de la Vidéo de Montréal,* Canada's oldest international cinema and video event. Between festivals, the theater screens intellectual and experimental films and operates *Café Meliès* next door (phone: 514-281-0525). The *Librairie Gallimard* (No. 3700; phone: 514-499-2012), Montreal's most prestigious multilingual bookstore, translates the spirit of a staid academic reading room into an ultra-contemporary setting designed by architect Shulim Rubin.

From food for thought to something more substantial, move on to Avenue des Pins (also known as Avenue Pine) for a European-style sausage at the *Zagreb Charcuterie* (3766 Blvd. St-Laurent; phone: 514-844-3265). Back on The Main, stop at *La Vieille Europe* (No. 3855) to sample the cheese selection before calling in at *Warshaw's Supermarket* (No. 3863), a landmark since 1935, when the Warshaw family left Poland to open a small grocery at the rear of a butcher shop. Another legend among Montrealers is the *Montreal Hebrew Delicatessen and Steak House* (3895 Blvd. St-Laurent; phone: 514-842-4813), commonly known as *Schwartz's* (see *Quintessential Montreal/Quebec* in DIVERSIONS). Old St-Laurent is Montreal's nosh strip, so loosen a notch on your belt and try one of the sandwich favorites here. A fixture on The Main since 1927, this crowded, steamy shrine to the smoked meat (similar to pastrami or corned beef) sandwich claims it's the last of the perfectionists in Montreal to smoke its own house special.

Cross Rue Napoléon for a look at *Moishe's Steak House* (3961 Blvd. St-Laurent; phone: 514-845-1696), where tenderly aged western Canadian beef comes in Texas-size portions. Moishe Lighter founded this granddaddy of Montreal steakhouses back in 1938, when cholesterol hadn't yet entered the culinary vocabulary.

Before continuing north into Montreal's Little Soho district (so named for its putative similarity to New York City's SoHo), turn east at Rue Rachel into Place des Amériques, which reflects the Latin American influence on this section of The Main. A small park farther up the block north of Rue Marie-Anne is a nostalgic reminder of the boulevard's Portuguese connection. *Parc de Portugal* lives up to its name, featuring a quaint little bandstand with colorful tiles lining its plaza, recapturing travel-poster memories of a village square back on the Iberian Peninsula.

Across the street, *Oslo Furs* (4316 Blvd. St-Laurent; phone: 514-499-1777) is one of The Main's outlets for quality fur and leatherwear. *Bagel-Etc,* just south of Marie-Anne, is a late-night, diner-style restaurant for chic insomniacs, featuring an eclectic menu and taped jazz. It's also a popular rendezvous for Sunday brunch. (For additional details, see "Eating Out" in *Montreal,* THE CITIES.)

Four blocks north, one of Montreal's great firehouses dominates the corner of Avenue Laurier and The Main. The baronial No. 30 station started life pretentiously in early French Renaissance style as the *Hôtel de Ville* (City Hall) for suburban St-Louis-du-Mile-End in 1905. Until the 1980s, the blocks between Avenues Laurier and St-Viateur were gray areas of small businesses and factories, corner variety stores, and quick lunch counters; today, the neighborhood boasts fashion outlets, design studios, and restaurants. *Eclectic* (No. 5133; phone: 514-270-9144) is an aesthetic black-and-white temple of unisex beauty that designers Jacques Bilodeau and Jean-Pierre Viau created for compulsive trendsetters. A hairstyling here includes a 10-minute scalp massage, wine or coffee, and a predictably high tab.

Just north of Avenue Fairmount, *LUX* set the tone for the old business area's new ambience when it pioneered the northern frontiers of Little Soho. Luc Laporte designed this quirky core of late-late nightlife on The Main to accommodate an inexpensive restaurant, bar, snack counter, magazine store, pastry shop, and T-shirt boutique under one leaded-glass roof. *LUX* is at its multicultural best after midnight, when the upstairs piano bar draws the young and the restless from all corners of the city. The magazine racks on the mezzanine gallery are stocked with publications from around the world, and the second-floor T-shirt collection features exclusive *LUX* creations you can't buy anywhere else in town. A local TV show is taped on the premises every Friday afternoon at about 5 PM. (For additional details, see "Eating Out" in *Montreal,* THE CITIES.)

Turn west off The Main at Fairmount to enter the heart of Mordecai Richler country. One of Montreal's most prominent citizens, the world-renowned author grew up on Rue St-Urbain in the 1930s, when the Fairmount–St-Urbain crossroads was the hub of Jewish community life. But the neighborhood he described so vividly in his best-selling novel *The Apprenticeship of Duddy Kravitz* has changed since Richler brought the irrepressible Duddy to life 36 years ago. Only a few memories of the Kravitz era linger in cosmopolitan Fairmount today, among them a scrap of film history regular customers know as *Wilensky's Light Lunch* (34 Fairmount, corner of Rue Clark; phone: 514-271-1247). Scenes from the 1974 movie version of Richler's novel were shot at this pokey little fast-food establishment. For a chapter of urban history, step inside this pint-size luncheonette, where the daily specials are marked up over a foggy mirror behind the counter and an all-male clientele perches on tipsy stools. The Main and its west-side arteries used to support one of these salami-and-seltzer parlors on every other corner, but they're now a dying breed.

Another old-timer on Fairmount is the *Bagel Factory* (phone: 514-272-0667), founded a few blocks to the south by Itzac Shalfman in 1929 and relocated at 74 Fairmount Ouest 20 years later. Shalfman's son and grandson still run the family business, which has served at least four generations of bagel mavens, all firmly convinced the Shalfman product is Canada's—if not the world's—most delectable.

Take time to pause at the corners of Fairmount's north-south intersections between Rue Clark and Avenue Park to admire the gentrification of a timeworn neighborhood. The prim little two-story houses, with their pointed dormers and Victorian trim, are flushed with the colors Greek and Portuguese newcomers splashed over weathered brick, stone, and wood when they moved up The Main. Rue Waverly is still lined with Montreal's famous balcony flats, with their steep outside staircases, and St-Urbain is now one of the district's most attractive streets. Walk up from the Fairmount intersection toward Avenue St-Viateur past modest homes where Portuguese residents mark their presence with religious pictures at the front door and an Orthodox synagogue that shares the block with a Buddhist house of worship and a Roman Catholic church. The Byzantine *Eglise St-Michel l'Archange* (Saint Michael the Archangel Church; 5580 St-Urbain) accommodated a predominantly Irish congregation when it was built in 1915; through World War II, it served Quebec's second-largest English-speaking parish. Now affiliated with a Polish mission, *St-Michel* celebrates mass bilingually—in English and Polish.

Walk west on St-Viateur past a kosher butcher, an Italian meat shop, and a Greek grocery to the *Bagel Shop* (No. 263; phone: 514-276-8044), also known as *Maison du Bagel*. Patrons of the aforementioned *Bagel Factory* and this St-Viateur shop have been engaged in a rivalry since the latter opened in 1956: Each claims to bake the world's best bagel.

Continue west to Avenue Park, where you can hop the No. 80 bus to the *Place des Arts Métro* station and return to the midtown hotel strip on Rue Sherbrooke. But before boarding, stop by Montreal's popular venue for French-fried potato freaks. *Frite Alors* (5235A Av. Park; phone: 514-948-2219) keeps busy on the lower floor of a renovated house across the street from *Club Soda*. While the daily bill of fare includes sausages, hot dogs, brochettes, and burgers, the house special is *frites*. Local connoisseurs claim this latest arrival on Avenue Park is the best thing that's happened to the spud in years. A small order may be all you'll have room for after your gastronomy-oriented tour of The Main.

Walk 4:
Parc du Mont-Royal

When Montrealers crave a breath of fresh air, they don't necessarily join the autoroute trek to the Laurentians. After all, they have a perfectly adequate mountain right at their doorstep. *Parc du Mont-Royal*'s 496 airy acres of natural woodlands, grassy dells, and sylvan paths are all within a 10-minute cab ride of the city center.

No one makes better use of a resident mountain than the citizens of Quebec's high-rise metropolis. They ski it, toboggan it, skate it, bird watch its woods, jog and cycle its paths, sail toy boats on its willow-banked lake, picnic in its maple-treed shade, and admire the view from the heights of its observation terrace. But mostly they simply walk on it, happy to escape the noise and tensions of urban life for an hour or so, feeding the squirrels and listening to the sing-song of the birds.

Visitors who've overdosed on Montreal's wealth of dining, shopping, and other temptations learn to love the mountain, too—once they find their way around. Fanciers of New York City's *Central Park* may notice some similarities in the design of the landscape when they get here. In fact, *Central Park*'s designer, American architect Frederick Law Olmsted, planned *Parc du Mont-Royal* in 1874 on the enduring premise that "the possession of charming natural scenery is a form of wealth."

There are many approaches to the mountain-crested oasis. The easy way to the top is by car, cab, or public transportation. If you have your own wheels, approach the western flank of the mountain via Côte-des-Neiges, driving north to Chemin Remembrance; turn right into the park just beyond the *Manège Militaire de Côte-des-Neiges* (Côte-des-Neiges Drill Hall). Chemin Remembrance leads to two meter-equipped public parking lots, one near Lac des Castors (Beaver Lake) and a second, larger facility farther east, where the road merges with Voie Camillien-Houde (named for one of the city's more controversial mayors of the 1930s and 1940s). Or board the No. 165 bus at the *Guy-Concordia Métro* station and transfer to No. 11 at the *Avenue Forest Hill* stop. No. 11, the park's only public transport service, follows Chemin Remembrance and the parkway along Mont-Royal's northern crest from Côte-des-Neiges to Avenue Mont-Royal, with stops at Lac des Castors and other points along the route.

The eastern approach for motorists is via Voie Camillien-Houde. This scenic route merges with Boulevard Mont-Royal, Avenue Mont-Royal, and Avenue Park just west of *Parc Jeanne-Mance.* The No. 11 bus embarks on its east-west parkway journey from the *Mont-Royal Métro* station.

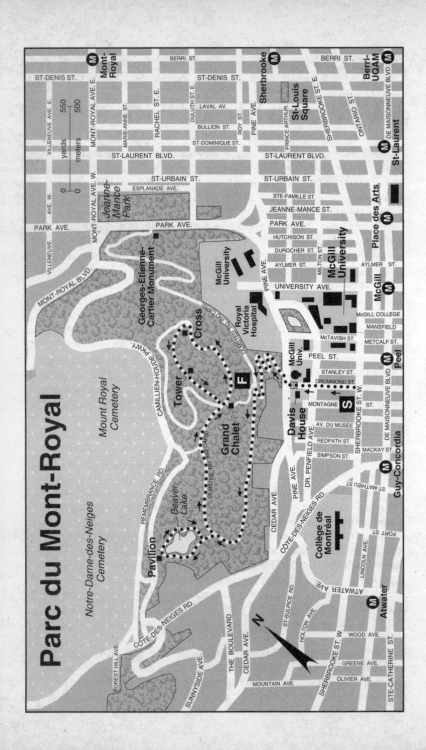

The parkway and Chemin Remembrance skirt the southern fringes of two city cemeteries, one Protestant and one Catholic, which spread over the north side of the mountain where hillside farms flourished until the 1850s. These were the first planned greenspaces in Montreal, the results of a 19th-century bylaw prohibiting burials within the city limits (no one at the time could have foreseen that the city would spread beyond this area). Opened 20 years before Olmsted designed the mountain park, Protestant *Cimetière Mont-Royal* (Mount Royal Cemetery) is a park in itself, with roadways and paths winding through a peaceful retreat of towering old trees and flowering shrubs.

Among the monuments to the soldiers, politicians, fur traders, explorers, and financiers who shaped 19th-century Canada, the modest grave of Mrs. Anna Leonowens is easy to pass by. If you've ever caught yourself humming "Shall We Dance?" or "Getting to Know You," take the time to visit it. Mrs. Leonowens was the spunky Anna, governess to the children of the King of Siam, whose story formed the basis of the musical *The King and I.* How she ended up in Montreal is a story in itself: After finishing her stint with the king in the 1860s, she returned to England, where she wrote two books, *English Governess at the Siamese Court* in 1870 and *Romance of the Harem* in 1872. She then journeyed to New York to seek her fortune by (unsuccessfully) trying to get the work adapted to the stage. Anna eventually moved to Halifax, where she became secretary of the *Halifax Council of Women,* a suffragette association, and helped form the *Victorian School of Art and Design.* She later moved to Montreal, where she died in 1915, never knowing how well known her story eventually would become. In 1943, Margaret Landon wrote *Anna and the King of Siam,* a popular book about Anna's life, which in turn inspired the play *The King and I,* first staged in 1951.

Next door is the Catholic *Cimetière de Notre-Dame-des-Neiges,* opened in 1854. Larger than its Protestant neighbor, this vast space is the final resting place of more than a million Montrealers, among them Calixta Lavallée, composer of Canada's national anthem ("O Canada"), two Fathers of Confederation, and Camillien Houde.

The Voie Camillien-Houde–Chemin Remembrance route is the park's only concession to motor traffic. Rue Olmsted, the old bridle path that loops around Mont-Royal from the *Monument à Sir George-Etienne-Cartier* on Avenue Park to the meadows above Lac des Castors and the *Grand Chalet* in the middle of the park, is reserved for calèche traffic, bikers, and strollers. Olmsted meets a footpath that follows the park's eastern threshold to the massive monument to French Canada's great statesman and Father of Confederation. The monument site marks the most convenient eastern access to Mont-Royal for walkers who'd rather putter along than pant up a series of steep pathways. A more challenging trek snakes up Rue Drummond to the southwest slopes above Avenue Pine, one of the most accessible park gateways for midtown hotel guests in the Rue Sherbrooke

Ouest area. Following this route, explorers will spend a good three hours on the mountain and its network of paths and trails.

Puffing uphill from the corner of Sherbrooke and Drummond, it's hard to believe the posh *Ritz-Carlton Kempinski* hotel and its neighbors mark a halfway plateau on Mont-Royal's long southwest slope. Now that it's paved and built over, most Montrealers forget their mountain's past, when the foothills' forest climbed upward from Rue St-Antoine not far from the riverfront. Jacques Cartier knew it well, however, in 1535, when he pushed up from the river through a majestic forest of red oak and maple to the mountainside Iroquois village of Hochelaga. "As beautiful as any forest in France," he gushed after his hosts led him to the top of their world and the summit of today's park.

The explorer who christened the "Royal Mountain" probably followed a trail a few blocks east of Drummond. Conjure up thoughts of that lost forest while ascending today's apartment-tower canyon to Avenue Dr.-Penfield. Cross at the light to the northeast corner of this traffic speedway, taking a breather by the landscaped terrace in front of the *Phytotron,* the greenhouse laboratory *Université McGill*'s biology department maintains for plant-development studies. The rotund tower overlooking the lab is the *Pavillon McIntyre de Médecine* (McIntyre Medical Building), another university property. Directly opposite is *Pavillon Davis* (Davis House; 3654 Drummond), a red-brick replica of an English manor house, built in 1909 for a prominent Montreal family; it now accommodates *McGill*'s department of physical and occupational therapy. The department also occupies the somewhat shabby sandstone mansion at 3630 Drummond. This once-opulent relic of the Beaux Arts building boom was the talk of the town in 1907, when it was built for Charles Rudolph Hosmer, who made his fortune developing a telegraph system for the *Canadian Pacific Railway.*

Drummond dead-ends at a steep flight of steps to Avenue Pine. At the top, cross Pine at the stoplight and bear right to the serpentine access to Olmsted. The shortcut path on the left cuts down the distance between the bridle path's elongated loops and a set of staircases halfway up the switch-back road, but it's easier to zigzag gradually up the slope and leave the bypaths to conditioned climbers. The loopy roadway coils up into the woods and the junction with Olmsted's namesake carriageway, where you'll meet lots of fellow travelers on bikes, calèches, and, in winter, horse-drawn sleighs jingling along on fat rubber wheels instead of traditional runners. To reserve an honest-to-goodness sleigh (available on special occasions), call 514-653-0751.

Turn left at the junction and stroll on past the old horse trough, following the road to Lac des Castors. En route, you'll pass through what's left of Jacques Cartier's forest. Some of the stands of red oak and maple, offspring of the Cartier-era groves, still attract bluejays, cardinals, chick-adees, and other representatives of the more than 150 feathered species that flutter through the park in their season. Most of today's coniferous and deciduous woodlands—mountain ash, chestnut, birch, wild cherry, spruce, and pine—are less than a century old. Replanting of the mountain forest began on a wide scale in the 1870s, before which time hillside residents cut into the forest for firewood. After one particularly severe winter, however, public outcry against the practice was so intense that city fathers invited Olmsted to create a mountaintop preserve in keeping with his conviction that unspoiled nature was the great healer of body and soul.

Since the 1950s, when the instigators of a public morality campaign tried to discourage amorous rendezvous by thinning out the maple groves and slashing away the thickets, more than 100,000 trees have been planted over the mountain's bald spots, including the stands of pine and spruce the *City Parks Department* introduced to Mont-Royal. Now, along with 600 species of herbaceous plants, the forest is home to not only chipmunks, squirrels, and rabbits but also groundhogs, skunks, and the occasional red fox.

A series of footpaths lead off the carriage road into the woods and a network of cross-country ski trails. If you climb the public staircase to the right, clamber up past the pumping station and turn right again at the first path. You'll be on the fast track to the *Grand Chalet* and its observation terrace, the *Belvédère Mont-Royal*. Continuing west along the Olmsted route, less adventurous mountaineers come upon the gentle slopes of the park's toboggan slide and rope-tow ski run. Follow the first path to the left beyond the drinking fountain; Lac des Castors will take its free-form shape below the hill. Skaters cut a fine figure here in winter, warming up over hot chocolate at the lakeside pavilion, where there's a fast-food restaurant, washroom facilities, and pay telephones. In summer, the circuit around the large, manmade pond is a popular promenade, and the shady groves above the water make for one of the city's coolest retreats. On weekends, taped music echoes through the trees to the open lawns where sun worshipers congregate, and toy boat armadas bob along in the breeze. The stage by the pavilion is the scene of free summer concerts and folk-dancing sessions in which all comers are invited to take a whirl.

After rounding the lake, return to Olmsted the way you came and strike out on a quarter-hour walk to the *Grand Chalet*. Olmsted, whose mission was to keep the mountain park as close to its natural state as possible, probably would not be amused by the intrusion of this vast, echoing hall constructed by the city in 1931–32. Lac des Castors, on the site of a natural beaver pond, was another Depression-era project.

The chalet is used primarily for civic functions and exhibitions, but between galas it's well used as a rest stop for park regulars. Washroom, phone, and snack-bar facilities are tucked tactfully into the rear of the hall behind a seigneurial fireplace bearing the city crest. Here you can admire an impressive interior decor of heraldic crests and murals depicting highlights of the city's early history.

Out on the brink of the observation terrace, *Belvédère Mont-Royal* (see *Quintessential Montreal and Quebec City* in DIVERSIONS) is usually lined with horizon scanners. US-born visitors with a pang of homesickness swear they can see the Green Mountains of Vermont on a clear day. The *Centre de la Montagne* (phone: 514-844-4928), a nature interpretive and education center, conducts guided walks from its headquarters next to the chalet. It also publishes a colorful walkers' map of Mont-Royal and other informative literature.

From the terrace, turn east and follow the inner circle of Olmsted toward one of Montreal's best-known beacons, the illuminated cross on the eastern summit of Mont-Royal. And if you're a bird watcher, take time for a detour along any of the small paths laced through the wooded slopes on the left. Depending on the season, your binoculars will focus on cedar waxwings and yellow-bellied sapsuckers, rock doves and red-breasted nuthatches, or even a few visiting pheasants on an excursion from their *Cimetière Mont-Royal* nesting grounds. The main track leads around the base of the cross, erected by the *Société St-Jean-Baptiste* (St-Jean-Baptiste Society) in memory of the long-vanished wooden original that Paul de Chomedy, Sieur de Maisonneuve, planted on the mountaintop more than three centuries ago. The city's founder carried a rough-hewn oak cross 3 miles up into the mountain wilderness on a bitter January day in 1643, just weeks after a flood had threatened to destroy his frail riverside settlement. De Maisonneuve had vowed to raise the cross in thanksgiving for Ville Marie's miraculous escape; for years, the symbol of the colonists' gratitude drew worshipful pilgrims up the mountain. Installed on *Christmas Eve* of 1924, the hundred-foot steel structure is illuminated in different colors on special occasions.

A footpath on the right side of Olmsted's way circles the cross and leads directly to Mont-Royal's highest point (763 feet) and Montreal's communications tower, the "mast" through which vital information about fire, crime, and road conditions is transmitted. Follow the path down through the spruce glades for a close-up view of the transmission tower of the Canadian Broadcasting Corporation (CBC). The candelabrum of antennae at the tower's tip, 1,100 feet above sea level, also transmits programs for other Montreal television and radio stations.

A short-cut path leads down from the tower to a curve in Olmsted where the carriageway's inner circle joins the main circuit, just west of the *Grand Chalet*. A right turn here leads to the large parking complex and the No. 11 bus stop, probably a welcome sight for flagging trailblazers. Turn left to return to the chalet. Hardier souls can take the pathway down from the east side of the observation terrace to the public staircase and the lower level of Olmsted. Turn left to take the long road back to Avenue Park (and add 45 minutes to the tour). A right turn at the foot of the stairs leads back the way you came, down the meandering route to Avenue Pine and the stairs to Rue Drummond.

Walk 5:
Université McGill/
Rue Prince-Arthur

Walking through the groves of academe is a pleasure *Université McGill* offers to anyone who cares to pass through its *Portail Roddick* (Roddick Gates). They're always open at 805 Rue Sherbrooke Ouest, a courtesy downtowners appreciate in a neighborhood of corporate towers, hotels, and apartment blocks, where greenspace is at a premium. The campus also is the departure point for one of the city's most interesting walking tours, from one seat of higher education to another. This two-hour stroll begins at *McGill* and ends at the *Université du Québec à Montréal (UQAM)*. It's a journey through changing times and neighborhoods, with a colorful pedestrian mall that bridges the gap between two student cultures.

The tour begins at the *McGill College* exit from the *McGill Métro* station. Walking up the broad boulevard of Avenue McGill College, you'll see the campus vista opening below a wooded mountain backdrop, the octagonal dome of its first on-site lecture hall crowning the historic *Pavillon des Arts* (Arts Building) at the end of a central driveway. The university's oldest building on campus didn't open its doors until 1839, 26 years after James McGill left his 46-acre mountainside estate and £10,000 to the *Royal Institute for the Advancement of Learning,* on the understanding that a university would be established in his name.

The founder was an enterprising Glaswegian who made his mark and wealth as a fur trader, merchant, army officer, and legislator. Unlike most of his Scottish contemporaries—who had left school early to seek their fortunes in booming 18th-century Montreal—McGill was a graduate of *Glasgow University.* Making a case for higher education in Quebec's business and financial capital was one of his priorities, and, dying childless, he bequeathed his beloved *Salle Burnside* (Burnside Hall)—the unpretentious country home he built on the south side of today's Rue Sherbrooke—to the cause. After years of litigation with other claimants, the *Institute* finally received its royal charter from King George IV in 1821, and the university's first college was founded. The first student body of 20 attended lectures in *Salle Burnside*.

The squire's garden grew opposite the site of the *Portail Roddick,* but the grand entrance and its carillon clock were a later bequest. The imposing Greek Revival gateway opened in 1924 as a memorial to Sir Thomas George Roddick, a benefactor and distinguished member of the universi-

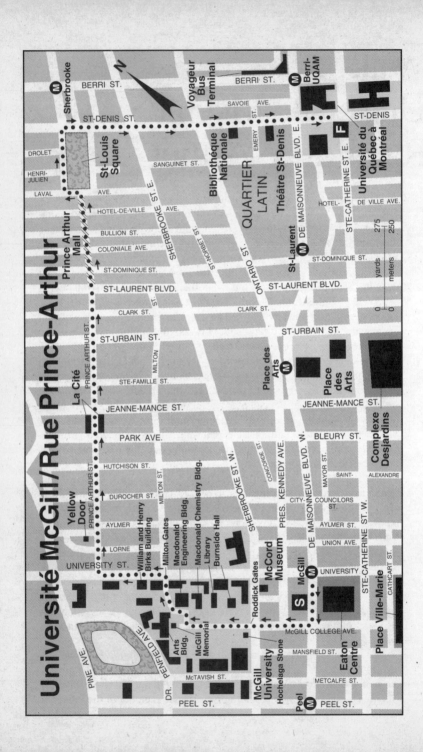

Université McGill/Rue Prince-Arthur

Université McGill

Rue Prince-Arthur

M Sherbrooke

BERRI ST.

Voyageur Bus Terminal

BERRI ST.

M Berri-UQAM

St-Denis

SAVOIE AVE.

ST-DENIS ST.

DROLET

St-Louis Square

SANGUINET ST.

Bibliothèque Nationale

EMERY ST.

QUARTIER LATIN

Théâtre St-Denis

F

Université du Québec à Montréal

HENRI-JULIEN

LAVAL

AVE.

Prince Arthur Mall

HOTEL-DE-VILLE AVE.

SHERBROOKE ST. E.

ST-NORBERT ST.

ONTARIO ST.

St-Laurent

DE MAISONNEUVE BLVD. E.

HOTEL-

STE-CATHERINE ST. E.

DE VILLE AVE.

BULLION ST.

COLONIALE AVE.

ST-DOMINIQUE ST.

M

ST-DOMINIQUE ST.

PRINCE ARTHUR ST.

ST-LAURENT BLVD.

ST-LAURENT BLVD.

275

yards

250

meters

La Cité

CLARK ST.

CLARK ST.

0

0

ST-URBAIN ST.

MILTON ST.

ST-URBAIN ST.

STE-FAMILLE ST.

Place des Arts

M

Place des Arts

JEANNE-MANCE ST.

JEANNE-MANCE ST.

Complexe Desjardins

PRINCE ARTHUR ST.

PARK AVE.

BLEURY ST.

CONCORDE ST.

PRES. KENNEDY AVE.

MAYOR ST.

SAINT-ALEXANDRE

Yellow Door

HUTCHISON ST.

MILTON ST.

DUROCHER ST.

SHERBROOKE ST. W.

CITY-COUNCILORS ST.

DE MAISONNEUVE BLVD. W.

AYLMER ST.

STE-CATHERINE ST. W.

AYLMER

UNION AVE.

William and Henry Birks Building

Milton Gates

Macdonald Engineering Bldg.

Macdonald Chemistry Bldg.

Library

Burnside Hall

LORNE

McCord Museum

McGill

M

UNIVERSITY

Place Ville-Marie

CATHCART ST.

UNIVERSITY ST.

Roddick Gates

S

Eaton Centre

STE-CATHERINE ST.

PINE AVE.

DR. PENFIELD AVE.

Arts Bldg.

McGill Memorial

McGill University

Hochelaga Stone

McGILL COLLEGE AVE.

MANSFIELD ST.

McTAVISH ST.

METCALFE ST.

PEEL ST.

Peel

M

PEEL ST.

N

ty's medical faculty. Walk through the gates, past the security guard's post, and turn left off the drive to the *Stèle Hochelaga* (Hochelaga Stone). The small granite boulder just inside the formal black iron fencing along Rue Sherbrooke commemorates the Iroquois village of Hochelaga, which was still thriving behind its wooden stockade when Jacques Cartier visited more than 450 years ago.

The Iroquois villagers had moved on by the time Montreal's first European settlers arrived, less than a century later, but *McGill* makes a point of remembering them. It also remembers the *Founder's Elm* with a plaque on the tree stump on the right-hand side of the main drive in front of the *Pavillon Macdonald de Physique* (Macdonald Physics Building; ca. 1890). Campus historians are convinced James McGill planted the tree himself in 1790, before anyone knew about Dutch Elm disease. The afflicted tree was cut down in 1976 but still is revered as part of the philanthropic Scot's legacy.

Turn back to the central drive and walk up toward the *Pavillon des Arts*. On the right is *Salle Burnside*, the modern computer center on the south border of the campus, just inside the fence, then the vintage physics building, home to the science and engineering library, followed by the *Pavillon Macdonald de Chimie* (Macdonald Chemistry Building; 1896) and the *Pavillon Macdonald de Génie* (Macdonald Engineering Building; 1908). On the left, the university's old playing fields sweep up to Gertrude Vanderbilt Whitney's charming statue group of the Three Graces, irreverently known around campus as "The Three Bares."

Continue up the drive to the *Monument Commémoratif de McGill* (McGill Memorial) in front of the *Pavillon des Arts,* where the founder's tomb rests under a quadrangular column topped by a funereal urn. (The monument, with McGill's remains, was moved from the Protestant cemetery on Square Dorchester when the old burial ground was closed in 1878.)

Return to the east branch of the drive, where neighborhood mothers bring their tots to play in the small children's park under the willow trees. Bear right past the *Pavillon McConnell de Génie* (McConnell Engineering Building) and pass through the *Portail Milton* (Milton Gates) onto Rue University. (For a more extensive tour, take advantage of guided excursions around the campus that *McGill* offers on 24 hours' notice; phone: 514-398-6555.)

You're on the threshold of the old student ghetto now, the never-never land of the 1960s and early 1970s, when flower children roamed between the campus and Avenue Park, Rue Sherbrooke, and Avenue Pine. Those were the Little Bohemia days, when students could rent affordable rooms in run-down houses and apartment buildings along Rues Milton and Prince-Arthur and the byways in between. Since then, the neighborhood has come an interesting full-circle to its genteel 19th-century beginnings.

Back in the 1850s, when *McGill* was developing according to the founder's plan, the area east of Rue University was still rural, sweet with apple orchards and hay fields. At about this time upwardly mobile citizens escaped from the crowded city below, moving into the fringes of uptown estate country in the shadow of Mont-Royal. Here the newly wealthy built substantial gray stone terrace houses with big back gardens and tidy front lawns. Yet this desirable enclave of Victorian- and Edwardian-era households started to disintegrate in the 1920s, as the old families sold out and the rooming-house operators moved in. Before long, student strays who weren't living in university residences discovered a good thing in inexpensive rented rooms and shared apartments—and a new community of blithe spirits was born. Now Montreal's young families have reclaimed this most convenient of midtown neighborhoods, gentrifying it beyond the means of the average student. They've renovated near-slums into cooperative housing, expensive condominiums, and single-family townhouses. Indeed, the old student ghetto is a prime piece of real estate today.

To explore one of its main thoroughfares, turn north from the *Portail Milton* and follow the west side of University up to Rue Prince-Arthur. This side of the campus boundary once was lined with mansion class housing, some of which *McGill* has salvaged or inherited. Other donations—such as the *Ecole de Service Social* (School of Social Work), *Ecole des Sciences Infirmières* (School of Nursing), and the *Pavillon William and Henry Birks,* on the left as you make your way uphill—were built in the collegiate Gothic style to the specifications of wealthy benefactors. Built around 1864, the gray stone row houses on the east side of University, most of which operate as rooming houses today, were built on a less imposing scale.

Turn east onto Rue Prince-Arthur. Originally designated Rue Bagg (for Stanley Clark Bagg, who developed much of the area's eastern suburbs), the 14-block street between Rue University and Avenue Laval was renamed for Prince Arthur, Duke of Connaught, son of Queen Victoria and a popular Governor-General of Canada. Pause at the first corner to look up Avenue Lorne, another loyal reference to the Crown, named for the Marquess of Lorne, the queen's son-in-law and another governor-general. Here's an example of suburban planning 1880s-style, with dignified rows of three-story houses leading to a charming residential crescent of the same name. Ignore the big apartment building on the west side of the street, and the block of snug Victorian buildings looks pretty much as it did more than a century ago, when a comfortable middle-income community took root here.

For a nostalgic step back into a more recent past, turn north at Rue Aylmer, where a landmark of the student-ghetto days remains in the *Yellow Door* (3625 Rue Aylmer; phone: 514-398-6243). Opened in 1967, it was a rallying point for disaffected young Americans during the Vietnam War and a stage for the folksongs of protest. Jesse Winchester enthralled some of his earliest audiences here, and folksinging is still the highlight of Friday-night gatherings.

The handsome, red brick house at 481 Rue Prince-Arthur has interesting student connections as well. The commodious relic—which dates from

1897—has served as a fraternity house, a Hare Krishna temple, and a youth hostel. But student activism was mild compared with the shock waves an earlier resident of that house sent through the neighborhood around the turn of the century. A leading civil rights advocate of the day, feisty Madame Benoit fought bravely for the feminist cause in a province that denied women a vote in Quebec elections until as late as 1940. Her former house, now in private hands, has been beautifully restored, from stepped gables to elaborate front gate and fenced lawn. Another Rue Prince-Arthur property with a long collegian connection is *Le Marché Campus* (No. 461). This convenience store started life as a stable (look for the upper-story hatch that once opened on the hayloft), but it's been a handy stop-and-shop for campus-area residents since the 1940s.

At the Rue Durocher intersection, you'll be on the corner of the district's oldest street; cut through farm fields in 1837 as a private road, it was later expropriated by city developers. The old farmhouse at the corner (3592 Durocher), gingerbread trim frilling the central dormer and an infelicitous aluminum awning over the front door, probably predates the road. The Beaux Arts building on the west corner (3612 Durocher) was a luxury hotel that failed even before the first guest registered. Converted to residential use in 1915, the *Halcion Apartments* are still an attractive presence on a tree-shaded street of period homes. Most of the unadorned, gray stone veterans of the neighborhood's earliest settlement—prim, red brick row houses with fussy Victorian trimmings and Edwardian latecomers with turret-topped towers and oriel windows—have been restored as single-family units or condominiums.

Return to Rue Prince-Arthur for an imposing view of the high-rise, high-rent complex of *La Cité*. Three apartment towers soar above their older neighbors on either side of Prince-Arthur between Rue Jeanne-Mance and Avenue Park, linked below the surface by a huge underground village of shops and services that includes a theater, a pool-equipped health club, a restaurant, and a bank. The *Hôtel du Parc* shares this underground facility with *La Cité* tenants (see "Checking In" in *Montreal,* THE CITIES).

Cross Avenue Park to the southwest section of the historic St-Louis district, which up-and-coming suburbanites colonized in the fields west of Boulevard St-Laurent in the 1870s and 1880s. Only a brisk, 10-minute jog from the *McGill* campus, the new neighborhood flourished as a solid middle class community of academics, merchants, and professionals, who settled into rows of three-story Victorian houses, with fashionable wood-trimmed gables and enclosed front porches. That image dimmed after World War I, as the population shifted to greener pastures beyond the city center; now, like the reincarnated campus zone, it's been adopted by a new wave of prosperous householders. Rows of neglected buildings destined for demolition have been transformed into cooperatives and condominiums, notably the onetime church on the corner of Prince-Arthur and Jeanne-Mance, now a condominium.

Continue east to Boulevard St-Laurent, where a welcome feature of a revived neighborhood opens up on the east side of the street. The five-block pedestrian mall between St-Laurent and Avenue Laval is one of the city's more successful experiments in urban renewal. The mall is really a legacy from the 1960s, when Prince-Arthur was known as "Hippie Alley," and a transient craftsperson could rent a store for $60 a month. Members of the flower-child generation who opened the original offbeat clothing outlets and bangles-and-beads boutiques drifted away once their casual agora turned acceptably trendy. But the carefree tone they set lingered on after the city transformed the blocks west of Laval into a village square for pedestrians in 1981.

Now that it's been dressed up with a fountain and flower beds, old-fashioned lamp standards, and Parisian-style "Morris" columns plastered with posters, the mall is a popular promenade for diners in search of an inexpensive meal in picturesque surroundings. Ethnic restaurants of every variety line both sides of the old residential street, and with the first breath of spring they set up sidewalk cafés along the brick-paved length of the plaza. In summer, clowns, magicians, and street musicians add more color to a lively street scene. The modest restaurants aren't as cheap as they once were, but the tradition of encouraging patrons to bring their own wine to the table has persisted. Check the house policy before arriving with your brown bag: Some of the new places are licensed.

With dozens of options on both sides of the mall, it's hard to make a choice—although half the fun of dining here is casing the territory, picking out a likely-looking spot, and then shopping around for an acceptable wine to accompany a meal of Greek, Italian, Polish, Vietnamese, Swiss, Japanese, or Québécois fare. *Donat Vezina Groceries* (27 Rue Prince-Arthur E.; phone: 514-842-8044) and *Marché Nascimento & Brito* (67 Rue Prince-Arthur E.; phone: 514-845-5751) carry inexpensive wines.

Walking west to east, you might be tempted by *Minerva* (No. 17; phone: 514-842-5451), a BYOW seafood house with a Greek accent, or *Coimbra* (No. 20; phone: 514-845-7915), a licensed Portuguese dining room featuring grilled specialties. *Le Prince-Arthur* (No. 54; phone: 514-849-2454) is a traditional French *brochetterie*. The Polish restaurant *Mazurka* (No. 64; phone: 514-844-3539) opened in 1964, making it the first kid on the block. *La Fondue du Prince* (No. 70; phone: 514-845-0183) caters to fondue enthusiasts but offers other appetizing choices. Another well-established Prince-Arthur landmark is *La Cabane Grecque* (No. 102; phone: 514-849-0122), a BYOW restaurant with a sidewalk café for people watching. *Pizza Mella* (No. 107; phone: 514-849-4680) is a good choice; *Vespucci* (No. 124; phone: 514-849-0202) outclasses most of its Italian neighbors in decor with a white-tablecloth dining room and a stained glass wall. In your browsing, don't mistake *Le Chat Botté* (No. 108; phone: 514-844-1850) for a pet-food store. It's been selling designer boots on Prince-Arthur since the pre-mall era. The *Vol de Nuit Bar Salon* (No. 14; phone: 514-845-6243) is a popular singles bar.

On the east side of Avenue Laval is the end of the mall and the beginning of Square St-Louis, which the city transformed from a reservoir into a park in 1867. Once the grass grew, a colony of prosperous French bourgeoisie built their Victorian townhouses and prudent three-family residences along both sides of an almost-private residential garden. Several generations of artists and poets favored the tranquil little sanctuary, with its bower of shade trees and playful fountain—and the square never quite lost its original cachet.

Here are formal, four-story Victorian buildings, some of which are still private homes with steep front staircases and ornamental balconies. Condo conversion has changed some of these historic structures, but many are house-size duplexes and triplexes, designed for a gracious, drawing-room era, with fine, high ceilings and long, park-view windows. In recent years, householders who've invested in expensive renovations have chafed at the decline in the state of the park, a nighttime haven for drug dealers and their customers and the homeless. But during the day Square St-Louis still evokes memories of a gentler society.

Take a turn around the square before heading south on Rue St-Denis (see "Special Places" in Montreal, THE CITIES) toward Montreal's legendary Quartier Latin, the scholars' domain that grew up around the *Université de Montréal* in the 1920s. Lately, the street evokes wistful visions of Paris, the Left Bank, and the café culture of Boulevard St-Michel. The heart of St-Denis's intellectual world throbs around the Rue Ste-Catherine intersection, where the *Université du Québec à Montréal* boasts a student body of 25,000. The newly fashionable blocks north of Rue Ontario Est draw more big spenders than thrifty collegians to their upscale bistros, boutiques, and haute cuisine restaurants.

One of the city's most expensive dining spots is on the east side of the street, just south of Rue Sherbrooke. At *Les Mignardises,* chef Jean-Pierre Monnet has transformed an elegant little 1880s townhouse into a temple of gastronomy (see "Eating Out" in *Montreal,* THE CITIES). This stretch of St-Denis was a preferred residential avenue for well-heeled French Canadian suburbanites who moved up the hill into subdivided estate country about the same time the new neighborhoods west of St-Laurent were settled. Walking south, note the gray limestone façades of their mini-châteaux, crowned with elaborate gables and turrets, camouflaged now by storefront additions and restaurant marquees. As you cross Rue Ontario, you'll sense a change of urban scene, one that began as early as 1876, when *Université Laval* opened a branch of the historic Quebec City institution in Montreal.

The Latin Quarter came to life with the university's decision to extend its faculties of law and medicine to sites around Rue St-Denis and with the construction of the *Ecole Polytechnique* in 1905. In 1920 *Laval*'s outpost of higher learning won its autonomy as the *Université de Montréal,* and an expanding student population took over the Victorian-era homes of southern St-Denis. Before the university moved to its new mountainside campus on the north slope of Mont-Royal in 1943, the stretch of St-Denis between Boulevard René-Lévesque and Rue Ontario was the intellectual and cultural nerve center of French-speaking Montreal. The focus changed when the largest French-language university outside Paris abandoned St-Denis—but not for long. The *UQAM* opened in 1969, and today a new generation of student activists, poets, and philosophers charts Quebec's future in the smoky bars and affordable *brochetteries* of a new Latin Quarter.

Stroll south from Rue Ontario; stop to admire the *Bibliothèque Nationale du Québec* (1700 St-Denis St.; phone: 514-873-1100). A Parisian-looking Beaux Arts building, it is one of three city centers associated with the province's national library. The *Edifice St-Sulpice* on St-Denis, which the Sulpician Order donated to the province in the 1960s, was built in 1912. Today it's the library's reference center and showcase for the collection of Canadiana the Sulpicians donated with the building. A variety of cultural activities takes place in *Salle St-Sulpice,* a period concert hall with exquisite stained glass skylights set into a beamed ceiling.

For a raucous change of pace, drop by the *Café de Picasso* (1621 Rue St-Denis; phone: 514-843-3533), a student hangout with a high-decibel approach to conversations. By mid-evening, this is the spot to hear young Montreal in full voice. Across the street, *Faubourg St-Denis* (1660 Rue St-Denis; phone: 514-843-4814) is another popular student rendezvous.

Before crossing Boulevard de Maisonneuve, inspect the Art Deco façade of the *Théâtre St-Denis* (1594 Rue St-Denis; phone: 514-849-4211). It covers the original 1916 face of a theater where Sarah Bernhardt won standing ovations; many traditionalists are not pleased with its new look. Thousands of visitors come here in the summer for such events as the *Festival International de Jazz de Montréal* and the *Festival Juste pour Rire* (Just for Laughs Festival). *Théâtre St-Denis* can accommodate such mega-productions as *Les Misérables* and French pop extravaganzas.

On the grounds of the *UQAM,* don't miss the *Eglise St-Jacques,* which enlightened architects saved from the wrecking ball when the university acquired the property. Instead of demolishing a Gothic Revival landmark that had stood its ground on Rue Ste-Catherine Est since 1860, the university integrated the highest church steeple in Montreal and the cathedral's south transept into the complex at 405 Rue Ste-Catherine Est (phone: 514-987-3125). *Place 350,* a park the city created on Rue Berri to celebrate its 350th anniversary in 1992, adds the requisite laid-back touch to the "all-business" student scene.

The university is linked to Montreal's Ville Souterraine (Underground City) through the *Berri-UQAM Métro* station, a boon to students who commute from all quarters of Montreal and beyond. Watch out for the traffic here, though. Students make up only a tiny proportion of the passengers who come through this hub of the Montreal subway system.

For a close encounter with Montreal on the move, turn into the *Métro* station on the west side of St-Denis opposite the university and join the flow. Four subway lines converge here on four different levels, and the rush-hour mob scene can be an eye-opener for strangers in town. Case-hardened regulars take it all in stride, so don't be surprised if you're the only one taking any time to admire the outsize stained glass window that covers an entire wall of *Berri-UQAM*'s underground art gallery.

The station is connected to the *Voyageur* bus terminal and *Les Atriums* shopping galleries, a seven-story complex with a waterfall cascading into a tropical garden. The multitiered mall is worth a visit before hitting the fast track to home base.

Quebec City Directions

Quebec's historic capital is Canada's most walkable city—its many charms are best discovered on foot. If you come to Quebec City by air, on arrival you'll probably be driven behind its walls by taxi, but that could be the last time during your stay that you travel in such a way. It's easy to get caught up in the spirit of the street here.

Indeed, using a car to navigate the maze of one-way thoroughfares in the confines of the ramparts is more nuisance than convenience. Public parking in Upper Town is limited, particularly on weekends and during the summer tourist season, when early birds snap up the available spaces and the local *gendarmerie* keeps an eagle eye on restricted parking zones. Sightseers from beyond the walls can avoid the frustration of traffic tie-ups and parking tickets by leaving the car in the hotel garage.

The historic *quartier* is an easy walk for hotel guests in the Colline Parlementaire (Parliament Hill)–Grande Allée district, and the No. 11 bus plies a regular course along Grande Allée, Chemin St-Louis, and Boulevard Laurier, linking the motel strip of suburban Ste-Foy to the heart of the walled city. Many of the larger Ste-Foy hotels operate a shuttle service to and from Upper Town. Parking is less of a problem in the Vieux Port area of Lower Town, where the facilities are new and expansive, but still it's best to leave the car behind: Much of Place Royale is restricted to pedestrian traffic in summer.

Uptown or downtown, walking through history is one of the great rewards of this compact, split-level city. It's almost impossible to get lost inside or outside the walls: The turrets and spires of the *Château Frontenac* hotel are a constant point of reference. Down by the river or out beyond the fortifications, head toward the *Château*'s high profile to find the way back to Place d'Armes and the heart of Upper Town.

Few cities in Canada make life easier for strolling visitors. From mid-June through *Labour Day,* bilingual tourist-information agents zip around both levels of the Old Town on bright green mopeds, on the lookout for confused wanderers. When in doubt, look for the little white flag with the big black question mark; at the crossroads of key pedestrian routes is a well-informed driver beneath the flying pennant.

Day or night, *la vieille capitale* is a safe city for strolling. Civic boosters take pride in Quebec City's low crime rate, pointing out the only real hazard on Vieux Québec's streets are the streets themselves. Plunging downward at unexpected corners or newly surfaced with historically correct paving stones, the lane-width roads of the *ancien quartier* call for stout walking shoes with good, thick soles. And keep an eye peeled for calèche traffic. The horse rules in traffic here, forcing rental-car drivers and local motorists alike to give way.

Walk 1: Vieux Québec/ Upper Town

For visiting history buffs, nothing in Canada surpasses the thrill of walking for the first time through *Porte St-Louis* into the Upper Town of Vieux Québec. There are other gateways to the only walled city in the US and Canada, but they don't lead back to the 17th century as dramatically as this western approach to the historic *quartier* of Quebec's provincial capital.

This is where guests from hotels outside the walls are one up on the insiders, who generally arrive by car or taxi through other breaches in the ramparts to check in to Upper Town accommodations. Caught up in the traffic stream, they miss out on the sensation of walking into history along the oldest tourist route in Canada. Years before modern-day explorers, native trappers followed this very trail down to what they called "Kebec" (Where the Waters Narrow) to observe the funny foreigners in their vulnerable riverbank settlement and do business at the new fur-trading post.

Today's visitors should leave the No. 11 bus at Avenue Dufferin so as to make the grand entrance to Vieux Québec on foot, on a centuries-old path. The neo-Gothic *Porte St-Louis* isn't as old as it looks. The original was built in 1693, along with nearby *Porte St-Jean,* as part of the colonial defense system, but both were located closer to the center of town. Moved several times during the French regime, today's imposing portal wasn't reconstructed until 1878. Still, it's easy to imagine it funneling frontier traffic into Upper Town's main thoroughfare and on to *Fort St-Louis* at the opposite end of the street where the *Château Frontenac* now stands.

Enter the upper reaches of this old split-level town to begin a walking tour of about two hours. Set back in the park on the left is the *Poudrière de l'Esplanade* (Esplanade Powder House); built in 1810, it's part of the *Fortifications de Québec,* a national historic site maintained by *Parks Canada.* The *Poudrière* is a reception and interpretive center, as well as the departure point for tours of the 3-mile wall circuit (see *Walk 3: Vieux Québec Wall Tour*). As you stroll, note that many of the windows in these old buildings have been covered over in brick or stone. In the 19th century, homeowners were taxed by the number of windows in their houses; the sealing of these openings not only saved on taxes but greatly reduced the need for extra firewood for heating.

Continue along the verge of the park to the intersection of Rues d'Auteuil and St-Louis and look to the right, up the picturesque slope of Avenue St-Denis, where rows of fine mid-19th-century homes are tucked under the wall of the *Citadelle* (see "Special Places" in *Quebec City,* THE CITIES). Turn left on Rue d'Auteuil at the *Monument de la Guerre des Boërs* (Boer War

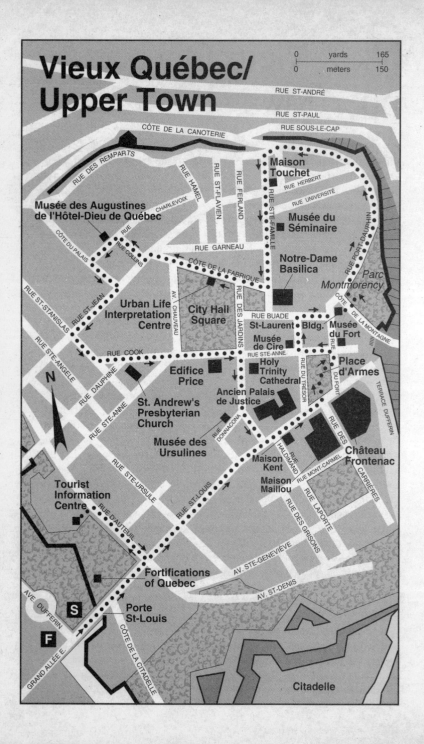

Vieux Québec/ Upper Town

| 0 | yards | 165 |
| 0 | meters | 150 |

RUE ST-ANDRÉ

RUE ST-PAUL

RUE SOUS-LE-CAP

CÔTE DE LA CANOTERIE

RUE DES REMPARTS

Maison Touchet

RUE HERBERT

RUE HAMEL

RUE ST-FLAVIEN

RUE FERLAND

RUE ST-... (RUE STE-FAMILLE)

RUE UNIVERSITÉ

Musée des Augustines de l'Hôtel-Dieu de Québec

CHARLEVOIX

RUE

Musée du Séminaire

CÔTE DU PALAIS

RUE COLLINS

RUE GARNEAU

CÔTE DE LA FABRIQUE

Notre-Dame Basilica

RUE PORT-DAUPHIN

Parc Montmorency

RUE ST-JEAN

RUE ST-STANISLAS

AV. CHAUVEAU

RUE DES JARDINS

Urban Life Interpretation Centre

City Hall Square

RUE BUADE

St-Laurent Bldg.

CÔTE DE LA MONTAGNE

RUE DE LA MONTAGNE

Musée du Fort

RUE STE-ANGELE

RUE COOK

Musée de Cire

RUE STE-ANNE

Place d'Armes

RUE DAUPHINE

Edifice Price

Holy Trinity Cathedral

RUE DU TRÉSOR

RUE DU FORT

TERRASE DUFFERIN

St. Andrew's Presbyterian Church

RUE STE-ANNE

Ancien Palais de Justice

RUE DONNACONA

Musée des Ursulines

Château Frontenac

RUE DES CARRIÈRES

RUE STE-URSULE

RUE ST-LOUIS

Maison Kent

RUE HALDIMAND

RUE MONT-CARMEL

RUE LAPORTE

Maison Maillou

N

Tourist Information Centre

RUE D'AUTEUIL

RUE DES GRISONS

AV. STE-GENEVIÈVE

Fortifications of Quebec

AVE DUFFERIN

S

Porte St-Louis

AV. ST-DENIS

F

GRAND ALLÉE E.

CÔTE DE LA CITADELLE

Citadelle

Monument) and follow the park to the *Tourist Information Centre* of the *Office du Tourisme et des Congrès de la Communauté Urbaine de Québec* (Greater Quebec Area Tourism and Convention Bureau; 60 Rue d'Auteuil; phone: 418-692-2471), a must stop. The bureau distributes free guidebooks, maps, brochures, and other tourist literature in French and English, and the bilingual staff has the answer to almost any question flustered newcomers may ask.

Return to the Rue St-Louis intersection to proceed down the most colorful street within the walls. Spring through fall, the eight-block link between *Porte St-Louis* and the *Château Frontenac* seems to be *en fête* (decked out) seven days a week. In summer, look up at the flashes of color coming from the old-style window boxes that brighten up historic stone façades and the baskets that hang from lampposts. Stop to smell the flowers in café window boxes and to admire the 17th-century buildings. In winter the spirit is different, but no less festive. In the cold and swirling snow, restaurant windows glow with welcoming light and warmth, and gaily painted doorways belie the friendliness and comfort that lies within.

Winter or summer, the restaurants always beckon: St-Louis is Quebec City's restaurant row. Write down the names of those whose looks you like, because there are many from which to choose. Start with *La Caravelle* (No. 68; phone: 418-694-9022), which serves traditional French and Spanish fare to the tunes of a dinner-hour troubadour (try the superb mussels with rosemary). Almost next door, at the *Café de Paris* (No. 66; phone: 418-694-9626), diners are beguiled by serenades of a resident *chansonnier,* while farther down the street is the *Restaurant au Parmesan* (No. 38; phone: 418-692-0341), which serves robust Italian fare to the accompaniment of Italian and French folksongs.

At the corner of Rue des Jardins, *Aux Anciens Canadiens* is Vieux Québec's most famous purveyor of traditional French Canadian cuisine. François Jacquet, a slate roofer, wasn't thinking in terms of a quaint restaurant when he built his little peak-roofed, stone cottage in 1675, but he'd probably be pleased to know his handiwork has withstood more than three centuries of war and weather. Though a dining spot nearby, *Le Continental* (No. 26), can't claim historic monument status, it is the dean of restaurant row's dining establishments. (See "Eating Out" in *Quebec City,* THE CITIES, for details on both restaurants.)

Cross to the opposite side of the street to the corner of Rue Haldimand, where *Maison Kent* (25 Rue St-Louis) has been a main-street landmark since 1650. Quebec's fate was sealed in this stately 17th-century home when the capital of French Canada officially surrendered to victorious British forces after the Battle of the Plains of Abraham in 1759. Just 32 years later, the proud relic of the old French regime adopted the name of a royal resident from England. The Duke of Kent, father of Queen Victoria, resided here as governor from 1791 to 1794. A few yards down the street (at No. 17), *Maison Maillou* houses the *Chambre de Commerce de Québec* (Quebec

City Board of Trade) in a handsome example of early Québécois architecture, built by Jean Maillou between 1736 and 1753.

This is the historic heart of Upper Town. Take a break in green, tree-shaded Place d'Armes, with its memorial fountain glorifying the faith of the early Récollet missionaries. Towering over the south side of the *place*, on Rue St-Louis, the *Château Frontenac* has commanded the strategic heights above the St. Lawrence River for more than a hundred years; built in 1883 by the *Canadian Pacific Railway*, it is the ultimate in Canadian grand hotels. Looking down from his statue column by the hotel's east corner, Samuel de Champlain surveys the site of the fortress he built in 1620 to defend his riverside colony at the base of the cliff. The *Terrasse Dufferin*, a terrace flanking the east side of the hotel, has obliterated all traces of *Fort St-Louis* (the founder died here in 1635), but the memorial statue of the Father of New France remains a focus of Upper Town life. Clowns, acrobats, and other street entertainers draw crowds around the monument base from early spring through the fall foliage season, and a fleet of calèches always is lined up on the nearby Place d'Armes to tempt footsore explorers. The nearly-hundred-year-old *Monument de Champlain* (Champlain Monument) now shares the *Terrasse Dufferin* with a much younger historic memorial—a sphere of bronze and glass that proclaims Vieux Québec a UNESCO World Heritage site.

West of the busy monument area, Place d'Armes came to life during the French regime as Grande Place, a combined speakers' corner and military parade ground. From here, sightseers can follow a path down to the square's northern boundary at Rue Ste-Anne. On the west side of the colonial meeting ground, look for the *Ancien Palais de Justice* (Old Courthouse), built over the site of a church and convent founded by the Récollet Order of Franciscan missionaries in the early 1600s. Next door, the east façade of the *Cathédrale Anglicane* (Holy Trinity Anglican Cathedral)—the first Anglican house of worship built outside the British Isles (1804)—faces the *place* from its churchyard in the old *Jardins de Récollet* (Récollet Gardens). Follow the chain of lamp-lined paths across the *place* to its eastern border on Rue du Fort, and continue north to the Rue Ste-Anne intersection. To the right is the *Musée du Fort* (10 Rue Ste-Anne; phone: 418-692-2175), a museum devoted to the six military sieges of Quebec. It's closed December 1 through *Christmas;* admission charge. (For details, see "Special Places" in *Quebec City*, THE CITIES.) Cross Rue du Fort, continuing along Rue Ste-Anne, a lively enclave of sidewalk cafés, bistros, and restaurants made even livelier in summer by wandering minstrels and other curbside performers. Compulsive brochure collectors may wish to visit the *Maison du Tourisme* (12 Rue Ste-Anne; phone: 873-2015), which the province operates in the former *Union* hotel. Back on the pedestrian section of the street, sort out brochures around the umbrella-shaded tables of *Auberge du Trésor,* a stalwart, half-timbered veteran of the 17th-century tourist trade that bills itself as North America's oldest inn (see "Eating Out" in *Quebec City*, THE CITIES).

On the corner of Rue du Trésor is the *Musée de Cire* (Wax Museum; 22 Rue Ste-Anne; phone: 418-692-2289), another vintage landmark of the French colonial period (1732), where a permanent collection of wax figures in period settings depicts major events in early American and Canadian history. It's open daily; admission charge.

Now turn down the narrow alley of Rue du Trésor, a casual outdoor gallery for street artists, who cover every inch of wall space with their work and sketch portraits from life on the spot. The cramped passage of cheery bohemia was not always like this. Once upon a time, disgruntled settlers tramped down this strip to the colony's tax bureau, where they paid their dues to the *Royal Treasury:* Hence the name Treasury Street.

At the bottom of the lane, turn right on Rue Buade. This shopping street adopted the family name of Louis de Buade, Comte Frontenac, the famous soldier-governor of Canada during the French colonial period whose title lives on in the city's best-known landmark. At the intersection of Rue du Fort, take a moment to window shop at *La Maison Darlington* (7 Rue Buade; phone: 418-692-2268), a long-established import outlet for British tweeds and woolens. Save selecting from *Darlington*'s stock of Shetland sweaters and mohair rugs for a shopping spree in Quebec City; instead, cross Rue du Fort to the *Edifice Louis-St-Laurent* (No. 3; phone: 418-648-4177). On the main floor, visit the displays in the *Parks Canada Exhibition Room* for a quick lesson in Canadian history. The building was named for Louis St-Laurent, one of Canada's most popular prime ministers (1948–57), affectionately known in Liberal Party circles (and most of Canada) as "Uncle Louis." The exhibits are open daily; no admission charge. Crowning the crest of a hill at Côte de la Montagne, the *Bureau de Poste* (Post Office Building) was erected in 1871 on the site of the old *Chien d'Or* (Golden Dog) hotel, immortalized in a 19th-century romantic novel of the same name set in New France. (The English-born author, William Kirby, who settled in Canada in the 1830s, was a popular writer of his day whose works include *Annals of Niagara* and *The U.E.: A Tale of Upper Canada.*) A relief on the façade shows a dog chewing a bone over a bitter little ditty that reflects the vengeful spirit of the universal underdog:

> *I am a dog that gnaws his bone*
> *I crouch and gnaw it all alone*
> *A time will come, which is not yet*
> *When I'll bite him by whom I'm bit.*

The statue opposite the *Post Office* on Rue Port-Dauphin is a monument to Monseigneur François-Xavier de Montmorency-Laval, the first Bishop of Quebec and founder of the seminary that became U*niversité Laval* (see "Special Places" in *Quebec City,* THE CITIES).

Cross Côte de la Montagne (with a sharp eye on the traffic taking the precipitous route down to Lower Town), and pause to enjoy the view from Bishop Laval's namesake park, *Parc Montmorency* (see "Special Places" in *Quebec City,* THE CITIES). The park ramparts are part of the city fortifications, and strollers can look down from this section of the wall to the town below—where the first settlers came ashore in 1608—and out across the St. Lawrence to the opposite shore. Greening the hill that divides Upper and Lower Town, this shady retreat was a wheat field in 1618; it was tilled by Louis Hébert, the first French Canadian farmer, whose statue stands in the park. The first official residence of the Bishops of Quebec was built on the park site from 1691 to 1696. The statue of Sir George-Etienne-Cartier, French Canada's great statesman and Father of Confederation, shares the hilltop greenspace with Hébert's monument.

Leave the park at the corner of Côte de la Montagne and Rue Port-Dauphin; the *Archeveché* (Bishop's Palace) has commanded this crossroads since 1844, when the Palladian-style residence replaced the original palace that was across the road. Rue Port-Dauphin changes its name to Rue des Remparts as it follows the wall around the heights past the cannon that once guarded the city's northern flank.

Now turn left into Rue Ste-Famille to one of Upper Town's best-preserved historic houses. *Maison Touchet* (No. 15) dates from 1774, reflecting in its high chimneys and steeply pitched roofline the traditional 18th-century building style. Continue to the intersection with Rue Université, and examine the eclectic collection of historic treasures at the *Musée du Séminaire* (Seminary Museum; 9 Rue Université; phone: 418-692-2843), which houses Canadian and European art, old coins, gold ornaments, and scientific instruments. It's closed Mondays; admission charge. (For additional details, see "Special Places" in *Quebec City,* THE CITIES.)

From the museum, return to Ste-Famille and proceed up to the corner of Côte de la Fabrique and the spiritual and intellectual heart of Catholic Quebec. The *Basilique Notre-Dame-de-Québec* and its historic seminary make up a venerable ecclesiastical complex at the intersection of Côte de la Fabrique and Rue Buade, opposite Place de l'Hôtel-de-Ville (City Hall Square).

To the left of the basilica, at 1 Côte de la Fabrique, an ornate wrought-iron gate—crowned with the monogram of the Paris Foreign Missions seminary—leads to the interior courtyard of the *Séminaire de Québec,* which was founded in 1663 by Bishop Laval to administer parishes and bring "The Word" to the first Canadians. At about the same time, a minor seminary trained young colonists for the priesthood. In 1852, seminary authorities founded *Université Laval,* North America's first French-language Catholic university; *Laval* relocated to suburban Ste-Foy in 1946, but the minor seminary serves today as a private high school for boys and a coed college. Guided tours of the seminary precincts include a visit to the *Chapelle Extérieure* (Outer Chapel), a Romanesque relic of 1888 that replaced an 18th-century original, and the 1950 memorial crypt of Bishop Laval. While touring the seminary, don't miss the bishop's kitchen and its original baronial fireplace and the former refectory. Visits to the seminary must be arranged in advance and are possible from June through August (phone: 418-692-3981). (For additional details, see "Special Places" in *Quebec City,* THE CITIES.)

Next door to the seminary, the *Basilique Notre-Dame* (main entrance at 16 Rue Buade; phone: 418-692-2533) ranks among the finest examples of Baroque architecture in all of Quebec. *Notre-Dame,* which started life as a humble parish church in 1647, was elevated to cathedral status 27 years later, when North America's first Roman Catholic diocese outside Mexico was established here under Bishop Laval. Indeed, the cathedral stands as a worthy symbol of the resilience and determination of the French people. Since it was first built, the cathedral was enlarged several times, bombarded during the British siege of Quebec in 1759, ravaged by fires (the latest in 1922), and always lovingly reconstructed on the same site. Four Governors of New France, including Comte Frontenac, and most of the Bishops of Quebec are buried in the crypt. Guided tours through the basilica and crypt are conducted daily from May through October (also see *Historic Churches* in DIVERSIONS).

Cross over to Place de l'Hôtel-de-Ville (at its center is a monument honoring Cardinal Taschereau, Canada's first cardinal), and follow Côte de la Fabrique to the *Centre d'Interprétation de la Vie Urbaine* (Urban Life Interpretation Center; 43 Côte de la Fabrique; phone: 418-691-4606) in the basement of the *Hôtel de Ville* (City Hall). The center's host building was built in 1895 on the site of a former Jesuit college. Maintained by the *Quebec Historical Society,* the basement museum interprets contemporary life in an old city with a large model of the capital as it looked in 1975. Video displays, electronic hands-on presentations, and other exhibitions tell the story of the growth of the modern city and its distinctive cultural life. It's closed Mondays and from *Labour Day* to June 23; no admission charge.

Côte de la Fabrique—the area north and west of the seminary that classical scholars from *Université Laval* traversed—was one of the main thoroughfares of Canada's first Latin Quarter. Slip into these scholars' shoes as you follow their original route to the corner of Rue St-Jean. On the right is Rue Collins, which leads to Rue Charlevoix and the *Musée des Augustines de l'Hôtel-Dieu de Québec* (Museum of the Augustines of the Hôtel-Dieu of Quebec; 32 Rue Charlevoix; phone: 418-692-2492). The museum is housed on the first floor of the *Monastère des Augustines,* which adjoins North America's first hospital. (Members of the Augustine Order founded the *Hôpital l'Hôtel-Dieu* in 1639.) Some of the personal effects and medical instruments of the first nursing sisters are on display in the small museum, along with paintings, antique furniture, and 17th-century ornaments. Guided tours are conducted on request through the church and into the deep, vaulted cellars where the nuns found shelter during the various bombardments of Quebec. The museum is closed Mondays; no admission charge.

Continue along Rue Charlevoix to Côte du Palais; turn left onto Rue St-Jean. Walk south along St-Jean to its intersection with Rue St-Stanislas, then turn left toward Rue Cook. The *Eglise Presbytérienne* (St. Andrew's Presbyterian Church; 1810), on the corner of Rues Cook and Ste-Anne, is a major symbol of the introduction of British ways after the conquest. Presbyterian sons and daughters of members of James Wolfe's army first worshiped here, yet many would marry French girls and raise Québécois families of their own. These roots are recalled today in such names as Jean-François Stewart and Sandy Larocque.

From the church, follow Rue Ste-Anne along the south border of Place de l'Hôtel-de-Ville toward Rue des Jardins. On the right is the Art Deco *Edifice Price,* Quebec's first high-rise office building. At the corner, turn right on Rue des Jardins and walk up the hill to Rue Donnacona. Just before the intersection is the main entrance to the *Cathédrale Anglicane* (Holy Trinity Anglican Cathedral; 31 Rue des Jardins; phone: 418-692-2193). A copy of London's *St. Martin in the Fields,* the cathedral was built by royal decree of British monarch George III, who personally donated many of the church's treasures, including the silver communion service. During the summer visitors can attend weekly organ concerts and a festival evensong every afternoon at 4:45 PM. Daily guided tours are conducted from May through the first week in October. Just around the corner is the *Musée des Ursulines* (12 Rue Donnacona; phone: 418-694-0694). Quebec City's most endearing small museum, it is dedicated to the Ursuline Order's more than 350 years of service. Adjoining the *Chapelle des Ursulines,* where the sisters founded the oldest school for girls in North America, the museum sits so modestly behind its plain, gray stone walls that many sightseers pass it by. But don't: The dimly lit interior, tranquil as a tomb, affords a poignant glimpse of French Canada's history, from the time three unflappable Ursulines set up their primitive two-room convent on Lower Town's waterfront in 1639 to the last days of the French regime. The nuns moved up to the Donnacona site three years later, and they've been conducting classes in the convent school ever since. The museum is closed Mondays and December; admission charge. The charming little chapel next door (10 Rue Donnacona) contains the tombs of Reverend Mother Marie de l'Incarnation, who founded the order with Madame de la Peltier, and General Montcalm, defeated leader of the French army in the Battle of the Plains of Abraham.

The Marquis Louis-Joseph de Montcalm owes his final resting place to a nosy little schoolgirl with a long memory. In the confusion and sorrow that followed the fateful battle, no one noticed nine-year-old Amable Dubé following the torch-lit funeral cortege through the streets to the *Chapelle des Ursulines.* She watched the burial of the fallen hero as his hastily built coffin was lowered into a grave near the chapel grating. Seventy-four years later Amable, then an Ursuline nun, told this story to nuns who were contemplating erecting a tomb to honor Montcalm. The only living witness to the burial, she was even able to point to the exact gravesite.

Take a peek into the adjoining *Centre Marie-de-l'Incarnation* (phone: 418-692-2569), which combines a bookstore with films about the order's cofounder and a collection of her personal belongings. The center is closed Mondays; admission charge.

If it's lunchtime, stop just down the street at the *Café de la Paix* (see "Eating Out" in *Quebec City,* THE CITIES). Frequent visitors make a point of dropping by Benito Terzini's intimate main-floor restaurant just to make sure he hasn't changed the comfortable clutter of lamp-lit tables, pastry carts, wine racks, and Desrosier landscapes.

After lunch, continue up the block to Rue St-Louis and head back toward the starting point at the town gate at the top of the street. Halfway up, on the corner of Rue Corps de Garde, look for the tree with remnants of a cannonball wedged into its lower trunk—a reminder that walls and fortified gates were one of life's necessities when Vieux Québec was a battleground in Europe's struggle for mastery of North America.

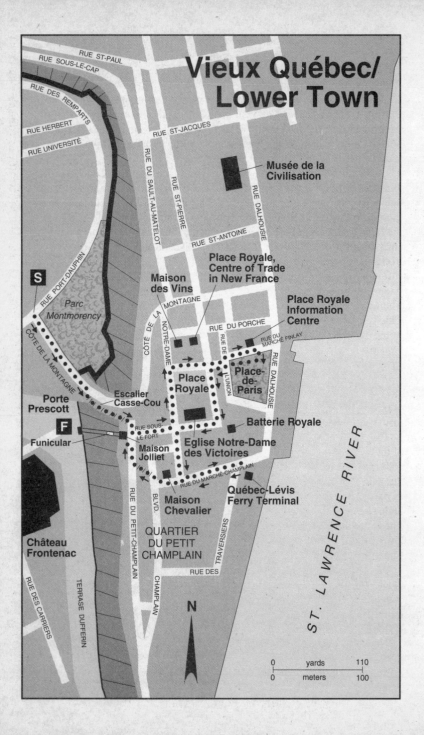

Walk 2: Vieux Québec/ Lower Town

There's an easy way down to the birthplace of Quebec City and a 90-minute walking tour of New France's first permanent settlement. A funicular at the north end of the *Terrasse Dufferin,* opposite the memorial statue of Samuel de Champlain, cranks passengers down over the rooftops to a safe landing in the heart of Lower Town in less than five minutes.

But that's hardly the historic way to go. The founder himself charted the original "road" between the new colony's upper and lower levels in 1623, three years after he built *Fort St-Louis* on the heights above the waterfront village. The Côte de la Montagne trail was hacked out of the sheer cliff face of Cap Diamant (Cape Diamond) to link port and fort. So conscientious historians generally leave the funicular for the return ascent, when an easy way up can be much appreciated. While going down, trace Champlain's route from the corner of Rue Port-Dauphin and still-precipitous Côte de la Montagne, following the grassy southern slope of *Parc Montmorency* to *Porte Prescott,* one of four remaining gateways to the walled city.

Porte Prescott suffered the same fate as other historic entries to town in 1871, when it was demolished along with its guardhouse to ease the kind of traffic congestion Champlain never imagined. A replica of the 18th-century original was erected on the site only 10 years ago.

Pass under the gate's arched bridge; to the left, a cross indicates the site of the settlement's first cemetery, opened after the first terrible winter of 1608–9, when at least 20 of the founding party died of scurvy. Halfway down the hill, to the right, the *Escalier Casse-Cou* (Break-Neck Staircase) isn't as dangerous as it sounds—and certainly nowhere near as taxing as the flights of 17th-century steps pedestrians climbed during the French regime. The city's first iron staircase replaced them in 1893; now wooden steps follow the iron-railed descent to the cliff in easy stages to Rue du Petit-Champlain.

At the foot of the stairs is one of the best seafood restaurants in Vieux Québec. Tucked into a centuries-old fieldstone building, *Le Marie Clarisse* has a devoted following of Upper Town regulars. Make reservations if you want to include a long, relaxed lunch in your Lower Town walking tour (see "Eating Out" in *Quebec City,* THE CITIES).

Next door, at the corner of Rues Petit-Champlain and Sous-le-Fort (Under the Fort), the *Maison Jolliet* is the funicular's Lower Town station. From the outside, the durable, white-plastered building maintains a traditional 1683 image, much as it was when Jolliet—the explorer who codiscovered the Mississippi River—came here to retire. Don't bother going inside: The all-too-commonplace souvenir shop features typical trinkets and T-shirts.

Walk down Rue Sous-le-Fort and turn left at Rue Notre-Dame, which leads into Place Royale. Entering Vieux Québec's earliest market square, you're probably walking over the site of Champlain's first *habitation*. Somewhere in the immediate vicinity, the founder, who arrived from France on July 3, 1608, with two shiploads of recruits, paced out a fortress plan on a stretch of level land between river and cliff. He set the shore party to work immediately, clearing the woods and building a storehouse and living quarters, surrounded by a stout palisade and ditch. But it was not all smooth sailing for the man who was to become known as the Father of New France. Within weeks malcontents were hatching a plot to assassinate him and to escape to sea with the company stores. Undismayed, Champlain promptly put down the mutiny, executed the ringleader, and carried on with preparations for the winter ahead.

Nothing remains of that first fragile outpost of French civilization in North America, but archaeologists have discovered the foundations of a second *habitation* (1624) under *Eglise Notre-Dame-des-Victoires* (Our Lady of Victories Church; Pl. Royale; phone: 418-692-1650). Indeed, the quaint, little, gray stone church on the south side of the *place* is literally the cradle of New France.

By the time *Notre-Dame* was built over the earliest settlement ruins in 1688, Champlain had died and left New France to his successors. Place du Marché had become Place Royale, a proper colonial setting for the bust of King Louis XIV that was installed at this crossroads of the young frontier town. Today's square, with its authentic, sole-testing paving stones and center-stage replica of the original Sun King effigy, remains an economic crossroads of sorts. Tourists—not furs or lumber—are the stock in trade, buzzing in and out of the district's boutiques, galleries, snack shops, and restaurants.

After admiring *Notre-Dame*'s beautifully restored interior and its unusual, castle-shape high altar, wine fanciers won't want to miss the *Maison des Vins* (House of Wines; 1 Pl. Royale; phone: 418-643-1214), on the opposite side of the square. Colonial merchant Eustache-Lambert Dumont had this substantial stone domicile built to order a year after *Notre-Dame* appeared on the Place Royale scene. Now his deep storage vaults, some of which predate the building, are stocked with a small fortune in rare vintage wines, which visitors are invited to inspect before getting down to business in the street-level retail outlet. Customers have a choice of a thousand bottles of wine at their disposal—anything from the ordinary table variety to oenophilic extravagances at $1,000 a cork. It's closed Sundays and Mondays; no admission charge.

Now look at the many historically correct restorations that envelop the square, in the spirit of the 17th and 18th centuries. Many of these buildings remain private homes, while others are business offices and crafts studios. Like their ancestors, Québécois live and work here, adding an infectious vibrancy to the historic *quartier*.

Visitors can see how colonial shoppers did their marketing when they stop by *Place Royale, Centre of Trade in New France* (phone: 418-643-6631), one of two Place Royale interpretive centers, next door to the *Maison des Vins*. At the sign of 17th-century merchant Nicolas Jérémie, three restored properties are devoted to exhibits and a multimedia show that trace the development of a young country during the halcyon days of the fur trade. The show is presented daily, June 7 through September; no admission charge.

From here, take Rue de la Place on the east side of the square to Rue St-Pierre. Turn right to cross the threshold of another reclaimed townhouse (25 Rue St-Pierre; phone: 418-643-6631). This colonial homestead has been converted to another interpretive center, *Place Royale, 400 Years of History,* whose exhibitions tell the story of Lower Town's early beginnings as a trading post through its prosperous heyday as the financial hub of New France to the present day. It's open daily, June 7 through September; no admission charge.

Return to the corner of Rue de la Place and head toward the river and Rue du Marché-Finlay. Here, at the *Entrepôt Thibodeau* (Thibodeau Warehouse), you can join a guided/audio tour of the neighborhood that is steeped in stories of Lower Town's past and get handy information about activities or entertainment on or around the *place*. The information center is open daily, June 7 through September (phone: 418-643-6631). It overlooks Place de Paris, where Champlain's settlers came ashore (the river was higher then) at the corner of Rues de la Place and de l'Union. A contemporary geometric sculpture, *Dialogue avec l'Histoire,* is believed to mark the exact spot of the first landing.

Also well worth a visit is *Batterie Royale,* south across Place de Paris, at the corner of Rues St-Pierre and Sous-le-Fort. Buried for years under a sprawl of wharf development, the original 1691 defense system was unearthed 18 years ago and rebuilt in the image of its 18th-century self, complete with gun ports and cannon. The battery was part of the city's defense during the siege of Quebec, when Wolfe's army lobbed 40,000 cannonballs and 10,000 fire bombs onto the capital.

Three stalwart neighbors of the battery escaped the worst of the enemy fire eventually to become a cultural center, maintained by the *Musée de la Civilisation.* To visit them, follow Rue Sous-le-Fort west to its intersection with Rue Notre-Dame and turn left toward Rue du Marché-Champlain, where the *Maison Chevalier* (60 Rue du Marché-Champlain; phone: 418-643-9689) offers a glimpse of 17th- and 18th-century Lower Town life. The trio of historic buildings that make up the complex was built by master mason Pierre Renaud for the Chenaye de la Garonne, Frérot, and Chevalier families between 1695 and 1752. All have been restored to their prime as handsome, five-story dwellings with massive chimneys towering over their steep, red rooflines. They were designed for safety and warmth to accommodate the leaders of Lower Town's merchant society, and Renaud used four-foot-thick stone for the walls. The *Maison Chevalier* is open daily mid-May to mid-October; no admission charge.

On the corner opposite the *Maison Chevalier, La Vieille Maison du Spaghetti* (Old Spaghetti House; 40 Rue du Marché-Champlain; phone: 418-694-9144) has adopted a row of refurbished 18th-century homes to house a reasonably priced pasta parlor. Warm-weather customers can sit out on the flower-banked terrace and think about the next leg of the tour over a fortifying pizza. From the umbrella-shaded tables, it's a short stroll back down Rue du Marché-Champlain to the waterfront and the *Québec-Lévis* ferry terminal (10 Rue des Traversiers; phone: 418-644-3704). Add half an hour to the excursion for a return trip across the river to the Lévis shore. The commuter service departs every hour on the half hour between 6 AM and 7:30 PM, less frequently in the evenings. Sightseers going along for the ride aren't expected to disembark with the commuters. From the ferry deck, passengers can enjoy a superb view of the city, the little gray port with the multicolored rooftops huddled at the base of the cliff, and the turrets and spires of the *Château Frontenac* dominating the heights.

Those who want to forgo the St. Lawrence and its views should walk west from the restaurant into Rue Cul-de-Sac, which forms a little shopping corner around the rear walls of the *Maison Chevalier* before it merges with Boulevard Champlain. Take the first staircase to the right, just beyond the *Anse aux Barques* restaurant (28 Blvd. Champlain).

At the top of the stairs is Rue du Petit-Champlain, the heart of Vieux Québec's first shopping street and the oldest of such streets in Canada. Once Quebec was established as a lucrative trading post, its waterfront settlement flourished as a busy port with plenty of opportunities for canny dealers and fortune seekers. Quartier du Petit-Champlain was the colony's main financial district, its namesake street lined with the homes, shops, and counting houses of newly prosperous tradesmen and ship owners. But the district fell into a decline toward the end of the 19th century, as residents moved onward and upward, abandoning Lower Town to the wharf and the businesses there. Thirty or so years ago, visitors determined enough to see all sides of Quebec rattled down Lower Town's old main drag in horse-drawn calèches and gawked at a sad little slum of a street, a narrow plank road where barefoot children scrambled around the tourist traffic begging for coins and candy.

Today, the old broken-down tenements and shanties have been restored to make Rue du Petit-Champlain Canada's oldest shopping center. These days the pedestrian route could pass for the High Street of a seaport village in France, flanked with interesting boutiques, galleries, and crafts studios. Take time to window shop both sides of the street, from the corner of Rue Sous-le-Fort down to the junction with Boulevard Champlain.

For a short shopping spree on this, Quebec City's best little shopping strip, stop first on the north side at *Pot-en-Ciel* (No. 27; phone: 418-692-1743), which displays the works of Quebec potters, ceramists, and carvers. Nearby, *Les Vêteries* (No. 31½; phone: 418-694-1215) features high fashion in wool, silk, mohair, and cotton. The following is a select list from which to choose, or visit them all—you won't be disappointed: *Atelier Ibiza* (No. 47; phone: 418-692-2103) is a reliable source of fine leatherwear, and *Le Jardin de l'Argile* (No. 51; phone: 418-692-4870) is Canada's only outlet for sweet, sleepy-faced "Lorteau" figurines, each an individual work of glazed clay in delicate pastel colors. The Quebec City artist creates just 300 pieces a year, which the store will ship to almost any address in the world. *Studio d'Art Georgette Pihay* (No. 53; phone: 418-692-0297) is the atelier-gallery of the popular Belgian-born sculptor. At *Le Fou du Roi* (No. 57; phone: 418-692-4439) are educational toys, domestic and imported. *Peau sur Peau* (No. 85; phone: 418-694-1921) offers high fashion in leather for men and women, and *O Kwa Ri* (At the Sign of The Bear; No. 59; phone: 418-692-0009) is a place for indigenous crafts.

Cross to the south side of the street for a look at the handmade dolls at the *Galerie Le Fil du Temps* (No. 88; phone: 418-692-5867); here, exquisitely crafted dolls can cost anywhere from $100 to $6,000. Or satisfy yourself with a chocolate fix at the *Confiserie d'Epoque Madame Gigi* (No. 84; phone: 418-692-2825). The *Théâtre du Petit-Champlain* (No. 66; phone: 418-692-2631) mounts regular French-language productions near *Le Lapin Sauté* (No. 52; phone: 418-692-5325), a modest but agreeable little café, open for breakfast, lunch, dinner, and after-theater supper. Pauline Pelletier's *Petite Galerie* (No. 30; phone: 418-692-4871) is a showcase for the works of this innovative Quebec ceramist and other regional artists who share the retail space with imported exotica from India, China, Thailand, and other faraway sources. *Créaly* (No. 26; phone: 418-692-4753) is a retail outlet for Quebec artists and artisans and a source of such unusual finds as decorative leather masks and costume jewelry set with semi-precious stones.

This walk has come full-circle back to the *Maison Jolliet.* Hardy souls may want to walk in the shoes of a typical 17th-century Canadian, but the funicular may seem a better way to go. Just pay your fare, crowd into the often-packed, glass-walled car, enjoy the view, and *voilà,* you're at the *Terrasse Dufferin.*

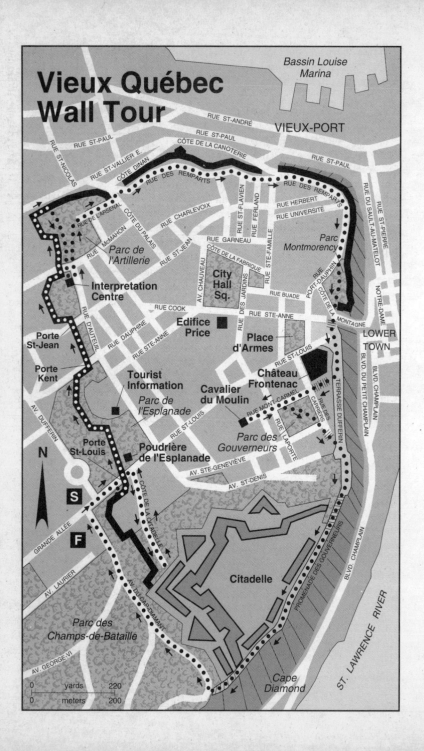

Vieux Québec Wall Tour

Bassin Louise Marina

VIEUX-PORT

RUE ST-ANDRÉ

RUE ST-PAUL

RUE ST-PAUL

RUE ST-NICOLAS

RUE ST-PAUL

CÔTE DE LA CANOTERIE

CÔTE DINAN

RUE ST-VALLIER E.

RUE DES REMPARTS

RUE DES REMPARTS

RUE ST-PIERRE

RUE DU SAULT-AU-MATELOT

RUE ST-PAUL

RUE DE L'ARSENAL

RUE CHARLEVOIX

RUE ST-FLAVIEN

RUE FERLAND

RUE HERBERT

RUE UNIVERSITÉ

Parc Montmorency

CÔTE DU PALAIS

RUE McMAHON

Parc de l'Artillerie

RUE ST-JEAN

RUE GARNEAU

CÔTE DE LA FABRIQUE

RUE STE-FAMILLE

RUE PORT-DAUPHIN

NOTRE-DAME

Interpretation Centre

AV. CHAUVEAU

City Hall Sq.

RUE DES JARDINS

RUE BUADE

CÔTE DE LA MONTAGNE

LOWER TOWN

Porte St-Jean

RUE D'AUTEUIL

RUE COOK

Edifice Price

RUE STE-ANNE

Place d'Armes

RUE ST-LOUIS

Porte Kent

RUE DAUPHINE

RUE STE-ANNE

Château Frontenac

BLVD. DU PETIT CHAMPLAIN

BLVD. CHAMPLAIN

AV. DUFFERIN

Tourist Information

Parc de l'Esplanade

Cavalier du Moulin

RUE MONT-CARMEL

RUE ST-LOUIS

TERRASSE DUFFERIN

Porte St-Louis

RUE ST-LOUIS

Poudrière de l'Esplanade

RUE LAPORTE

Parc des Gouverneurs

N

S

F

CÔTE DE LA CITADELLE

AV. STE-GENEVIEVE

AV. ST-DENIS

GRANDE ALLÉE

AV. LAURIER

AV. DU CAP-DIAMANT

Citadelle

PROMENADE DES GOUVERNEURS

BLVD. CHAMPLAIN

ST. LAWRENCE RIVER

Parc des Champs-de-Bataille

AV. GEORGE-VI

Cape Diamond

| 0 | yards | 220 |
| 0 | meters | 200 |

Walk 3: Vieux Québec Wall Tour

Doing your own version of sentry duty on the ramparts of Vieux Québec is a unique tourist attraction: No other Canadian city—no North American one, for that matter—is enclosed by historic walls on which you can walk. No longer protection against invading armies, Quebec City's walls are open to all who care to trace the course of the city's history—although they're closed from December through February, when ice and snow make the route hazardous. At other times, though, visitors are welcome to walk on top of a long, western section of the fortifications as they make the traditional 3-mile circuit of *la vieille capitale*'s defense system. Allow three hours for this tour, taking time out to explore the military highlights along the way and to savor the magnificent views from the heights.

The logical departure point for a wall walk is the *Citadelle* (on Côte de la Citadelle), the star-shaped fortress commanding the city's critical southern flank. The "Gibraltar of North America" wasn't part of the 17th-century defense network French army engineers started in 1690. The French had intended to encircle the entire capital with a protective wall, but when New France fell to the British in 1759, only the western section between Cap Diamant and Côte du Palais was finished. After the conquest, the British followed the original plan for 63 years, building ramparts and fortified gates; from 1820 to 1832 they constructed their own "Gibraltar," 350 feet above the St. Lawrence River.

Today the fortifications, part of a national park administered by *Parks Canada*, have been designated a historic monument. The *Citadelle*, from which a hostile shot has never been fired, is the largest manned fortress in North America; home of the Royal 22nd Regiment, the legendary "Van Doos"; and Quebec residence of Canada's governors-general. Although the Van Doos—a phonetic approximation of the French word for 22 *(vingt-deux)*—have not been called upon to defend Canada at home, they have distinguished themselves in battle in both World Wars and are regarded as one of the country's most valiant regiments.

From the *Porte St-Louis* entrance to Upper Town, turn right into Côte de la Citadelle and continue up the hill to the fort's visitors' entrance. The military complex includes 25 buildings, the *Redoute Cap-Diamant* (Cape Diamond Redoubt; 1693), and five heavily fortified bastions. Tour guides lead visitors around the public areas, through the *Regimental Museum*, located in a former powderhouse (1750), and into an old military prison. The big treat here is the changing of the guard ceremony (mid-June to *Labour Day*), when the Van Doos in their natty red tunics and bearskin busbies put on a daily show at 10 AM, weather permitting. The citadel and museum are closed December through February, except to groups with reservations (write to the *Musée de la Citadelle,* CP 6020, Haute-Ville, QUE G1R 4V7); open during *Carnaval.* Admission charge (phone: 418-648-3563). For more information about the *Citadelle* and the fortifications, see "Special Places" in *Quebec City,* THE CITIES.

From the citadel, retrace your steps down to Rue St-Louis and cross to the *Poudrière de l'Esplanade* (Esplanade Powderhouse), a reception and interpretive center just inside *Porte St-Louis* (see *Walk 1: Vieux Québec/Upper Town*). Conducted tours of the fortifications begin here. If you prefer to explore on your own, go back through the gate toward Grande Allée and climb the staircase to the wall on the citadel side of the street. Follow the footpath west over *Parc de l'Esplanade, Porte Kent,* and *Porte St-Jean* to *Parc de l'Artillerie,* a strategic defense site for more than 250 years. This oldest section of the wall owes its life to Lord Dufferin, a farsighted Governor-General of Canada who took office just as Quebec was preparing to demolish the entire defense system to further urban sprawl.

With the departure of British troops from the citadel in 1871, a change in the landscape of Old Quebec occurred when federal authorities, bowing to public pressure, had the walls torn down; at the same time, they lowered the eastern ramparts. The decision angered the governor-general of the day, Lord Frederick Temple Hamilton-Temple-Blackwood, the First Marquess of Dufferin and Ava. Realizing the value of the fortifications, he had the decision overturned and launched a salvage operation to preserve the walls and rebuild some of the gates.

Leave the wall via the stairs at the northwest end of *Parc de l'Artillerie* at Rue de l'Arsenal, and walk back across the green to the interpretive center (2 Rue d'Auteuil; phone: 418-648-4205). Three buildings are open to visitors here—the center itself, where, among other educational exhibits, an intricate scale model of Quebec reproduces Upper and Lower Town as they were in 1808; the *Redoute Dauphine* (1712–48); and the 1820 officers' quarters. The center is closed Monday mornings April through September; closed weekends the rest of the year; no admission charge.

Return across the park to the intersection of Rue de l'Arsenal and Côte du Palais, and turn left to the junction with Rue des Remparts. Follow the north section of the fortifications at sidewalk level, pausing to look across the wall to the Vieux Port restorations, its farmers' market, and the *Bassin Louise* marina.

Turn away from the view and the cannon-mounted walls at 51 Rue des Remparts and look for the plaque on the left side of the house that marks the *Maison Montcalm,* the residence French General Montcalm occupied for only a year until he fell in the Battle of the Plains of Abraham. In recent times the house has been decked out in ways that doubtless would not amuse the aristocratic seigneur of the *Château Candiac.* Montcalm's old lodgings seem to change color with the seasons. Currently, the private house is painted an eye-popping purple.

Continue around the northeast curve of the defense works into *Parc Montmorency,* a restful spot to find a park bench under the trees at the halfway mark on the tour (see *Walk 1: Vieux Québec/Upper Town*). The wall rings the east side of the cliff-top park and continues over the Pont Porte-Prescott (Porte Prescott Bridge) across Côte de la Montagne to the *Escalier Frontenac* (Frontenac Staircase), one of 25 stairways that link one level of the Old City to another. From the top of the stairs you'll see the *Terrasse Dufferin,* the broad boardwalk promenade that follows the ramparts along Upper Town's eastern approach.

The brainchild of colonial Governor Lord John George Lambton Durham, the terrace emerged in 1838, an expansive version of an English seaside "prom," and was extended 40 years later with pavilions for gull's-eye viewing above the chest-high walls by order of Governor-General Lord Dufferin. That work was done by architect Charles Baillairgé, the designer of the current façade of *Notre-Dame-de-la-Paix de Québec,* Quebec's basilica. Spring through fall (the breezy terrace is a bone-chiller in winter), the boardwalk is the capital's most popular rendezvous, as much a part of Quebec City's tourist image as the *Château Frontenac.*

Follow the promenade south, past the *Monument de Champlain* (Champlain Monument) and *Château Frontenac,* toward Cap Diamant and the *Citadelle.* If hunger strikes, this may be the time to stop by the *Château's Café de la Terrasse,* where window-table customers can watch the passing parade in comfort. Look for an entrance to the *Terrasse* at the hotel's northeast corner by the ice-cream counter. (For details on the restaurant, see "Eating Out" in *Quebec City,* THE CITIES.) The hotel's main entrance is a few yards away, off Rue St-Louis at 1 Rue des Carrières. For strollers who prefer to snack while walking or while seated on a boardwalk bench, refreshment is also available at a couple of outdoor stands along the way.

Find a spot along the boardwalk for a peek over the wall at Lower Town below and beyond to the ocean-bound river traffic that shares the St. Lawrence River with fleets of local sailboats. On clear days you can see downriver as far as Côte de Beaupré and Ile d'Orléans, and well beyond the Lévis skyline on the opposite shore.

From the river-view ramparts, turn inland at the south corner of the *Château* and mount the steps to Rue Mont-Carmel. At the west end of the street is the *Cavalier du Moulin* (Windmill Outpost), a pretty, tranquil park, located on land that once was a strategic military site. Named for the windmill that once stood here, it was converted to a military outpost in 1693, with orders to destroy the *Redoute Cap-Diamant* and the *St-Louis* bastion if either fell into enemy hands.

Turn back from the park on Rue Mont-Carmel, and cut across *Parc des Gouverneurs* toward the boardwalk. When the *Château St-Louis* stood at the north end of the terrace, residents of the colonial governor's palace claimed the park as their private garden. Now it's the peaceful setting for an unusual war monument, dedicated to two opposing generals—James Wolfe and Louis-Joseph, Marquis de Montcalm. In one of history's bitter quirks, both were personal losers in the battle for Quebec. British commander Wolfe died on his field of victory. The defeated French general was carried off the battleground mortally wounded. He died the following day, thankfully proclaiming, "I shall not live to see the English masters of Quebec."

At the park's southeast corner—where Avenue Ste-Geneviève meets Rue des Carrières—at the end of a row of fine old 19th-century houses is the *US Consulate* (2 Pl. Terrasse-Dufferin; phone: 418-692-2095). Once occupied by officers from the citadel garrison, nearly all of the houses have been converted to small private hotels. Take the first set of steps down to the terrace and continue south to the staircase and Promenade des Gouverneurs. The view from the stairway clinging to the rim of the cliff is well worth the climb. The governors' walk extends along the east flank of the citadel to the tip of Cap Diamant, where hardy souls can press on into *Parc des Champs-de-Bataille* (Battlefields Park)—or save that excursion for another day.

From the Cap Diamant lookout, follow the park path or Avenue du Cap-Diamant down the grassy hillside, past the citadel's southwest bastions, to the city wall and *Porte St-Louis,* where the fortifications tour began.

Walk 4: "New" Quebec

Newcomers to Quebec's famous walled city often get so caught up in the romance of the *quartiers historiques* that they overlook life beyond the walls. Many leave thinking they have seen what there is to see, like someone who visits central London and the theater district and then "ticks" London off as an experience.

The story of the provincial capital is a tale of two cities. Old Quebec, the 323-acre UNESCO World Heritage preserve, includes the community within the ramparts and the waterfront village below the fortifications where the first settlers arrived in 1608, while "New" Quebec, which took shape in the early 1800s when prosperous townsfolk began moving out toward the country villages of Sillery and Ste-Foy, covers a vast area of residential neighborhoods, industrial zones, government and corporate office towers, and suburban shopping malls. But here too is where the most fateful battle in Canadian history took place, and where the National Assembly, the legislature for the province of Quebec, is charting the province's strategy in its constitutional negotiations with the rest of Canada.

Porte St-Louis is the traditional gateway to New Quebec, the start of this four-hour walk from the Old World to the new along Grande Allée. This gracious avenue, which Quebeckers proudly compare to the Champs-Elysées, is a charming section of Route 175, the main link between Vieux Québec and Ste-Foy.

Beyond *Parc des Champs-de-Bataille* (Battlefields Park), Grande Allée becomes Chemin St-Louis and, beyond Sillery, Boulevard Laurier. But its eastern section, just beyond the walls, is one of the capital's most beguiling strolling venues. Once Quebec City's most prestigious residential enclave, the thoroughfare is lined on both tree-shaded sides by stately Victorian and Edwardian mansions, most of which have been converted to restaurants, bars, and discos. In summer, when every restaurant opens bright umbrellas and awnings over its sidewalk café, the stretch of conviviality between Place George-V and Place Montcalm is transformed into a round-the-clock block party. Compulsive party animals prowl here until the last bar closes, and daytime strollers can always find a lively *terrasse* oasis for people watching.

As you cross Avenue Dufferin onto Grande Allée, you'll be following a trail that native trappers tramped out of the wilderness in the early 1600s, when they brought their furs to the French trading post of Kebec. During the French regime, this was the colony's longest road, the main link to other frontier outposts. Walking in the same direction, you'll pass an entrance to *Parc des Champs-de-Bataille* (at Av. George-VI); just beyond the park entrance, modern buildings with Orwellian-sounding names—like *Complexe H* and *Complexe J*—house the offices of Quebec's premier. On the oppo-

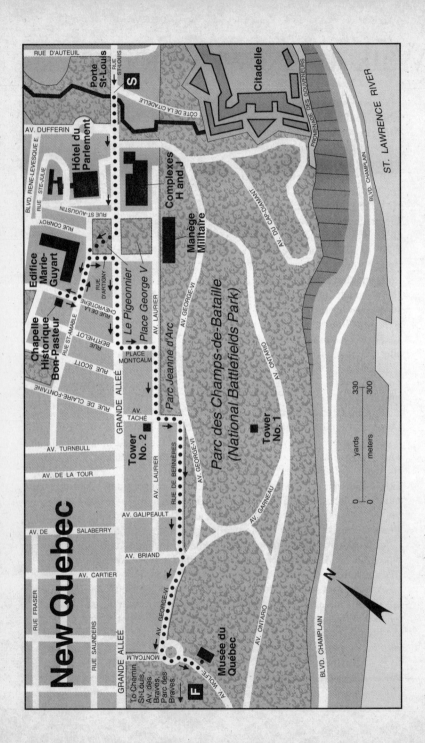

New Quebec

RUE D'AUTEUIL

RUE ST-LOUIS

Porte St-Louis

S

AV. DUFFERIN

CÔTE DE LA CITADELLE

Citadelle

ST. LAWRENCE RIVER

PROMENADE DES GOUVERNEURS

BLVD. RENÉ-LÉVESQUE E.

RUE STE-JULIE

Hôtel du Parlement

RUE ST-AUGUSTIN

Complexes H and J

Manège Militaire

AV. DU CAP-DIAMANT

BLVD. CHAMPLAIN

RUE CONROY

Edifice Marie-Guyart

RUE D'ARTIGNY

Le Pigeonnier
Place George V

AV. LAURIER

AV. GEORGE-VI

Chapelle Historique Bon-Pasteur

RUE DE LA CHEVROTIÈRE

RUE ST-AMABLE

RUE BERTHELOT

RUE SCOTT

PLACE MONTCALM

Parc Jeanne d'Arc

Parc des Champs-de-Bataille
(National Battlefields Park)

RUE DE CLAIRE-FONTAINE

GRANDE ALLÉE

AV. TACHÉ

AV. TURNBULL

Tower No. 2

AV. LAURIER

RUE DE BERNIÈRES

AV. GEORGE-VI

AV. ONTARIO

Tower No. 1

AV. DE LA TOUR

330
300

AV. GALIPEAULT

yards
meters

AV. DE SALABERRY

AV. BRIAND

0
0

AV. GARNEAU

AV. CARTIER

AV. GEORGE-VI

RUE FRASER

MONTCALM

N

RUE SAUNDERS

GRANDE ALLÉE

To Chemin
St-Louis,
Av. des
Braves,
Parc des
Braves

AV. WOLFE

AV. GEORGE-VI

Musée du Québec

AV. ONTARIO

BLVD. CHAMPLAIN

F

site side of the Allée, the *Hôtel du Parlement,* home of Quebec's National Assembly, dominates the landscaped greens of Colline Parlementaire (Parliament Hill) at the corner of Avenue Dufferin and Grande Allée.

New France's first legislative assembly was housed in the bishop's palace on the site of today's *Parc Montmorency* (see *Walk 1: Vieux Québec/Upper Town*). In 1869, when the legislators for the then two-year-old province decided they had outgrown their *palais épiscopal* accommodations, they chose a place beyond *Porte St-Louis* where the English once played cricket; the seat of government still exists. A modified version of the *Louvre* in Paris, the *Hôtel du Parlement* was designed and built between 1877 and 1886 under the direction of architect Eugène-Etienne Taché, whose place in Quebec history was assured when he personally carved *"Je me souviens"* ("I remember") into the building's provincial crest, a quotation the latter-day province has adopted as its motto.

Guided tours are available for visitors who'd like to see the *Legislative Council Chamber* and the Renaissance-style *National Assembly Chamber* where Quebec's elected representatives meet. *Le Parlementaire* (phone: 418-643-7239), the parliamentary restaurant, is open to the public between noon and 9 PM when the Assembly is in session.

The bronze statue facing Grande Allée from the legislature lawn is of Maurice Duplessis; the most dominant man in the history of Quebec politics, he ruled the province between 1936 and 1939 and again from 1944 until his death in 1959. Beyond Colline Parlementaire, Grande Allée bisects two small parks: *Place George-V* and *Le Pigeonnier* (Pigeon Park). Bird-loving Québécois maintain a heated birdhouse and feeder in the center of *Le Pigeonnier;* local pigeons seem to like the cuisine, but few stay the night. From *Place George-V* you'll see the *Manège Militaire* (Drill Hall) in *Parc des Champs-de-Bataille,* another Eugène-Etienne Taché work, dating from 1888. Militia units still perfect their parade-ground technique here.

Detour off Grande Allée by cutting across *Le Pigeonnier* to Rue St-Amable, and turn right at the corner of Rue de la Chevrotière. Stop at No. 1037 for the best panoramic view in Quebec City. *Galerie Anima G* (phone: 418-643-9841) is on the 31st floor of *Edifice Marie-Guyart (Complexe G),* the city's highest observation point; visitors can tour an exhibition of works by Quebec artists and enjoy views of the city and the river flowing beyond.

From *Complexe G,* cross the street to the *Chapelle Historique Bon-Pasteur* (1080 Rue de la Chevrotière; phone: 418-648-9710). Here, tour the Romanesque-Baroque chapel of the sisters of Bon-Pasteur de Québec (1868), leaving plenty of time to admire the intricately carved and gilded high altar and works of art by members of the order (see "Special Places" in *Quebec City,* THE CITIES). Next, return to Rue St-Amable and walk back toward *Le Pigeonnier,* where on a summer day you're likely to happen upon an outdoor concert.

Follow the west side of the park along Rue d'Artigny to Grande Allée; this is the threshold of the Allée's most sprightly R & R area. At the corner, *Vogue* (1170 Rue d'Artigny; phone: 418-647-2100) is a split-level rendezvous, with a café-bar on the ground floor and a disco upstairs. *Sherlock Holmes* (phone: 418-529-9973), one of the new breed of British pubs to make the capital scene, shares the premises. Around the corner, *Brandy* (690 Grande Allée; phone: 418-648-8739) is a popular hangout for the thirtysomething crowd. Now follow the lineup of outdoor terraces (they're open on sunny days till the end of September) to *L'Express Minuit* (No. 680; phone: 418-529-7713), another hot spot for young and young-at-heart discomaniacs.

Le Bonaparte (phone: 418-647-4747), a veteran of Grande Allée's top-ranking restaurant colony, shares the address, if not the spirit, of *L'Express Minuit.* Diners can enjoy classic French cuisine on *Le Bonaparte*'s terrace or in the formal dining room indoors.

A few steps along the Allée, the *Auberge Louis Hébert* combines a small, upper-floor hotel of 10 rooms with a street-level restaurant and summer terrace. Across the street, *Au Petit Coin Breton* serves reasonably priced crêpe specialties indoors and out. Back on the opposite side of the Allée, *Le Paris-Brest* has contrived a winning combination of traditional French fare and Art Deco flair. (For details on all three eateries, see "Eating Out" in *Quebec City,* THE CITIES.) The terrace of *Loews Le Concorde* is a striking, tomorrow-designed presence on the stately home strip of 19th-century Quebec, topped by *L'Astral,* the city's only revolving tower restaurant (see "Checking In" in *Quebec City,* THE CITIES).

Cross Grande Allée here, where a statue of French General Montcalm stands at the head of Place Montcalm. It's a replica of the original monument in Candiac, the Provençal estate near Nîmes, France, where Louis-Joseph, Marquis de Montcalm, was born in 1712. The defeated general died within the walls of Old Quebec, but he suffered his fatal wounds not far from here on the historic battlefield above Cap Diamant.

Walk down Place Montcalm to Avenue Laurier to the verge of the Plaines d'Abraham (Plains of Abraham), the undulating expanse of wheat fields and pasture land where British General James Wolfe and soldiers under his command clashed with the French defenders of Quebec on a sunny September morning in 1759. The land, first cleared by a Scot, Abraham Martin, more than a century earlier, was still open farmland on that day when the English surprised the French so close to the walls of the city. The skirmish—involving some 9,000 soldiers—was over in 20 minutes, as New France fell to England and both sides lost their military leaders.

Today the battlefield has healed into *Parc des Champs-de-Bataille,* a national park encompassing 250 acres of green meadows, woodlands, and gardens laced with paths and scenic motorways. Since 1908, when the battlefield was landscaped in its current form, the land has become a haven for cyclists, joggers, picnickers, and park-bench readers in summer, and cross-country skiers in winter. Calèche drivers take passengers through the park in every season. Commemorative plaques, stones, and artillery pieces trace the course of the conflict, but they're scattered throughout the park, easily missed in grassy hollows and wooded glades.

Continuing along the avenue, you'll pass *Jardin Jeanne d'Arc,* with its flower-banked equestrian statue of the warrior saint; this is the site where, in 1880, "O Canada" was played for the first time. At the corner of Avenues Taché and Laurier, *Tour* (Tower) *No. 2,* one of the four Martello towers Britain added to its Quebec defense arsenal between 1801 and 1811, still stands guard over the plains, in line with *Tour No. 1,* closer to the cliffs above the St. Lawrence River. Both are open during the summer.

Turn left on Avenue Taché and continue along Rue de Bernières to Avenue George-VI, a scenic parkway that leads to the *Musée du Québec* (see below). At the Grande Allée end of the avenue, a monument to General Wolfe marks the spot where the 32-year-old commander died in a sheltered dell behind the lines. Wounded three times as he led the charge, he lived just long enough to hear of the French defeat. "God be praised, I die happy," he sighed, with his last breath.

But the French do not associate the Plaines d'Abraham with only defeat. Six months after the battle, the French fought for—and very nearly won back—their beloved city. Under Gaston-François, Chevalier de Lévis, Montcalm's second in command, a force of 7,000, some armed with no more than hunting guns and knives, captured Ste-Foy and whipped the overconfident British on the plains before laying siege to the town. Only the arrival of the British fleet dashed hopes of further victories, and Lévis was forced to lift the siege and retreat to Montreal, where he was soon surrounded by superior forces. The final capitulation, signed the following September, officially ended France's regime in Canada.

Leave the plains now for the *Musée du Québec,* which stands at the opposite end of Avenue Wolfe-Montcalm. Four years ago, the original 1933 neoclassical building was linked to the Old Quebec jail next door to create a stunning complex of galleries and administrative offices, with a modern library and auditorium. Art lovers may decide to end the tour here and spend the rest of the day viewing a collection of Quebec art that spans the centuries, from the early French colonial period to the 1990s. International and other Canadian artists also are well represented.

The glass-roofed *Salle Grand* opens on an attractive restaurant and terrace café overlooking the plains, where weary walkers can map out the next stage of the tour over lunch or tea, while history buffs who haven't yet had their fill will want to stop first at the *Parc des Champs-de-Bataille* exhibition room on Level 1 of the *Pavillon Baillairgé,* where they can locate important battle sites on a model of the plains. Strollers who've wound up their tour admiring the art in one of the museum's 11 galleries will want to stop in its well-stocked gift boutique for cards, books, and gift items. The museum is closed *New Year's Day, Christmas,* and Mondays from September 7 to May 16. No admission charge Wednesdays (phone: 418-643-2150).

In summer, a free shuttle-bus service departs from the museum area for guided tours of the battlefield. Determined walkers should follow Avenue Montcalm out to the *Terrasse Earl-Grey* for one more dramatic view of the river before wandering back to town through the park. Or leave the national preserve at the junction of Avenue Montcalm and Chemin St-Louis (the extension of Grande Allée) and walk two blocks west to Avenue des Braves. At the end of the avenue, a monument in *Parc des Braves* (Park of the Brave) recalls Lévis's short-lived victory of 1760. Avenue des Braves intersects with Chemin Ste-Foy, an old colonial road, where strollers who've decided to call it a day can catch the No. 7 bus back to the walled city via *Porte St-Jean*. Those whose arches have held up can walk back to town along Grande Allée and on to Rue St-Louis and the heart of Vieux Québec.

Glossary

Useful Words and Phrases

Unlike their European counterparts, French Canadians are almost unfailingly cordial and helpful, especially when you attempt to speak even a few words of their language. So don't be afraid of misplaced accents or misconjugated verbs—in most cases you will be understood.

The list below of commonly used words and phrases can help you get started.

Greetings and Everyday Expressions

Hello, goodbye, cheers, good luck!	*Salut!*
Good morning! (Hello!)	*Bonjour!*
Good afternoon, good evening!	*Bonsoir!*
How are you?	*Ça va?*
Not bad.	*Pas pire.*
No better than that?	*Pas plus que ça?*
I feel bad, eh?	*Je suis mauvais, la?*
Pleased to meet you!	*Enchanté!*
Good-bye!	*Au revoir!*
See you soon!	*A bientôt!*
Good night!	*Bonne nuit!*
Yes!	*Oui!*
No!	*Non!*
Please!	*S'il vous plaît!*
Thank you!	*Merci!*
You're welcome!	*De rien!*
Excuse me!	*Excusez-moi!* or *Pardonnez-moi!*
It doesn't matter.	*Ca m'est égal.*
I don't speak French.	*Je ne parle pas français.*
Do you speak English?	*Parlez-vous anglais?*
Please repeat.	*Répétez, s'il vous plaît.*
I don't understand.	*Je ne comprends pas.*
Do you understand?	*Vous comprenez?*
My name is . . .	*Je m'appelle . . .*
What is your name?	*Comment vous appelez-vous?*
You're very nice.	*Vous êtes bien gentil/gentille.*
Where is the men's/ladies' room?	*Où est le petit coin?*

French resident of Quebec	*Québécois/e*
old pioneer stock	*la vieille souche*
100% French lineage (also, pure wool)	*pure laine*
miss	*mademoiselle*
madame	*madame*
mister/sir	*monsieur*
open	*ouvert*
closed	*fermé*
entrance	*entrée*
exit	*sortie*
push	*poussez*
pull	*tirez*
today	*aujourd'hui*
tomorrow	*demain*
yesterday	*hier*
Help!	*Au secours!*
ambulance	*l'ambulance*
Get a doctor!	*Appelez le médecin!*

Checking In

I have (don't have) a reservation.	*J'ai une (Je n'ai pas de) réservation.*
I would like . . .	*Je voudrais . . .*
a single room	*une chambre pour une personne*
a double room	*une chambre pour deux*
a quiet room	*une chambre tranquille*
with bath	*avec salle de bain*
with shower	*avec douche*
with air conditioning	*une chambre climatisée*
with balcony	*avec balcon*
overnight only	*pour une nuit seulement*
a few days	*quelques jours*
a week (at least)	*une semaine (au moins)*
with full board	*avec pension complète*
with half board	*avec demi-pension*
Does that price include breakfast?	*Est-ce que le petit dejeuner est inclus?*
Are taxes included?	*Est-ce que les taxes sont compris?*

Do you accept traveler's checks?	Acceptez-vous les chèques de voyage?
Do you accept credit cards?	Acceptez-vous les cartes de crédit?

Eating Out

bottle	une bouteille
cup	une tasse
fork	une fourchette
knife	un couteau
spoon	une cuillère
napkin	une serviette
plate	une assiette
menu	le carte
wine list	le carte des vins
ashtray	un cendrier
(extra) chair	une chaise (en sus)
table	une table
coffee	café
black coffee	café noir
coffee with milk	café au lait
cream	crème
fruit juice	jus de fruit
lemonade	citron pressé
milk	lait
mineral water	
non-carbonated	l'eau minérale
carbonated	l'eau gazeuse
orangeade	orange pressé
tea	thé
water	eau
beer	bière
port	vin de porto
sherry	vin de Xérès
red wine	vin rouge
white wine	vin blanc
rosé	rosé
sweet	doux
(very) dry	(très) sec
cold	froid
hot	chaud

bacon	*bacon*
bread	*pain*
butter	*beurre*
eggs	*oeufs*
soft boiled	*à la coque*
hard boiled	*oeuf dur*
fried	*sur le plat*
scrambled	*brouillé*
poached	*poché*
omelette	*omelette*
ham	*jambon*
honey	*miel*
sugar	*sucre*
jam	*confiture*
juice	*jus*
orange	*jus d'orange*
tomato	*jus de tomate*
pepper	*poivre*
salt	*sel*
Waiter!	*Monsieur!* (Never *Garçon!* in Quebec.)
Waitress!	*Madame!* or *Mademoiselle!*
May I check my coat?	*Est-ce que je peux vous laisser mon manteau?*
I'll have . . .	*Je vais prendre . . .*
a snack	*une bouchée*
a glass of	*un verre de*
a bottle of	*une bouteille de*
a half bottle of	*une demie-bouteille*
a liter of	*un litre de*
a carafe of	*une carafe de*
The check, please.	*L'addition, s'il vous plaît.*
Can you change a $20?	*Avez-vous du change pour vingt piasses?*
Is the service charge included?	*Le service, est-il compris?*
I think there is a mistake in the bill.	*Je crois qu'il y a une erreur dans l'addition.*

Shopping

bakery	*boulangerie*
barber	*barbier*

bookstore	*librairie*
butcher store	*boucherie*
camera shop	*magasin de photographie*
clothing store	*magasin de vètements*
convenience store	*dépanneur*
delicatessen	*charcuterie*
department store	*grand magasin*
drugstore (for medicine)	*pharmacie*
grocery	*épicerie*
jewelry store	*bijouterie*
newsstand	*kiosque à journaux*
outfitting company for outdoor sports	*pouvoirie*
notions shop	*mercerie*
pastry shop	*pâtisserie*
perfume (and cosmetics) store	*parfumerie*
pharmacy/drugstore	*pharmacie*
shoestore	*magasin de chaussures*
supermarket	*supermarché*
tobacconist	*bureau de tabac*
cheap	*bon marché*
expensive	*cher*
large	*grand*
larger	*plus grand*
too large	*trop grand*
small	*petit*
smaller	*plus petit*
too small	*trop petit*
long	*long*
short	*court*
old	*vieux*
new	*nouveau*
used	*d'occasion*
handmade	*fabriqué à la main*
Is it machine washable?	*Est-ce que c'est lavable à la machine?*
How much does this cost?	*Quel est le prix?/Combien?*
What is it made of?	*De quoi est-il fait?*
camel's hair	*poil de chameau*

cotton	*coton*
corduroy	*velours côtelé*
filigree	*filigrane*
lace	*dentelle*
leather	*cuir*
linen	*lin*
silk	*soie*
suede	*daim*
synthetic	*synthétique*
wool	*laine*
wood	*bois*
brass	*cuivre jaune*
copper	*cuivre*
gold (plated)	*or (plaqué)*
silver (plated)	*argent (plaqué)*

May I have a sales tax rebate form?	*Puis-je avoir la forme pour la détaxe?*
May I pay with this credit card?	*Puis-je payer avec cette carte de crédit?*
May I pay with a traveler's check?	*Puis-je payer avec chèques de voyage?*

Getting Around

north	*le nord*
south	*le sud*
east	*l'est*
west	*l'ouest*
right	*droite*
left	*gauche*
straight ahead	*tout droit*
far	*loin*
near	*proche*
map	*carte*
airport	*l'aéroport*
automobile	*le char*
bus	*autobus*
bus stop	*l'arrèt de bus*
gas station	*station service*
subway	*le métro*
trams	*le petits chars*

gasoline	le gaz
regular (leaded)	ordinaire
super (leaded)	super
unleaded	sans plomb
diesel	diesel
Fill it up, please.	De plein, s'il vous plaît.
tires	les pneus
oil	l'huile
train station	la gare
gate	porte
track	voie
one-way ticket	aller simple
round-trip ticket	un billet aller et retour
sleeping car	le char dortois
in first class	en première
in second class	en deuxième
no smoking	défense de fumer
Does this subway/bus go to . . . ?	Est-ce que ce métro/ bus va à . . . ?
What time does it leave?	A quelle heure part-il?
Danger	Danger
Caution	Attention
Detour	Détour
Dead End	Cul-de-sac
Do Not Enter	Défense de stationner
No Parking	Défense de garer
No Passing	Défense de doubler
No U-turn	Défense de faire demi-tour
One way	Sens interdit
Pay toll	Péage
Pedestrian Zone	Zone piétonnière
Reduce Speed	Ralentissez
square (plaza)	carré (place)
Steep Incline	Côte à forte inclination
Stop	Arrèt
Use Headlights	Allumez les phares
Yield	Cédez
Where is the . . . ?	Où se trouve . . . ?
How many kilometers are we from . . . ?	Combien de kilomètres sommes-nous de . . . ?

Personal Items and Services

aspirin	*aspirine*
Band-Aids	*pansements*
bath	*bain*
bathroom	*salle de bain*
beauty shop	*salon de coiffeur*
condom	*préservatif*
dentist	*dentiste*
disposable diapers	*couches*
dry cleaner	*nettoyage à sec* or *teinturerie*
hairdresser	*coiffeur pour dames*
laundromat	*laundrette* or *blanchisserie automatique*
post office	*bureau de poste*
postage stamps (air mail)	*timbres (par avion)*
razor	*rasoir*
sanitary napkins	*serviettes hygiéniques*
shampoo	*shampooing*
shaving cream	*mousse à raser*
shower	*douche*
soap	*savon*
tampons	*tampons*
tissues	*mouchoirs (en papier)*
toilet	*le petit coin*
toilet paper	*papier hygiénique*
toothbrush	*brosse à dents*
toothpaste	*pâte dentrifrice*

Days of the Week

Monday	*lundi*
Tuesday	*mardi*
Wednesday	*mercredi*
Thursday	*jeudi*
Friday	*vendredi*
Saturday	*samedi*
Sunday	*dimanche*

Months

January	*janvier*
February	*février*
March	*mars*
April	*avril*
May	*mai*
June	*juin*
July	*juillet*

August	*août*
September	*septembre*
October	*octobre*
November	*novembre*
December	*décembre*

Numbers

zero	*zéro*
one	*un*
two	*deux*
three	*trois*
four	*quatre*
five	*cinq*
six	*six*
seven	*sept*
eight	*huit*
nine	*neuf*
ten	*dix*
eleven	*onze*
twelve	*douze*
thirteen	*treize*
fourteen	*quatorze*
fifteen	*quinze*
sixteen	*seize*
seventeen	*dix-sept*
eighteen	*dix-huit*
nineteen	*dix-neuf*
twenty	*vingt*
twenty-one	*vingt-et-un*
thirty	*trente*
forty	*quarante*
fifty	*cinquante*
sixty	*soixante*
seventy	*soixante-dix*
eighty	*quatre-vingts*
ninety	*quatre-vingt-dix*
one hundred	*cent*
1995	*mille neuf cent quatre-vingt quinze*

Colors

black	*noir*
blue	*bleu*
brown	*brun*
gray	*gris*

green	*vert*
orange	*orange*
pink	*rose*
purple	*violet*
red	*rouge*
yellow	*jaune*
white	*blanc*

WRITING RESERVATION LETTERS

Restaurant/Hotel Name
Street Address
Quebec City or Montreal, Quebec
Postal Code, Canada

Dear Sir:	*Monsieur:*
I would like to reserve a table for (number of) persons for lunch/dinner on (day and month), 1995, at (hour) o'clock.	*Je voudrais réserver une table pour (number of) personnes pour le déjeuner/dîner du (day and month) 1995, à (hour using the 24-hour clock) heures.*
or	or
I would like to reserve a room for (number of) people for (number of) nights.	*Je voudrais réserver une chambre à (number) personne(s) pour (number of) nuits.*
and	and
Would you be so kind as to confirm the reservation as soon as possible?	*Auriez-vous la bonté de bien vouloir me confirmer cette réservation dès que possible?*
I am very much looking forward to meeting you. (The French usually include a pleasantry such as this.)	*J'attends avec impatience la plaisir de faire votre connaissance.*
With my thanks,	*Avec tous mes remerciements,*
(Signature)	(Signature)

(Print or type your name and address below you signature.)

Weights and Measures

APPROXIMATE EQUIVALENTS

	Metric Unit	Abbreviation	US Equivalent
Length	1 millimeter	mm	.04 inch
	1 meter	m	39.37 inches
	1 kilometer	km	.62 mile
Capacity	1 liter	l	1.057 quarts
Weight	1 gram	g	.035 ounce
	1 kilogram	kg	2.2 pounds
	1 metric ton	MT	1.1 tons
Temperature	0° Celsius	C	32° Fahrenheit

CONVERSION TABLES

METRIC TO US MEASUREMENTS

	Multiply:	by:	to convert to:
Length	millimeters	.04	inches
	meters	3.3	feet
	meters	1.1	yards
	kilometers	.6	miles
Capacity (liquid)	liters	2.11	pints
	liters	1.06	quarts
	liters	.26	gallons
Weight	grams	.04	ounces
	kilograms	2.2	pounds

US TO METRIC MEASUREMENTS

	Multiply:	by:	to convert to:
Length	inches	25.0	millimeters
	feet	.3	meters
	yards	.9	meters
	miles	1.6	kilometers
Capacity	pints	.47	liters
	quarts	.95	liters
	gallons	3.8	liters
Weight	ounces	28.0	grams
	pounds	.45	kilograms

TEMPERATURE

Celsius to Fahrenheit	$(°C \times 9/5) + 32 = °F$
Fahrenheit to Celsius	$(°F - 32) \times 5/9 = °C$

Index

Index

small	petit
medium	moyen
large	grand